Teacher Identity Discourses

Negotiating Personal and Professional Spaces

Teacher Identity Discourses

Negotiating Personal and Professional Spaces

Janet Alsup

Purdue University

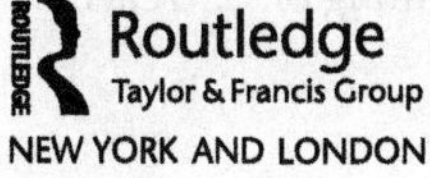

NEW YORK AND LONDON

First published by
Lawrence Erlbaum Associates, Inc., Publishers
10 Industrial Avenue
Mahwah, New Jersey 07430
www.erlbaum.com

This edition published 2013 by Routledge

Routledge
Taylor & Francis Group
711 Third Avenue
New York, NY 10017

Routledge
Taylor & Francis Group
2 Park Square, Milton Park
Abingdon, Oxon OX14 4RN

Routledge is an imprint of the Taylor & Francis Group, an informa business

Cover design by Tomai Maridou

Library of Congress Cataloging-in-Publication Data

Alsup, Janet.
Teacher identity discourses : negotiating personal and professional spaces / Janet Alsup.
p. cm.
(NCTE-LEA research series in literacy and composition)

Includes bibliographical references and index.

ISBN 0-8058-5632-3 (cloth : alk. paper)
ISBN 0-8058-5853-9 (pbk. : alk. paper)

1. High school teachers—Training of. 2. Teachers—Professional relationships. I. Title.
LB1777.A48 2005
373.1102—dc22 2005040155
CIP

ISBN 978-0-805-85853-2

I dedicate this book to Kit Glover,
the first person to show me that teachers are,
above all, people.

Contents

Foreword

Deborah P. Britzman
York University

The drama of student teaching is also the drama of being a student teacher. Its stage and its staging are overpopulated with the instructions from actual and imagined others. There one first confronts, and hopefully may learn to play with, the contents of one's own educational archive. Curiously, it is the history of one's own making and, until it can be spoken, it remains a hidden force. Our opening scene contains these tensions and we may sense how the beginning of learning a profession is chaotic, disorganizing selves in the search for meaning. Educating others while being educated is where the student teacher must begin. It can take a good long while to understand that the work of learning to teach and then the work of trying to teach also encompass belonging to a profession that can and should question its own authority. Yet, for beginners, the question may be which authority to question. One may feel disloyal or worry about losing oneself in doubt. At times, these doubts that seem to take center stage create and then star the character of self-blame. What then becomes dramatic is the figure of the teacher in our educational archive, who returns to berate the mind of the newly arrived for all that she or he lacks. And the student teacher must then ask this demanding question: Am I meant to be a teacher?

As Janet Alsup constructs this tale, there are emotional events stirring the work of learning to teach, adding more questions, rendering old strategies useless and, perhaps, conditioning the need for a new language. There are tensions in this world. One of the most poignant concerns the experience of having to convey how one feels without knowing what to do. And in this borderland of limits and hopes, the way feelings are conveyed in the crowded world of student teaching tends to wander into and animate our earliest archive: good and bad, right and wrong, success or failure. What to do with our march of stories that begin with bad days, bad grades, and bad student teacher, and then end with bad future? Have we even left the past? How are we to be competent when we learn before we understand? For teacher educators and for student teachers, Alsup argues, these painful questions are relevant places to begin if they are not to be their own private education.

In Alsup's view, one more turn is required to even begin to reflect on what is taken for granted. It concerns how everyone involved in teacher education listens to the peripheral world of self-doubt, of not knowing, and of irrelevant and desperate questions without being buried, or burying them, by an avalanche of educational cliches. A student teacher desperately asks her class too early on a December morning, "Does anyone remember what dramatic irony is?" as she misses the irony of that question and gives a punishing quiz. Another student teacher worries if she will be mistaken for a boy as she rehearsers how to dress in the costume of a woman teacher. Must she wear frilly things, even if they feel wrong on her body? A third imagines the "cutting edge" as a dangerous weapon and takes a knife as a metaphor of teaching. There are so many double edges, but one that stands out for this reader is the idea that influencing others can also be a way to hurt them. A fourth student teacher worries about getting caught up in events, almost drowning in a sea of incidences that may be of her own making. Her metaphor becomes a river, or a stormy sea. Another student teacher sees teaching like the weather: subject to sudden changes, storms, maybe even the hoped-for snow day. How, then, to think about what is going on?

Alsup reminds the reader that to glimpse the world of student teaching, and to make from this glimpse a glimmer of understanding, means being open to an encounter with the ridiculous and the sublime. To learn from this combination, Alsup suggests, is to tolerate the humanity of doubts and wishes that are also education. She may be saying to our field that teaching can be a defense against learning unless we consider the most vulnerable places where this idea lives, namely in the lives of student teachers and in the structures of experience they encounter. Then we might understand the power of language in teacher education. This is a language that is not given to an other, but rather one developed because student teachers are invited, urged, even required to talk to one another and to freely associate their worries with their wishes.

As readers enter this world of student teaching in secondary English education and the teacher educator who provokes talk, we meet the literary events of learning. By this I mean the emotional excess of knowledge and the idea that knowledge itself also embodies its limits. Alsup poses this dilemma as one of discourse, usually in the form of an unthought desperation made from feeling that one has to choose between personal selves and professional selves. A key tension in this study of secondary teacher education, perhaps even another character in this crowded world, is discourse, or the idea of thinking about the structure of language from the vantage of the choices it naturalizes, the positions it offers its speakers and listeners, the events that are foreclosed there, and its normative images of how life should be. We borrow the very thing we feel authored by and that we then author. When we analyze discourse, we are also trying to understand who is doing what to whom. The tension is that in speaking of symbolic systems that preexist a speaker, that divide a speaker from herself or himself and from the thing to which discourse then congeals, agency divides as well. Alsup may be read as suggesting that if we are driven to discourse, we can also notice there is no perfect communication because there is no perfect subjectivity. And yet, this lack does wreak havoc on our profession, where we dream of the good teacher, the best education, the excellent lesson, an education without having to learn.

The pressing problems in this study are many, but one of the key ones concerns identity, what a teacher is and does, what a teacher looks like, and whether the teacher's body is a normal teacher's body. If these concerns seem close to adolescence, it may also be because adolescence, including one's own in the case of the secondary teacher, is never very far away. Something about schooling calls for the immature. We are affected by the worlds we try to affect; our sense of identity may telegraph this human condition. But in the world of education, one feels both the pressure of these thoughts and the anxiety that these thoughts are not normal. In this difficult context, Alsup offers a way to think about a language of teaching and learning, one she calls the world of borderland discourse. This must remain a strange geography charted anew by each participant. Alsup puts the tension beautifully when she observes that borderland discourse gives evidence and then contains the tensions between the personal and the social, the imaginary and the reality. We need not choose, provided that we open ourselves to the existential in pedagogical relations. Attention to how the teacher's identity develops from something like teacher education, Alsup suggests, is itself an education.

A creative turn in this study, as it documents the development of some secondary education English student teachers, is found in Alsup's development and discussions of course assignments. They are designed to contain and give relief to some of the confusions of learning to teach. Although old assignments, such as the famous "What is your educational philosophy?" are critiqued, new ones are on offer. And their power emerges from valuing creative expression, a strategy in English education. We might see this aesthetic approach as beginning with a faith in language, that expressing how one thinks and feels matters to one's capacity to think for oneself in relation to others. This design of English education should affect the larger world of teacher education. Alsup demonstrates the importance of metaphor to how we see the world; through visual metaphor we approach the approximating self. Notably, the assignments Alsup invites are tied to the body: feet, shoes, soda pop, wild and exciting animals, objects for defense. The assignments provide a way into this research, documenting as it does a developing teacher education.

One of the oldest ideas this study leads to is the Socratic imperative "Know thyself." It is difficult to argue against this advice, for surely we in education understand that our naked subjectivity is the only means we have to relate to others. Additionally, in thinking about the qualities of relations we make—what it is to influence and be influenced, what it means to care about something and to recognize what the other cares about, and how our preconceptions of events may work as defenses against being affected—in all of these immaterial events, each individual learns of her or his knowing self. To know thyself can be understood as an ethical question, to learn what one cares about, what is tolerable and intolerable, when one breaks meaning and tries its repair, and even to understand something about the limits of one's own understanding. To know thyself is a paradox. It is to know that one must meet, again and again, the unknown other and, in so doing, the unknown self.

Alsup's study puts a great deal of pressure on teacher educators. After all, these people create the conditions for the particular learning that composes a learning profession. I can't help but think that a comparable world of emotional disarray and bad days, harried hopes and passionate ideas also are a part of the teacher educator's world. Alsup gives us a clue with almost a throwaway line: "Teacher educators do not feel comfortable with the emotional lives of their students." It may be that this discomfort speaks to the idea that emotional worlds are not easily tamed by our methods, our rules, or even our assignments. The discomfort may arise because the other's emotion can render the self helpless and emotional. And yet, we are left with a question: How can any teacher educator "know thyself" if she or he eschews the very qualities that are required to even notice how one is affected in the world of discourse and in the world of others? The problem is that knowing thyself is not a corrective experience but instead one of the awareness of constructing experience. To foster this awareness, Alsup supposes, means to think of teacher education in very generous and large ways, to rid the world of teacher education of tacit normalization and to be curious about the conditions of awareness. It may mean to take our educational clichés so seriously that they become our objects of research, so that we analyze how they come to limit thinking and feeling. The principle is that the imperative and responsibility of self-knowledge is an inclusive address that implicates everyone.

Preface

Americans have been told since the 1950s that their children can't read, can't write, can't think, and can't keep up with the rest of the world. They have also been told that most of this failure is due to a lack of educator "accountability"—teachers and administrators are choosing not to work hard enough, do not care enough, and often are not even qualified to do their jobs. In my 7 years as a high school teacher and my 7 years as a teacher educator, this egregious deficit has not been what I've found in my dealings with secondary teachers. Although there are certainly individuals who are less motivated or not as prepared as others, I have found the majority of teachers to be motivated, caring, and diligent. When they either quit the profession or stop working so hard, it is usually because they have become frustrated with the lack of respect and/or support they are receiving, or because they feel overwhelmed with educational discourse that disregards their individuality and expertise.

I began the research project described in this book in the fall of 2000, because my experience as a secondary and postsecondary teacher, as well as a teacher educator, had demonstrated that being a successful secondary teacher is much more complex than is normally recognized or shared with teacher education students. Learning the "skills" of teaching and disciplinary content, although important, is not enough to create a happy and successful secondary school teacher. Preservice secondary teachers also need a teacher education that provides them with opportunities to develop satisfying professional identities, so that they can live and work in challenging institutional environments. One way of providing this support involves learning what kinds of discourse facilitate professional identity development, and then encouraging this discourse in university methods classes. In this book, I call such transformative discourse "borderland discourse"—discourse in which there is evidence of integration or negotiation of personal and professional selves. It is at the discursive borderlands, and by association at the borders of various subjectivities or senses of self, that preservice teachers can discover how to move from being students to being teachers, and can learn how to embody a workable professional teacher identity without sacrificing personal priorities and passions.

Many before me have also argued that a teacher's identity is a combination, or a mixture, of the personal and the professional (Britzman, 1991; Bullough, Knowles, & Crow, 1992; Danielewicz, 2001). To ignore either part of the mix can result in an overly simplistic, essentially unsuccessful teacher education. The integration of personal aspects of the self and professional expectations or demands is more complicated than simply bringing together two binary opposites (i.e., the self and the other); such a synergy involves bringing together, mixing and merging, and even welcoming a collision between personal ideologies and perceived professional expectations. For some teachers, such a merging or meeting of subjectivities is relatively simple—their personal lives and sense of self are more or less parallel to the conservative expectations of most secondary and elementary schools. For example, they *are* White, female, heterosexual, and suburb dwellers. However, for others, such a satisfying combination of the self and the professional other is more of a challenge. What happens if you are a student teacher and you don't look like the teachers in the school where you are working? Or act like them? Or value what they value? How do you develop a teacher identity that is both accepted by the school and palatable to you? How do you get and keep a job without giving up the very essence of who you are?

I never encourage my students to capitulate—to give up the personal beliefs that are often the very basis for why they became teachers in the first place—in order to "fit in" with the stereotypical culture of many American schools. However, I have also worked with students who have decided not to be secondary school teachers because of the perceived demands and expectations based on a narrow set of beliefs. Sometimes these "nontraditional" teacher education candidates who decide to follow other professional paths demonstrate the most potential for implementing many of the critical pedagogical reforms that teacher educators hold dear; however, these candidates can't figure out how to uphold these ideologies while also working within the socially conservative, politically correct, and increasingly litigious institution of the public school.

To complicate matters even further, teacher education—or the much more mechanized phrase "teacher training"—is usually focused on the future students of the preservice teacher, not on the development of the teacher him- or herself. When concepts such as multicultural education, identity construction, personal growth, and even the learning of new content are addressed, they are discussed in terms of how preservice teachers can encourage such learning on the part of their future students. I don't think such a focus is completely misplaced—new teachers should, of course, be concerned with what their students are learning. However, this externally focused approach tends to assume that the teacher is already self-actualized, already emotionally and affectively prepared to assume the teacher identity, with few personal challenges left to face. I argue that this assumption is rarely accurate, and teacher educators and new teachers should be more selfish and take care of themselves first, in order to better take care of others later.

I wrote this book for new and preservice teachers, who—like my six research participants Linda, Janeen, Lois, Carrie, Karen, and Sandy—have embarked on the journey of becoming a teacher. I also wrote this book for the many practicing secondary and elementary school teachers who struggle with the development of a holistic and satisfying professional identity in an institutional climate that too often rewards conformity and stagnancy, as well as for the teacher educators, mentors, and supervisors who wish to nurture and encourage the new teachers who bring wonderful idealism and boundless energy into their classrooms. It is my hope that all of these potential readers find something of value in this book.

Chapter 1 describes my personal experiences in developing my teacher identity and how reflection on these experiences led to my interest in this project. Chapter 1 also provides brief biographical sketches of the six preservice teacher participants in the study. Chapter 2 outlines some of the major historical developments in the history of elementary and secondary teaching and teacher education in the United States. It also provides an overview of how I define both discourse and borderland discourse, and describes the qualitative methodology of my study.

Chapters 3–7 describe how the preservice teacher participants used narratives to speak about their developing teaching lives. Narrative was by far the most frequent genre engaged in by my participants—as there were a total of 354 stories told by the participants over the 2½ years of the study. In chapters 3–7, I examine narratives of tension, experience, embodiment, family and friends, and borderland narratives, respectively. In chapters 8–9, I look at two other genres of significance—the metaphor and the philosophy statement—to describe the teaching life. The visual metaphors created by the student participants were the most transformative type of borderland discourse in which they engaged over the time of the study. The last chapter of the book summarizes major findings and reviews implications for the teacher educator, the new teacher, and the educational community at large. In appendix A, I provide eight assignments to be used in the English methods class to support professional identity development. These assignments provide opportunities for students to engage in borderland discourse, the weaving together of various discourses and associated subjectivities to create a professional teacher identity with which they can live and work as new teachers. Finally, in appendix B, I include a glossary of key terms used throughout the book.

ACKNOWLEDGMENTS

I would like to acknowledge several people and organizations who have made this book possible though their hard work, support, and encouragement. First, I thank the senior editor at Lawrence Erlbaum Associates, Naomi Silverman, and the senior editor at the National Council of Teachers of English, Zarina Hock, for their support of my scholarship. I also thank the early reviewers of my book, including Bob Yagelski (SUNY-Albany), who provided insightful feedback helping me improve my manuscript. I humbly thank Professor Deborah Britzman, both for her brilliant work that inspired and informed mine, and for generously contributing the foreword to this volume.

I thank the Purdue University Department of English, and specifically the English Department Head Professor Irwin Weiser for his consistent encouragement and support during the time I researched and wrote this book. I am grateful to the Purdue University College of Liberal Arts (CLA) for both financial support received through the CLA Research Incentive Award Program and release time provided by my appointment to the CLA Center for Undergraduate Instructional Excellence. I thank the College of Education at Purdue University for awarding me the assistance of a very capable undergraduate research trainee at the beginning of the study, and I thank Beth May for wonderfully accurate and speedy transcriptions of interviews.

I offer my deepest gratitude to my friend and colleague Margaret Morris —exemplary writer, editor, and research assistant. Margaret, your sympathetic ear and sage advice during the writing process were irreplaceable. Thanks for offering smart revision suggestions (even when I didn't want to hear them!) and lifting me up when I was down.

I extend heartfelt thanks to the co-editors of the Research Series in Literacy and Composition, Professors Andrea Lunsford and Beverly Moss. Thank you, Andrea and Beverly, for believing in my work and for your many insightful and perceptive suggestions for revision as I wrote. Thank you for your close attention to my project and your commitment to making it the best book possible. It's truly an honor to be the author of a book in your series.

Finally, I thank my students, past, present, and future, for all they continue to teach me.

Chapter **1**

A Teaching Life: How and Why This Project Came to Be

borderlands
do you wander
the borderlands
while we stand sentinel
the Greek chorus aligned
and despairing
reciting our mute plea
"Come back. Come back."

perhaps you converse
with shadows
of consciousness
you dream of swallows
and messengers
and wild places of youth
before the crows came
and took your sight
pecked and worried at you
til you retreated to
the borderland
where time flows
a lugubrious stream
until the final heartbeat
And it stops.

the swallows flee
crying "Come back, Come back."

as we, robed in our crow's garb,
worry at fallen petals
that garland you now
heavy burden of soul's husk
lies rigid, motionless,
Durer's figure carved out
in wax
this mask is still
but the air shimmers
alive with whispered tendrils
and there is no room for tears
"I am here. I am here."

(Katrina Imison-Bowker, 2004)

This project really began in the fall of 1989, when I took my first teaching job at New Bloomfield R-3 High School (NBHS) in New Bloomfield, Missouri. This school was very near my hometown of Mokane, and both towns were quite small—fewer than 500 residents, including those who lived outside the city limits. It's a joke that small Midwestern towns only have one, blinking yellow light; well, New Bloomfield didn't have that. It had a stop sign. The school at New Bloomfield was small as well, with K–12 in the same building, and the elementary and junior high/high school separated only by a long hallway.

I interviewed for the job and accepted it before I graduated with my bachelor's degree in English Education from the University of Missouri—Columbia, so I spent the summer after graduation preparing to teach my first year. My classroom was relatively large, with the standard type of student and teacher desks, but it also had windows along one wall that looked out toward the shop and automotive department as well as the graveled parking lot. There were low bookshelves, under the windows, that had been built by the boys in the woodshop classes, and two long chalkboards. It was only a short walk out the back door to get to the baseball field and concession stand where parents volunteered to cook hot dogs and sell sodas every Friday afternoon when there was a ball game. Sports were big in New Bloomfield—much bigger than learning English.

Even though I was very nervous when I walked into that first classroom, I was also relatively confident in my preparation. I had had inspirational professors during my undergraduate program, and I felt intellectually ready to teach. After all, I had graduated with a near-perfect GPA, so surely I was prepared. However, I didn't feel affectively ready. My level of self-confidence—or sense of personal and professional identity—needed space for development. Only 22 years old then, I assumed that my qualms would simply fade once I started teaching—this was, after all, my "calling."

When school began, routines formed relatively well. I had seventh and ninth through twelfth graders, and the principal had given me the extra roles of newspaper advisor and cheerleading coach. I was busy. I planned and graded and "performed" for 100 students every day, and then often rode game buses until late into the night—maybe even midnight or 1A.M. before returning home to start all over again the next day. Now, whenever I return to my home state I have flashbacks to the small, rural school gymnasiums in the tiny Missouri towns I frequented as a cheerleading coach.

As the school year progressed, the students began to take advantage of my fledgling professional identity. Cruel comments or disruptive behavior on the part of the NBHS adolescents could bring me close to tears and often made me question my preparedness. Students sometimes acted out when I was trying to help other students or groups. One notable time, several "problem" boys broke apart ink pens, smeared the ink on the bottom of their shoes, and proceeded to walk about the room leaving large, blue footprints. I spent an hour after school trying to clean the ink off with Fantastik before the unappreciative custodians found out. This incident foreshadowed many of my early teacher experiences that form the base of much of my knowledge regarding the institutional constraints placed on preservice teachers. To make matters worse, the principal didn't really support me—on the contrary, I "got in trouble" as much as the students did, it seemed to me, whenever I sent one of them to the office for chastisement. In those situations I would have to defend my reasons for referring the student to the office, as if I was to blame for the situation.

At year's end, I took another job at the high school I had attended as a teenager, South Callaway R-2 in Mokane, Missouri. However, the first couple of years there were only a little easier, as I continued to struggle toward a professional identity. I vacillated among teacher personas. The first few years, I chose between alternating tactics: either the strict, no-nonsense teacher or the "teacher as friend." Both of these situated identities had good days and challenging days, but each only offered a fragment of a full professional identity. I don't think I harmed students irrevocably, but I certainly wasn't the teacher I wanted to be—in fact, I didn't completely know what or who that teacher was yet. I saw other teachers around me whom I wished to emulate, but I could never step into another's professional identity de facto. When I did try to emulate their actions or their interactions with students, some element would not fit. Burning questions remained. How could I bring *me* into my teaching life? How could I be a good teacher and not always feel like I was playing a part, trying to "put on" a persona that was not me? After 7 years of teaching high school and earning a Master's degree, I decided to return to graduate school full time to seek my PhD—and answers.

My struggles to attain a metacognitive, holistic teacher identity drove me down a path of personal and professional identity development, and eventually to conduct research and write this book about the processes surrounding preservice teacher identity growth. I can't say that when I started this project I knew what it would look like upon its completion. As Helene Cixous (1993) noted about the writing process, "It's the book of the Act of Writing .... How can it be written? With the hand running. Following the writing like the painter draws: in flashes. The hand leads to the flowers. From the heart where passions rise to the finger tips that hear the body thinking: this is where the Book ... springs from ..." (p. 156).

With my own "hand running" and responding to my passions, I knew that I wanted to learn something about teacher identity, and as a teacher educator I wanted to understand how teacher identity development could be an important component of learning to teach. In my undergraduate years, my professors' approaches had seemed to assume that I was learning something on my own that I simply wasn't. For an even longer time, I believed that my early teaching experiences were unique. The longer I taught preservice teachers and mentored new teachers, however, the more I became convinced that my experience was almost universal.

As my metacognitive awareness of my teacher self increased, I began to wonder why university teacher education programs didn't directly address issues of professional identity development. Most teacher education programs talk about issues of professional demeanor, dress, and communication. However, these are not the professional "identity" issues that concern me the most. The issues I'm worried about are the aspects of identity development that involve the integration of the personal self with the professional self, and the "taking on" of a culturally scripted, often narrowly defined, professional role while maintaining individuality.

Overall, the role of the university teacher education program seems to be to provide knowledge about learning theories and pedagogical approaches, not help the new teacher develop an identity. However, my own experiences taught me that such knowledge is not always enough. I now see my preservice teacher students struggle with similar identity issues (as shown in the experiences of the six students in this research study). One reason I think identity concerns are rarely addressed in teacher education courses is that they are difficult to tackle, and are often uncomfortable for the instructor or mentor to talk about. How do you have a discussion about personal and professional identity integration in a methods course? How do you help students engage in transformative identity discourse?

To answer such questions, I followed six preservice English education students to test my hypothesis about the centrality of forming (or failing to form) a workable teacher identity. As a result, I have created a theory about the intersection of various types of discourse within the process of professional identity development. This theory became the foundation for specific suggestions for assignments in methods courses that teacher educators can use as is or adapt to their own contexts. I worried over the decision to include assignments. On the one hand, such assignments may reflect a simplistic, reductive approach to developing teacher identity. Readers might assume that completing a few assignments could *create* an identity that might, in actuality, take a lifetime to develop. I didn't want to codify or simplify the process of teacher identity by implying that it can be achieved through a few select assignments. I know that the process of identity development is difficult, messy, and complex, and that it must be exactly this way to be successful. On the other hand, I was determined to apply the theoretical concepts the book explores to classroom practice. Frankly, I feel a responsibility to my teacher-educator readers to provide them with real-world applications. Otherwise, all I have done is create another abstract theory about teacher education that has no real-world correlative.

The classroom applications grew directly out of the focus on discourse that developed as I analyzed my prolific data. One of the most exciting things about my research results is that they culminated in the description of various genres of discourse that can be applied to classroom assignments to facilitate the expression of "borderland discourse," that transformative teacher identity discourse allowing preservice teachers to develop integrated, holistic professional selves. These genres of discourse are powerful for the teacher educator because discourse, in its various forms, is what we engage in during a class—be it written, oral, performative, or cognitive discourse. Identifying characteristics of transformative discourse has tremendous potential to assist the teacher educator in addressing issues of identity formation in education courses. Therefore, for the purpose of improving teacher education, I hope readers will recognize and respect the delicate balance I try to maintain between so-called "reductionism" and practical application. The assignments appear in appendix A, and I welcome readers to apply these assignments and modify them to suit.

THE HOLISTIC NATURE OF TEACHER IDENTITY

Similar to my dilemma about including sample assignments, I felt some tension about naming the discursive genres I identified during my qualitative coding or analysis process. Primarily, this tension applies to my naming of "borderland discourse," which is an organizing concept of this book. I hesitated to name such complex, even ambiguous, discourse because of the fear of reducing it to something more simplistic than it really is. The problem with naming something like a form of discourse that facilitates identity formation is that readers may think it is stable, always similar, and easily identifiable across time and space. But, of course, that is not an accurate description of borderland discourse, or any other kind of discourse. In this book, I often find myself describing examples of borderland discourse by discussing its cognitive, emotional, and psychological power rather than its linguistic or stylistic characteristics. I chose to name it because although naming risks oversimplification, it also allows discussion and heightened meta-awareness of a concept. I hope that by the end of the book, the reader can understand borderland discourse as complex, rich, and context dependent, a view that the examples throughout the book support. My goal was not to esssentialize the experience of teacher identity development, but rather to explore, explain, and improve how we educate teachers.

Borderland discourse, as a transformative type of teacher identity discourse, reflects a view of teacher identity that is holistic—inclusive of the intellectual, the corporeal, and the affective aspects of human selfhood. Within borderland discourse there is evidence of contact between disparate personal and professional subjectivities, which can lead to the eventual integration of these multiple subject positions. Such integration through discourse is vital for the developing teacher, who must negotiate conflicting subject positions and ideologies while creating a professional self. Cultural expectations and definitions of "teacher" can exaggerate the challenges of such negotiation. I spend a great deal of time and space in chapter 2 talking about these cultural expectations and how teacher educators might counteract pervasive cultural scripts and stereotypes of teachers reproduced and disseminated through movies, TV shows, books, visual images, and even within the narrative memories of each and every one of us who has been to school and who chooses to remember selected aspects of "teacher."

An interesting study conducted by Weber and Mitchell (1995), asking participants of various ages and cultural backgrounds to "draw a teacher," revealed that many people depict teachers similarly and with stereotypical markers (pointers, chalkboards, authoritative poses, female, Caucasian, etc.), demonstrating the pigeonholing of teacher identity. The problem arises when young people (particularly young women) become teachers and they don't view these stereotypes as problematic—they may *want* to be the prim, feminine young teacher who has a firmly entrenched place in society that doesn't challenge existing gender stratifications or social norms. This stereotypical role is attractive because it seems to be free of conflict and contradiction. For many working-class students, this image even represents a rise in status rather than a reductive expression of an oppressive stereotype, because it represents admittance into the accepted societal norm. But regardless of this initial attraction to the scripted identity, many find it hard to actually take on this persona and simultaneously be true to themselves— they may result in tension, frustration, and sometimes abandonment of the profession. To avoid these consquences, the student becoming a teacher must carve out an identity space for him- or herself. Often this space is in the so-called borderland between identity positions or situated discourses, and is a space of continual becoming rather than an endpoint culminating in a singular identity construction.

Such a singular identity is where I thought I was headed when I graduated from my undergraduate program, and I was disillusioned when I didn't take on or "own" that illusory teacher identity easily and quickly, as I thought I should. Frankly, no one ever told me that such identity work would be hard to accomplish, and all the images of teachers in my cultural landscape appeared to be at ease, whole, and untroubled by inner demons. What I didn't realize is that taking on this professional identity may be more difficult for some new teachers than for others, due to their outsider or marginalized status in society. If a new teacher is not a member of the middle class, White, female, and heterosexual, the difficulty of the transition is exaggerated. Coming from a working-class family, I felt tension between my personal experiences and beliefs and my new professional expectations. For example, I had more difficulty establishing myself in a position of authority in the classroom because I had never experimented with such a role before.

Teacher educators must talk to preservice teachers about the difficulty of professional identity development, even under the best of circumstances, even though it might be uncomfortable for us and such a discussion might mean revealing some of our own perceived weaknesses. We must bring issues of identity into the methods class if we want to slow the exodus of young teachers from the profession, and sometimes this curricular change necessitates that personal information belonging to both teacher and students be exposed. Please realize that I'm not advocating an Oprah Winfrey-like classroom in which Foucauldian "confessionals" abound, but rather I am supporting the expression of (and reflection on) individual quests for professional identity through a variety of discursive genres. Making such experiences explicit in the form of narratives, metaphors, and philosophy statements, for example, and then critically analyzing their relationship to one's developing personal pedagogy, is essential to professional identity formation and the making of a good teacher.

The expression of such discourse in the methods class means that, as a teacher educator, you might sometimes hear about that third-grade teacher who slapped students' knuckles with a ruler, that uncomfortable conversation with a father about professional choices, or even a serious illness or catastrophic life event that led to a professional awakening. The six participants in this study commonly told such stories, and although the stories told to me in a one-on-one setting during interviews and not in front of an entire class, if teacher identity is privileged in whole-class instruction such stories might be shared there as well. The teacher educator doesn't need to judge these stories—he or she simply needs to listen, demonstrate respect, and ask questions relevant to the students' developing professional identity. For example, such questions could include, "How did this event affect your feelings about teaching?" "Your pedagogical preferences?" and "Your teaching beliefs and/or philosophy [what I prefer to call *personal pedagogy*]?" Such questions can lead to critical analysis and identity growth.

WHAT IS DISCOURSE?

There are many ways to define discourse. There are multiple theorists, researchers, and philosophers who have expounded on the concept over the years, including many who are well known to academics: Foucault (1972, 1973, 1977, 1978), Berkenkotter and Huckin (1995), Miller (1984), Bourdieu (1991), and Geertz (1973). When reading about various theories of discourse and methods of discourse analysis, I found the work of Jim Gee (1999) to be particularly powerful. Gee's definition of discourse was broad and is politically and socially oriented. His understanding of discourse took into consideration the holistic nature of human expression and encompassed the effects of discourse on the material world and on individual lives. In my work with preservice teachers, his approach seemed to have the most potential for creating positive change within the educational community.

Discourse is not only spoken or written language, and it was certainly more than that for the participants in my study. Gee defined discourse (what he called discourse with a capital "D") as:

> different ways in which we humans integrate language with non-language "stuff," such as different ways of thinking, acting, interacting, valuing, feeling, believing, and using symbols, tools, and objects in the right places and at the right times so as to enact and recognize different identities and activities, give the material world certain meanings, distribute social goods in a certain way, make certain sorts of meaningful connections in our experience, and privilege certain symbol systems and ways of knowing over others. (1999, p. 13)

As you can see from this definition, according to Gee, discourse incorporates many activities and actions, both internal and external, along the mind-body-spirit continuum. Gee's conception of discourse is subtly different from Foucault's, whom many postmodern theorists turn to for the definitive word on discourse. Foucault viewed discourses as more like what we would call "disciplines," while Gee, a reading educator and sociolinguist, saw them as "situated identities" (1999, p. 38). To Foucault, discourses were what constrains or "maps out" the terrain in which certain writing, speaking, or thinking can be done. So, for example, the larger realm of the "discourse of education" determines the kind of speech an educator can engage in on a daily basis and still be a part of that community. Therefore, when an individual claims to be part of a community and thus engages in its discourse, a certain subjectivity or situated identity (synonyms in Gee's work), such as "teacher," results.

Although Gee agreed that there are larger disciplinary or social/cultural discourses that affect people, he seemed to see an individual's participation in discourse as more active or engaged than Foucault. In Gee's definition of discourse, the individual brings certain subjectivities to a discursive act, while, at the same time, the discourse affects the individual engaging in it. There is the possibility that a discursive act would actually involve multiple subjectivities, and the individual owning them could at any given moment decide which one he or she will enact within the discourse. In short, I believe that, for Gee, discourse had more significance for identity formation and enacting local change and less, perhaps, for politics and the interaction of global, ideological communities. This isn't to say that Gee wasn't concerned with the localized political power of discourse. On the contrary, he explained how, by carefully participating in opposing discourses, for example, the individual can speak to a certain community and enact change. However, it's important to understand that Gee was not talking about "pretending" to be a believer in a certain discourse, or simply "playing the game" of being a teacher when you really feel like a fake the whole time. Instead, one must find the borderland between two (or more) discourses in a sincere way and speak from this new space, this site of alternative discourse, to enact change in a particular community. Finding and inhabiting these borderlands between discourses occurs as the result of cognitive dissonance and often results in increased metacognitive awareness and identity growth.

One problem with the borderland metaphor is that it implies a "crossing over" as the goal—eventually moving *from* one discursive space to another (e.g., from student to teacher). This is the simplistic view of teacher education, the notion of professional identity as simply learning a new set of rules for behavior. However, reaching the in-between ground, the place of becoming, the space of ambiguity and reflection, *is* the goal—this is the space with which we want our preservice teachers to experiment. In this book, I explain borderland discourse by showing examples of when I believe it occurred for the six students in my study. These examples of borderland discourse occurred when they (a) did not completely repudiate their own discourses and (b) accepted (in perhaps modified form) some of the discourses of the "other," or of the educational community they were entering as young professionals. It was when they changed their minds, the moments when they realized they didn't know it all, or realized that they indeed knew something (depending on their level of self-confidence), that they became teachers without giving up themselves. They had found their "teacher within" (Palmer, 1998, p. 29).

Consistent with the understanding of teacher identity as holistic and borderland discourse as an expression of an intellectual-emotional leap, the expression of metaphor was essential to the identity development of the research participants. I asked the students to create textual and visual metaphors that represented their teaching identity and/or philosophy. The visual metaphors (the photographs that I describe in chap. 8) were, according to the standards of my analysis, the most powerful genre of teacher identity discourse in which the students engaged. The visual metaphors were examples of borderland discourse more often than were the textual metaphors, narratives, or the philosophy statements. This was a surprise to me. From reading I had done and my own experiences as a teacher, I believed that metaphors were a powerful form for identity creation and a catalyst for personal growth. As an English teacher and a lover of poetry, I understood the power of metaphor and other figurative language. However, if you had asked me to hypothesize before the analysis of the data, I would have said that the narratives would be the most powerful form of teacher identity discourse, because stories form the core of human expression. However, the metaphors proved me wrong. They were able to reach a higher plane, a place of true wisdom perhaps, about self. The part of the brain that produced the metaphorical images allowed access to thoughts and feelings that other genres did not. As a result, I think we need to regularly incorporate metaphor creation and visual thinking/composing into our methods courses.

There is, of course, institutional discourse that is expressed by school administrators, teaching colleagues, parents, textbook companies, school boards, and so on that affects the professional identities of new teachers. Unfortunately, I cannot explore all of these discourses in this book. Therefore, the school settings in which the six students worked during their student teaching are not intimately described in this book, and much institutional discourse these students may have experienced is not analyzed. I did not spend a great deal of time at their school settings, nor did I ask participants a lot of questions about their administrators' styles, school rules, school environment, and so on. If the reader is interested in studies that confront such issues in more depth, I would recommend both *Disturbing Practice: Reading Teacher Education as Text* (2002) by Avner Segall and *Contradictions in Teacher Education and Society: A Critical Analysis* (1988) by Mark B. Ginsburg. My focus was on the six individual preservice teachers and how they expressed their developing identities to their mentors, themselves, their students, and me.

DOING BORDERLAND DISCOURSE

I taught a graduate seminar in the spring of 2004 called "The American Teacher: The History of Teacher Preparation 1821–Present," and in this seminar the students shared many stories, metaphors, and philosophy statements about their teacher selves. The seminar title was perhaps an unfortunate choice, because it omitted the phrase "teacher identity," which is actually what the course was about. It's interesting to me that I omitted the phrase when proposing the course and creating its title. I think at that time I still questioned the relevance or intellectual rigor of studying teacher "identity," and thus I was fearful of putting it out there for all to see. The course did investigate historical events that affected teacher identity and cultural definitions of teachers over time, but we spent most of our time reading and discussing thinkers and teacher educators including Deborah Britzman, Jane Danielewicz, Sandra Weber and Claudia Mitchell, Avner Segall, Richard Lipka and Thomas Brinkthaupt, bell hooks, Parker Palmer, and Lisa Delpit, who write, in part, about the lives of teachers. The graduate seminar, which I taught while writing this manuscript, grew directly out of my research and what I learned from its student participants.

The graduate students taking the class came from a variety of disciplinary and teaching backgrounds: there were Master's and Ph.D. students in curriculum and instruction and rhetoric and composition, elementary school teachers, university teachers, high school teachers, a professional development coordinator for a large school district, and a preservice teacher who was completing her Master's degree prior to going on the job market. For their final seminar papers, many of the students chose to write "auto-ethnographies" exploring their teacher identities and their lives as teachers on the American educational landscape. In class, we read some book-length examples of teacher auto-ethnographies written by Mike Rose, Jane Tompkins, and Vivian Paley, among others, and we read about what ethnography is as a research methodology and as a genre.

Then, the students wrote, and what they wrote often surprised me with its power and poignancy. These auto-ethnographies were multigeneric, and combined personal narratives, poems, pictures, drawings, music, theoretical expositions, and even analyses of action research. The students presented their projects in class the last week of the semester, and then turned them in to me. Within these projects, many of the students voluntarily shared very personal parts of their lives that they deemed important as they integrated personal and professional identities and reflected on the progression of their teacher lives. These narratives, poems, pictures, and so on, although personal, were not revealed for the sake of pure voyeurism or as part of an isolated, out-of-context "personal narrative" assignment. Instead, they were shared for a reason—for the purpose of their analysis, for critical thinking about the students' teaching lives. And these teaching lives were inherently linked to the students' personal lives, to their core identities. There was no clear separation that could be made between private and public, creative and logical, student and teacher. After reading the projects, I realized that they were living examples of borderland discourse inspired by the auto-ethnography assignment. Following are some examples.

From Katrina:

> As I write this I am struck by the thought that much of my life can be summarized by a few clichés, and yet even so they represent the truth for me: I loved school; I was obsessed with reading and researching; I had a "thirst for knowledge" that sometimes put me at odds with my friends; I enjoyed working on projects and put forth significant effort not only to please my teachers (I was very much the "good girl" in school although I found some ways to quietly rebel), but because I genuinely enjoyed the process. None of this has changed for me over the years and perhaps that is why, despite other "adventures" outside teaching and academia, I keep finding myself drawn back to that familiar world. At times I have fought against remaining a teacher—frustration and burn-out encroach—but it seems to me that there is something internal that makes me a teacher and resists my occasional attempts to carve out a new career. Perhaps ultimately, we cannot change what we inherently are. Perhaps my own teacher identity goes far deeper than the external accoutrements of manner, dress, attitude, to that personal, spiritual grain within us all, that the poets might describe as our essence. I am what I am. And for today, at least, I am a teacher.
>
> Given intellectual freedom and space to wiggle cognitively (quite apropos when I picture my first grade class), students at all stages of their development can express themselves lyrically and evocatively through poetry. Most powerful for me, however, is the fact that poetry allowed my students—as it allows me—to grapple with some of the deep philosophical questions of humanity: who am I?; what is my place in the world?; what is my experience of the world? Poetry allows us to explore the at times mundane, the minutiae of everyday life, transforming brief moments of experience or interaction with the environment into something richer, deeper, and more profound. Temporal life becomes an adumbration of the existential and spiritual.

From Shannon:

> I realize that my desire to reach out to students and [pique] their interest in their own academic prowess will be met with opposition just from the process of them learning about themselves and struggling to figure out how to apply the idea that they are "the captain of their own ship" to their academic development. Looking back into my own athletic development, there were times that I was too stubborn to learn from my mistakes, which sometimes caused tension in my relationships with my coaches. It took a lot of personal reflection and failure to figure out how to actually apply what I had learned about training in order to advance in my athletic career. Without taking charge of my own actions and how the actions of others affected

me, I have found that abilities can be discounted and lost if the will to succeed is not strong enough. Deborah Britzman's book *Practice Makes Practice* [1991] makes reference to getting caught up in events and losing the ability to use reflection as a tool for improvement as she describes student teacher experiences: "... because they took up the myth that everything depends upon the teacher, when things went awry, all they could do was blame themselves rather than reflect upon the complexity of pedagogical encounters" (p. 251). Through this explanation of student teachers' reactions to outcomes of lessons, it is evident that there will be trial and error periods in teaching and that you can either make the choice to be defeated by failures or view mistakes as an opportunity for improvement. My own choice to view failures as opportunities for improvement allowed me to continue swimming despite a supposed career-ending injury, and I believe the failures I will encounter as a first year teacher will be easier to handle because I have been down that road athletically and I now know how to deal with adversity in a positive way.

From Mingyan:

Looking back to these so many years that I walked on the path of being a teacher, I am grateful. I am grateful to my father who initiated my interest of being a teacher, I am grateful to my brother who set up a role model and exerted so much pressure to me so that I learned how to hold on when all the world is against you; I am grateful to my students in China who gave me the attention and trust that made me whole in personality; I am grateful to my students in America who challenged me and presented me a different world that I would like to explore. I am not admiring those engineers who could devote their life to their career any more; I find teaching can be just the great career that I would like to devote myself to. Life is no longer a meaningless existence when I find I could inspire my students' love for learning, and my encouragement made them feel their dignity as a person is respected. All these years teaching taught me that being a blessing to other people is a more profound experience than getting a blessing from other people. Now I am no longer struggling between my self-expectation and the reality. I have accepted myself via my students. With my students, I am also living harmoniously with the world in which I am dwelling.

From Amah:

In the meantime, however, looking back on my life, I realize that I have always been on a quest to understand. Through this last experience, I understood that one is indeed the magic number because humanity is one—we are from the same source, and must therefore cultivate humanity and navigate life with our human senses as well as our spirit. No thing can separate us and we cannot limit ourselves or others ... we simply are. To define someone and box them up in categories as we in America are fond of doing sets that person's identity in stone as predetermined and fixed and, seeing that God is indefinable and is our source, we too should not be touched. However this is precisely what we do ... we condition ourselves and our children into thinking that some things are more important than others (i.e., capitalism, consumerism, pop culture), and the result is a diorama of compromised beings.

> The seizure and the other experiences discussed in this essay have shown me that beauty and power that comes with knowledge, the need for role models, understanding individuality, and spirituality. The knowledge I have gained from school and life has given me the tools with which I make sense of humanity, of "truth," of myself as a human being, a man, and of reality as has been defined and presented to me. Through education, I was and am able to go on an inner journey toward an honest, "truthful," and subjective way of seeing and of being in the world, and I realize that my ideas, feelings, and my own definition of what it means to be human and male are as real, powerful, and valid as the physical world that surrounds me.
>
> To separate "Amah" from Mr. Medard the teacher is impossible, for it would be reductive and depreciatory (Danielewicz, 2001; Palmer, 1998). My background in acting has taught me that every moment is important (the stagnant, the depressing, the enthralling, et al.) and is filled with learning and growing opportunities. I have had to teach myself and others many things; thus, my "inner teacher" is an integral part of who I am and my teaching identity has already been forged (Palmer, 1998). It is a composite of my experiences, my deepest human desires, the need to be surrounded by what inspires me, and to create meaningful experiences—both for myself and for my students.

As you can see from these examples, teacher identity is indeed holistic. It incorporates the cognitive, the emotional, the bodily, and the creative. To not allow students to talk about such issues, to not teach them how and why such issues are important to their teaching lives, to not give them the opportunity to speak and take the time to hear them, we are doing preservice and inservice teachers a disservice—we are leaving out, we are forgetting or choosing to forget, an important (if not the most important) part of being a teacher: the teacher identity.

Katrina wrote the poem, called "borderlands," that begins this chapter. One of the excerpts I shared from Katrina's auto-ethnography spoke of her belief in the power of poetry to help her understand herself and her place in the world. Katrina's poetry often depends on metaphor, as shown in "borderlands." In this poem, the narrator speaks to another individual who seems to be living at the "borderlands" of life, where she is able to "converse with shadows of consciousness," "dream of swallows and messengers and wild places of youth," and "where time flows a lugubrious stream." This borderland is the target of both fear and longing for the narrator, who throughout most of the poem seems not to be living at the borderland but instead at some distant place where she "stands sentinel" waiting for a reunion with the one already there. In Katrina's poem, the borderland is a mysterious place of dreams and shadows, fallen petals, shimmering air, and flowing time. It is a place one might want to be, but is not a place of complete ease or unattenuated joy. It seems to be a space of enhanced wisdom where one arrives only after experiencing pain. Arriving at the borderland means goals have been met, life lessons have been learned—growth has been achieved.

I hope this chapter has provided a brief glimpse into the reasons why I wrote this book and what I hope it can provide both for teacher educators and teacher education students. I believe that in order to become successful teachers, university students must develop a holistic understanding of their personal and professional identities and the intersections and contradictions among them. Such understandings can be realized though the expression of borderland discourse that facilitates the critical interrogation of conflicting subject positions or expressions of self, which can be primarily emotional, physical, intellectual, or even spiritual. Gloria Anzaldua (1987) described a similar borderland experience in her book about her life living on the "border" between U.S. and Mexican culture. Her definition of the Chicana borderland included cultural, physical, spiritual, sexual, and discursive interactions and integrations. She wrote in her preface that "[T]he Borderlands are physically present wherever two or more cultures edge each other, where people of different races occupy the same territory, where under, lower, middle and upper classes touch, where the space between two individuals shrinks with intimacy" (p. 19).

Although Anzaldua did not, of course, discuss the teacher identity, her experiences living on the so-called borderland were parallel in many ways to the borderland experiences of the participants in my research study and the experiences of many other preservice teachers. They, like Anzaldua, find themselves living at the intersection of multiple worlds and multiple ways of knowing. Ideally, their goal is not to minimize or erase these borders, but instead to learn to occupy the space between them. The borderland is no longer defined as a gap or an absence of identity, but rather as a space in which to experience a richer, fuller, and more complex understanding of self and other.

Throughout this book, I explore borderland discourse by describing and theorizing the experiences of six preservice English teachers in my university program and how they experienced professional identity development. In the following section I provide brief, introductory case studies of these participants for your referral as you continue through this volume.

PORTRAITS OF STUDENT PARTICIPANTS

I have chosen pseudonyms for the student participants to protect their privacy. Because I chose to structure the book around the genres of discourse they engaged in rather than write case studies of each of them as preservice teachers, I decided these short vignettes could be a useful point of reference. In recent years there have been numerous case studies of teachers that have added much to the knowledge of our field; however, rather than add to this existing body of such cases, I chose to structure this book around several genres of discourse that can help create a teacher.

Linda

Linda, 21 years old at the start of the study, was raised in a teacher family. She grew up in a small town in west central Indiana, and went to a rural school with approximately 500 students. Both her mother and grandmother were teachers, and Linda had known since high school that she wanted to follow in their footsteps. Linda was seeking a license to teach both English and social studies in middle and high school. I first met her when she enrolled in a course I taught at Purdue in the fall of 2000, called "Composition for Teachers."

Linda's mother was a fifth-grade teacher during most of Linda's life, and her father was a landscape contractor. She served as a "cadet teacher" (or teacher's aide) in her mother's class when she was a high school student, and she credited that experience for her decision to teach. Linda knew a lot about the teaching life from growing up and hearing her mother's discourse about being a middle school teacher. Many times, Linda talked to me about issues such as salary contracts, unions, discipline, and curriculum; she often sounded like a teaching veteran, and in a sense she was. Because both her mother and grandmother were teachers, she was comfortable and familiar with the "teacher life" and with teacher discourse; she was confident that she fully understood what being a teacher means. Linda believed that the methods classes she took at the university were a little unrealistic, when compared to her other teaching knowledge.

Similarly, Linda also seemed to know where her personal life would take her. Throughout most of the study, she was planning to get married the summer after graduation and begin her family life in a relatively traditional manner. After graduation, Linda took a job at a school near Indianapolis teaching seventh- and eighth-grade writing.

Janeen

I first met Janeen in the same class in which I met Linda—the "Composition for Teachers" course I taught in the fall of 2000. In fact, Linda and Janeen were roommates and best friends until they went separate ways to student teach. Janeen was a bridesmaid in Linda's wedding. Janeen was 21 years old at the beginning of the study, and came from a midsize town in northern Indiana where she had attended a large high school of approximately 1600 students. Her father was a union pipe fitter, and her mother a dental hygienist.

Janeen also was born into a "teacher family." Her brother was a social studies teacher, and her grandmother, an aunt, and an uncle were also teachers. Janeen began at the university as a pre-law student before deciding to become an English teacher, mostly because she said she realized the inadequacy of her own English preparation. To put it simply, she felt she could do a better job preparing college-bound students than her teachers had. Janeen was labeled "gifted" in elementary and secondary school, and her intelligence was obvious. However, she told stories of being bored in school and being given endless "busy work" that was not challenging for her.

Janeen student taught at an affluent school near the university that was well known for its high test scores and college attendance rates. Janeen had a positive relationship with her mentor teacher and tended to identify more with the practical ideologies apparent in the real school site, rather than with those prescribed in her education courses. Like Linda, she also took a teaching job after graduation, but at a large, urban high school in northeastern Indiana.

Lois

Lois was born and raised in southern Indiana, close to the Kentucky border, which accounted for her almost-southern accent. She was 21 years old at the beginning of the study, and she had two sisters who were close to her in age and with whom she communicated often. Her mother was a nurse, and her father worked as a lineman for an electric company, even though he had a degree in education. Lois started her university education as a pharmacy major, but switched to English education when she realized that she most enjoyed her English classes. She chose to teach primarily to be employable.

Lois loved school and learning, and enjoyed her student teaching. Lois studied abroad in England the summer after her junior year, and this experience was life changing for her. She talked about the experience to me often, and credited it, in part, for her desire to be a lifelong learner. She wanted to continue to travel, to learn new things, and to grow.

Lois had one of the most successful student teaching experiences of anyone in the study, and she and her mentor teacher had a positive working relationship. Lois was honest with her mentor teacher from the beginning about her perceived strengths and weaknesses, and this honesty enabled them to work together more effectively and for Lois' betterment. Lois did so well that she was offered and accepted a job the following year at the same school, "filling in" while her former mentor teacher went on a sabbatical. A year later, Lois decided to go to law school, and she was accepted at a small school in the upper Midwest. She stressed that this decision was not because of any negative feelings about teaching—she was just not yet done being a student.

Carrie

Carrie was a 21-year-old senior when she joined the research study. She joined a year later than the rest of the participants. I asked her to join the study because she appeared to be a thoughtful, reflective student who was struggling with her teacher identity. She came to the university to study computer engineering, but once here she decided to become a secondary English teacher, primarily because of her positive high school memories. Despite such positive experiences in high school, Carrie had a difficult time as a college student, struggling with persistent depression and feelings of inadequacy. She opted out of student teaching (and the education profession) at the last minute, graduating with an English degree only and eventually working for a moving company.

Carrie grew up in a midsize town in Massachusetts, and had 240 students in her graduating high school class. Carrie was from a working-class family; her mother was a single mother and worked as a secretary, and her two brothers were high school dropouts with blue-collar jobs. Carrie's mother was funding Carrie's education with a certain amount of sacrifice, of which Carrie was well aware. This financial hardship increased Carrie's desire to graduate on time, and it exacerbated her guilt when she decided not to pursue the career for which her education had prepared her. Carrie struggled with embodying a teacher identity, and her frustrations were often connected to her sexual orientation. Carrie was a lesbian who came out in high school. She was worried about how her "butch" or masculine appearance would be accepted in the teaching community. This concern about fitting into the culture created anxiety about teaching and a lack of self-confidence in the classroom.

Karen

Karen was 22 years old at the beginning of the study, and married to a student in computer engineering at the university. Her father was a supervisor at a local factory; her mother was a housewife. Like Carrie, Karen never student taught and decided not to teach after graduation—at least in the traditional way. Karen was from the same small town in which the university was located. She went to a midsize high school near the university, with 364 students in her graduating class. She was the mother of a young daughter, and, at the end of the study, she was pregnant with her second child.

Karen articulated tension between her personal and professional subjectivities, namely how to balance her family and career. She had multiple ideas about how she would integrate these two worlds. At different times she told me she would be a high school teacher, a bookstore owner, a graduate student in American studies, a creative writer, and an adult educator. At the end of our series of interviews she seemed settled on the bookstore idea. She thought the bookstore could be a venue for the facilitation of family literacy, and she believed she could include her own family in the enterprise.

In addition to the tensions between family and career, Karen's spiritual and political ideologies conflicted with her perception of public education. She couldn't see herself working in a system that she deemed overly politically correct, censored by left-wing bureaucrats, and even biased against poor, working-class, or minority students. A few months after the study ended, Karen told me that she had decided to pursue a Master's degree in adult education at another university. She was continuing her struggle to integrate her personal ideologies with her professional identity.

Sandy

Sandy was a 22-year-old junior when she began the study. I met her, along with Linda and Janeen, when she took the "Composition for Teachers" course in the fall of 2000. She excelled in this course because of her tutoring experience in the university writing lab. Sandy was from a small Indiana town an hour north of the university campus, and she had attended a rural high school with only 66 students in her graduating class. Her father was the manager of a fertilizer plant; her mother worked in human resources at a farm co-op. Her brother was also a high school teacher and coach, and she often sought him out for advice.

Sandy had a "mixed" student teaching experience. Although she was successful overall, she did not have a positive relationship with her school-based mentor teacher, and she lost some confidence in herself as a teacher because of the experience. She did not feel as if she received much support or guidance.

Sandy was a very good writing tutor by all accounts, and she often compared her feelings about being a tutor with those of being a teacher. She found that she was more comfortable being a tutor than she was teaching because, in part, she did not have the final call on students' grades, nor did she have to prepare daily lessons to teach in class. She preferred this more indirect role of "facilitator," which seemed to her to be an interim space between the "student" and "teacher" identities. Interestingly, after graduation, Sandy took a job with an educational company that provided tutoring to young people with reading problems. At this point in her professional and personal identity development, Sandy found tutoring to be more comfortable than teaching.

Chapter 2

What Does It Mean to Be a Secondary School Teacher?

> In our rush to reform education, we have forgotten a simple truth: reform will never be achieved by renewing appropriations, restructuring schools, rewriting curricula, and revising texts if we continue to demean and dishearten the human resource called the teacher on whom so much depends. (Palmer, 1998, p. 3)
>
> I'm not a box person. (Karen, preservice teacher participant)

Those who have been high school or middle school teachers know that secondary school teaching is demanding work. They have taught 130-plus adolescents per day, have spent weekends and evenings grading papers and planning lessons, and have negotiated the competing demands of various stakeholders including administrators, community leaders, colleagues, and students. They also know that the profession is often perceived, both by "insiders" and "outsiders," as being *more* than a job—instead, as a way of life or a "calling." A teacher is defined as an individual who should go above and beyond the call of duty for the benefit of the young people with whom he or she works, with no expectation of extra reward, much less even adequate compensation.

This definition of teaching as calling has both positive and negative consequences for those in the profession. On the bright side, cultural conceptions of teachers as heroes should mean that they are revered and respected. A recent series of television ads, for example, featured a voice-over urging young people to "Be a hero. Teach." Coffee cups and bumper stickers proclaiming "Teachers Make a Difference" are ubiquitous. However, the dark side, and also the fundamental irony, of such constructions is that only rarely are teachers the recipients of such reverence in American culture. Because standards of performance are so high, and the price of service is so great, few teachers are awarded this hero status; the rest are labeled mediocre at best, or simply inadequate. The "standards" movement that was born in the 1980s and the current push for "accountability" that began in the 1970s with Leon Lessinger's *Every Kid a Winner: Accountability in Education* (1970) were, in part, results of these harsh, public judgments of teachers. The prevailing opinion is that teachers and administrators in the public schools are slacking off and nobody is doing anything about it; therefore, the tax-paying American public must step up and make sure that educators do their jobs.

The first few years of teaching are even more difficult than remaining in the profession as an experienced teacher. According to Dwight L. Rogers and Leslie M. Babinski (2002), much has been written about the problems of new teachers, and ample research has been conducted on the topic (Bell & Gilbert, 1994; Bullough, 1987; Feiman-Nemser, 1983; Fuller, 1969; Grant & Zeichner, 1981; Kestner, 1994; Ryan, 1970; Veenman, 1984). Yet, Rogers and Babinski stated, "despite all of the research and all of the books and articles written about the difficulties endured by beginning teachers, the first year of teaching continues to be an exceptionally difficult time for most of them" (p. 2). All of the research and writing conducted by educational researchers, although published by respected journals and academic presses, has not really helped the new teacher. In fact, only 50% of new teachers' careers last longer than 5 years (Gordon, 1991; Huling-Austin, Odell, Ishler, Kay, & Edelfelt, 1989). And, if that isn't bad enough, Robert Bullough (1987) noted, "many of the teachers who remain in classrooms end up teaching in ways that are inconsistent and even contradictory to their initial pedagogical beliefs, goals, and expectations" (quoted in Rogers & Babinski, 2002, p. 3). They cannot find ways to teach as they were taught during their university education, so they revert to lifesaving measures that simply keep them afloat in the classroom, such as traditional teacher-centered methods of lecture and closed questioning.

Some international research supports Bullough's findings about discrepancies between university education courses and real-life experience. For example, German educational research has shown that preservice teachers become more cynical about students and schools, as well as more conservative and authoritarian, as their teacher education progresses. The greater the discrepancy between what these preservice teachers learned in college and what they experienced in field settings, the greater was this trend to negativity (Hans Gerhard Klinzing, in Tisher & Wideen, 1990, p. 94). Kenneth Zeichner (1987), an American educational researcher, has studied connections and disconnections between field experiences and educational coursework and has suggested that teacher educators consider how their program goals and philosophies are manifested in field sites as well as in the college classroom. Otherwise, it may seem to preservice teachers that their university professors are completely unaware of the challenges they face in real secondary classrooms, and they may choose to disregard university knowledge as irrelevant. As shown later in this text, some of the students in this study made just such a choice as they confronted contradictions between university- and field-based knowledge.

The cyclical rhetoric of educational failure and reform began in the United States in the 1950s, when the launch of *Sputnik* first caused Americans to fear international academic competition, especially in math and science. In 1955, the publication of Rudolph Flesch's *Why Johnny Can't Read—and What You Can Do About It* prompted a furor of anger against public schools and public school teachers, who seemed to be failing "Johnny" by not teaching phonics. Three decades later, *A Nation At Risk* (National Commission on Excellence in Education, 1983) was published by the National Commission on Excellence in Education appointed by President Reagan's Department of Education Secretary Terrel H. Bell, and a number of reports were unleashed about the "failure" of American elementary and secondary schools. After *A Nation at Risk*, more than 30 similar reports followed within the next 10 years, sponsored by special interest groups, commissions, and professional organizations (Pulliam, 1991).

Gerald W. Bracey, author of *What You Should Know About the War Against America's Public Schools* (2003b), wrote an article for the *Phi Delta Kappan* reflecting on the 20th anniversary of *A Nation at Risk* (2003a). He argued that at the time of the report's publication, there was a deliberate political effort, spearheaded by James Baker, Ronald Reagan's chief of staff, and Mike Deever, Reagan's close advisor, to deliberately suppress any good news about America's public schools and to attempt to correlate low test scores with lack of international competitiveness. Bracey called this connection "hokum" and provided evidence that the authors of *A Nation at Risk* stated incorrect and even nonexistent statistics, and that Deputy Secretary of Education David Kearns suppressed other positive reports of educational progress, such as the "Sandia Report" (Carson, Huelskamp, & Woodall, 1991). This report was compiled in 1990 by engineers at Sandia National Laboratories in Albuquerque, and presented evidence supporting the theory that "there was no systemwide crisis" in public education (Bracey, 2003a, p. 617). However, public belief in the failure of American education seemed to suit political agendas. As Bracey wrote:

> Alas nothing else is new, and, indeed we must recognize that good news about public schools serves no one's reform agenda—even if it does make teachers, students, parents, and administrators feel a little better. Conservatives want vouchers and tuition tax credits; liberals want more resources for schools; free marketers want to privatize the schools and make money; fundamentalists

want to teach religion and not worry about the First Amendment; Catholic schools want to stanch their student hemorrhage; home schooling advocates want just that; and various groups no doubt just want to be with "their own kind." All groups believe they will improve their chances of getting what they want if they pummel the publics. (2003, p. 621)

Such rhetoric of failure continued throughout the phonics/whole language debate of the late 1980s and early 1990s. It continued into the 21st century with George W. Bush's No Child Left Behind Act (2001), which reauthorized and modified the Elementary and Secondary Education Act of 1965, proclaiming the failure of teacher education and heralding the need for improving "teacher quality" as well as student achievement. Bracey called No Child Left Behind a "weapon of mass destruction" (2003, p. 621) against the public school system. The semantics of these reports are so ideologically loaded that they almost preclude rational debate: Who would argue for leaving a child behind? Who wouldn't want "Johnny" to be able to read? Well, no one, of course, and perhaps least of all the classroom teacher.

The practicing teacher has experienced (been subjected to) many local and regional educational initiatives associated with these larger political debates. For example, since the 1970s there have been scrambles to "align" curriculum and "train" teachers in methods of "mastery learning," "outcomes-based" education, "performance-based" education, and finally "competency-based" education. In the 1980s, the Council for Basic Education (founded by the Moral Majority) was formed, and its call to arms was "back to the basics." In 1978, the Supreme Court ruled that the National Teachers Exam (NTE) was not discriminatory against African Americans, despite the uneven test scores, and most states began to use it to license teachers (Pulliam, 1991, p. 219). Also, since the 1970s, there has been an undeniable trend toward more accountability for teachers, less trust in their professional and intellectual abilities (leading to a decrease in the professional ethos of the secondary teacher), and increased attempts to control education by government, civic, or religious organizations.

It is easy for a teacher, new or experienced, to become cynical about all of these initiatives, especially those top-down mandates from state or federal departments of education with little additional funding to support extra work. Kenneth M. Zeichner and Daniel P. Liston (1996) addressed the bureaucratic control of elementary and secondary education:

Rules, regulations, and mandates outside of teachers' control and influence often exert severe constraints on the freedom of teachers to act on the basis of their own practical theories. A good deal of literature has accumulated in recent years specifying in much detail the various ways in which teachers have been constrained by cultural and institutional forces, including attempts to micromanage schools by state departments (Wise, 1979), the influence of textbook companies (Apple, 1993), school district policies on curriculum, in-

> struction, and staff development (Lieberman & Miller, 1991), the structure of teachers' work, which includes such factors as large class sizes, and little planning time (Freedman, Jackson, & Boles, 1983), and the forms of reasoning and rationality that underlie these and other efforts to control teaching and teachers (Popkewitz, 1991). (p. 43)

If the media coverage of education is any indication, being a teacher in America grows even *more* difficult because the general public seems increasingly suspicious of the teacher. Television news and made-for-TV movies seem particularly eager to tell stories about the teacher who failed, sometimes in extreme and scandalous ways. Consider the cases of Mary Kay Letourneau, the teacher convicted of having an affair with a 13-year-old student, and Tanya Hadden, a San Bernardino science teacher who ran off to Las Vegas with her 15-year-old student. Although no one advocates or supports these clearly inappropriate and illegal acts, the national media attention about them reveals something about the cultural expectations for a teacher and the public eagerness to point out failings. In other words, the hero has fallen, so the rest of us are somehow made better in the face of his or her decline.

To be fair, the media spotlight sometimes falls on the stories of hero teachers, the teachers who are clear successes and therefore represent the ideal to which all "good" teachers strive. However, these stories are also problematic for American educators who struggle with developing a professional identity. These hero teachers show up in news stories about teaching awards or in "human interest" segments that sentimentalize how they have worked overtime, or spent their own money, or otherwise sacrificed for their students' benefit. Although I am happy that such recognition is given, I wish it weren't quite so rare and given primarily to showcase personal sacrifice. The hero teachers have common characteristics of selflessness and complete dedication to their pupils—but often enough at the expense of their personal lives, families, economic stability, and emotional/mental health. Hero teachers, according to our prevailing cultural myth, are willing to sacrifice themselves in order to dedicate their lives to students.

A binary is at work in the definition of teacher identity: The teacher is depicted as failure or hero, villain or angel. Most people I have met can tell stories about both types of teachers from their educational histories. They have ready, internalized narratives for each contrasting characterization of "teacher," which they can relate on demand and in support of the educational argument du jour. The 2-year research process I describe in this book provides a deeper perspective on teachers' struggle to transcend this binary, and urges a recognition of the various and sometimes contrasting subjectivities and associated ideologies that are present as teachers enact their professional selves.

There is another fundamental paradox in the cultural model of teacher in the United States, one that affects teacher education: For a teacher to be a hero, our society says he or she must be selfless; however, only the teacher who has developed a rich, well-rounded identity, or sense of self, is truly successful in the classroom. Thus, the successful teacher must be selfless and selfish at the same time, a seemingly impossible seesaw to balance. Among the participants in my study, only the preservice teachers who had a strong sense of their personal identity and its connection or disconnection with their professional identity were able to successfully transition into the profession. In other words, they needed to be "self-actualized" (to use the phrase coined by Abraham Maslow in 1962 and later used by bell hooks in 1994) to whatever extent possible. Self-actualization refers to self-awareness and reflexivity about the intersections of various aspects of self—namely the intellectual/cognitive, the emotional/affective, and the physical/material. Among the participants in my study, if such self-actualization had not occurred, the preservice teacher chose not to enter the profession immediately, and if she did take a teaching job, she was likely to experience future professional identity crises.

Perhaps most readers of this book will not argue with this premise of self-actualization as precursor to professional success; in fact, perhaps some, especially the elementary and secondary teachers, will see it as self-evident. The problem is that often teacher educators do not enact or engage in holistic pedagogies that encourage this more comprehensive model of growth. Instead, methods, pedagogy, or education courses might focus on the acquisition of discrete knowledge or skill sets that preservice teachers should know to be successful (e.g., state educational standards, lesson planning, adolescent psychology, canonical texts, etc.). Such knowledge and skills are relatively easy to teach and assess, and in this age of accountability and standards, the easier-to-implement partial models of preservice education are taking on an ever-increasing importance, to the neglect of a more comprehensive model. For example, at my institution, state and national standards for teacher education must be "mapped" or connected to our curricula, and our success in teaching them is evaluated by the NCATE (National Council for Accreditation of Teacher Education) every 7 years. This method of assessment really only measures the knowledge base and skill sets being taught, which, although important, are not necessarily a satisfactory evaluation of the total preparedness of our preservice teachers.

Additionally, teacher educators, most often university professors, have been indoctrinated to accept the Cartesian mind–body split and, hence, tend to value the intellectual over the emotional or physical. Knowledge is sometimes misunderstood as being purely intellectual or cognitive because the mind is what is valued in academe, so long dominated by patriarchal and scientific paradigms of rationality and logic. The building of holistic teacher identity is complicated further because of this stratification by default. Women educators historically have been associated with the bodily or physical and the emotional aspects of knowledge, whereas men have been identified as possessors of the superior intellectual or rational capabilities. These hypotheses of male/female teacher identity are clearly reductive in their binarism. Because teachers since from the mid-19th century have been predominately women,[1] the profession of teaching, as well as the individual female teacher, has often suffered the tyrannies of gender discrimination. In modern times, administrators (mostly male) and teacher educators have tried very hard to counteract this stereotype and convince others that they are *not* focused on the affective or the bodily more than on the intellectual or cognitive, given that these ways of knowing are not historically privileged in a patriarchal society. Hence, such attempts at defending professional integrity and intellectualism have led, in part, to the suppression and devaluing of multiple and alternative ways of knowing.

Despite nearly 30 years of postmodern thought, many academics still operate in the land of the binary, accepting a hierarchal division between the intellect and the affect. Even when they are aware of the recent theoretical rejection of this oversimplified binary heralded by poststructuralist thinkers such as Derrida, Foucault, and Deleuze, sometimes there is not much change in their pedagogy. And when there is change, it can seem to be a superficial nod to the notion of holistic education. Teacher educators, often relegated to lower faculty status in the university environment, seem particularly tentative about including anything in their curricula that could be perceived as anti-intellectual, a perception that they are eager to neutralize. Thus, coupled with the fact that most teachers are comfortable staying on the intellectual plane and not dealing with the "messy" emotional or bodily aspects of growth and learning, the teaching of teachers has focused on developing the intellect, the cognitive aspect of learning to teach, without recognizing that to separate the intellectual from the affective or the physical is unproductive, even impossible. New teachers will either have to figure out how to connect these multiple ways of knowing and being on their own, or they will fail. Although teaching in America may be one of the most difficult professions in existence today, teacher educators can make the induction phase of the new teacher easier through assignments that encourage the expres-

[1]A survey of public school teachers conducted in 1996 by the National Education Association showed a total of 2,164,000 public school teachers in American schools, of which 74.4% were women, 90.7% were White, and 75.9% were married (NEA Research, 2004).

sion of various genres of teacher identity discourse leading to the development of a holistic teacher identity.

A SHORT HISTORY OF TEACHER EDUCATION AND THE TEACHER

To return to the opening questions: What does it mean to be a secondary school teacher in today's America? What do teachers need to know and be able to do? What knowledge and behavior most consistently result in effective teaching? Since the 19th century and the appearance of the first public high schools and Normal schools (training schools for teachers), dozens of theorists, researchers, and teacher educators have attempted to answer these questions. Some theorists have asserted that being a teacher has something to do with having many practical experiences in the field on which one can reflect (Borko, Eisenhart, et al., 1992; Clift, 1990; Dewey, 1938/1963; Schon, 1983). Others say that to teach means knowing your disciplinary content thoroughly (Bodenhausen, 1989; Ferguson & Womack, 1993; Goldhaber & Brewer, 1998) or being able to "control" or manage a class of 30-plus adolescents (Rosiek, 1994). Still others believe that being a good teacher necessitates pedagogical preparation and the development of a certain type of teaching philosophy or approach, whether that stance be critical, progressive, behaviorist, constructivist, or traditional, or requires certain knowledge about educational psychology and adolescent cognitive development (Freire, 1970/1993; Giroux, 1997; Grossman, 1989; Hawk, Coble, & Swanson, 1985; Shor, 1987). Of course, there are the most ambitious teacher educators who think *all* of these characteristics are essential for effective teaching.

These types of professional knowledge are neither unimportant nor unnecessary; however, I argue that in addition to and perhaps more important than any of the above traits, secondary school teachers must develop a sense of professional identity that successfully incorporates their personal subjectivities into the professional/cultural expectations of what it means to be a "teacher." This incorporation, this merging, this professional identity formation happens through a new teacher's participation in various genres of discourse that facilitate a dialogic engagement with students, mentors, teacher educators, family, and peers, and even internal dialogues with other personal subjectivities or ideologies. Such discourse, as it becomes more complex and sophisticated, results in a more effective physical and emotional embodiment of teacher identity as well as increased intellectual competence. This is not to say that the eventual goal of the teacher is to iron out all ideological tension; such unity of subjectivities is not likely, or even necessarily desirable. However, the various identity strands making up the teacher's self should be able to coexist to the extent that a professional life—for example, the teaching life—can be enacted efficiently and effectively—at least most of the time.

As I write this, teacher education is being hotly debated as President George W. Bush and Secretary of Education Rod Paige have endorsed the No Child Left Behind Act that calls for improving teacher quality through a reform of teacher education institutions and increased accountability (i.e., student testing).[2] The goal is to make sure that all teachers are "highly qualified" by the year 2006. On my desk sits a 117-page call for proposals for the "Improving Teacher Quality State Grants" authorized under Title II, Part A of the No Child Left Behind Act. This grant funds professional development and related activities to increase the quality and preparedness of elementary and secondary teachers. The techniques and strategies deemed effective by researchers should be supported by "scientific" research, which the grant document defines as "research that applies rigorous, systematic, and objective procedures to obtain valid knowledge relevant to improving student academic achievement" (p. 6). These procedural options include experimental or quasi-experimental research designs, such as control groups, randomized assignments, empirical methods, measures of reliability and validity, and acceptance in peer-reviewed journals.

The implication is that high-quality teachers can be created through the application of teacher education and professional development that has been "scientifically" proven to be effective. However, many who have worked in education for years are skeptical about the kind of knowledge that such research yields. Although it might be helpful to a certain extent,[3] scientific research seems to be lacking when it comes to understanding the complexity and variety of students in secondary school classrooms and how to best meet their educational and personal needs. For example, it is difficult to scientifically "prove" that a particular pedagogical method causes improved reading "skill" or that the method's use translates to improved scores on standardized tests. How do you control other variables that may be affecting the students' learning, including home environment, peer in-

---

[2]The No Child Left Behind Act was not the first government proposal to criticize and suggest revisions to teacher education. Following *A Nation at Risk* in 1983, there were several proposals published calling for reforms and improvements to teacher education, often through increased state-sponsored accountability, including the Carnegie Task Force on Teaching as a Profession's *A Nation Prepared: Teachers for the 21st Century* (1986), the Holmes Group's *Tomorrow's Teachers: A Report of the Holmes Group* (1986), the National Commission on Excellence in Teacher Education's *A Call for Change in Teacher Education* (1985), and the National Consortium for Educational Excellence's *An Agenda for Educational Research: A View from the Firing Line* (1984).

[3]For example, scientific research has led to some useful understandings of memory and retention. Also, miscue analysis—a quantitative approach to reading assessment—can yield much useful information for a classroom teacher.

teraction, and motivation? It is more difficult to devise a scientific experiment when the subjects are human beings.

An opposite approach to evaluating good teaching is equally oversimplified. In many middle and high schools, it seems that the definition of a good or successful teacher is quite straightforward and requires no supporting research: A successful instructor keeps his or her students under control (quiet, "on task") and seldom approaches the principal with problems or difficulties. Additionally, the students of this ideal teacher should score high on state tests so as not to cause any concern on the part of administrators or parents. In other words, *invisibility* to these administrators and stakeholders is rewarded. The better a teacher does his or her job, the less that teacher should be seen and heard; the greater the visibility of a teacher, the greater the likelihood that he or she is a troublemaker or incompetent. Teachers should teach alone, with doors closed; if they are called to the office, or if a parent phones, it is usually not good. The teacher, like the student, can be chastised for being disruptive.

An example of such bad behavior is a teacher strike, and the most questionable teachers are those involved with unions. The general public, school administrators, and teachers themselves routinely villainize the teacher's union.[4] The idea of teachers being political simply does not "fit" with the idealized vision of the selfless, sacrificial teacher. A story in *The Washington Times* described a report released on February 26, 2003, by the 11-member Koret Task Force on K–12 Education that "primarily blames the National Educational Association (NEA) and the American Federation of Teachers (AFT), the two main teachers unions, for hampering school improvement" (Archibald, 2003, p. A06). The reason asserted is the overriding agenda of the unions in retaining teachers, at any and all costs.

Preferred and rewarded invisibility has been a dominant characteristic of the cultural model of teacher over the last century of American public schooling. Even though teachers were being criticized and alarm bells were ringing about U.S. education, the individual teacher was rewarded for keeping quiet. One of the recommendations of *A Nation at Risk* was to have "better prepared, better rewarded, and more highly respected teachers" (National Commission on Excellence, 1983, p. 97), although there were few stated strategies for realization, and even fewer ideas with state or federal funding attached.

Educational critiques and rhetorics of educational failure were evident decades before *A Nation At Risk*. In 1963, James D. Koerner argued that the "inferior intellectual quality of the Education faculty is the fundamental

[4]See *The Worm in the Apple: How the Teacher Unions Are Destroying American Education*, by Peter Brimelow (2003). Additionally and more recently, then Secretary of Education Rod Paige called the NEA (National Education Association) a "terrorist organization" during comments made to the nation's governors at a private White House meeting on February 23, 2004.

limitation of the field" (p. 238) when speaking of American public school teachers. Even earlier in U.S. history, in the first half of the 19th century, two Normal school administrators in Massachusetts—Horace Mann and Cyrus Peirce—expressed disappointment with the quality and motivation of their teacher education students who were mostly young, previously uneducated, working- or middle-class women seeking social advancement (Warren, 1989). Since the mid-1900s, the teaching profession has been dominated by White women, often young single women, using teaching as a space filler until marriage, or even as explicit preparation for marriage and childrearing. According to some sources I consulted (Hoffman, 2003; Warren, 1989), they were often not educated enough to demand professional respect, and even when they were, their status as young females made it unlikely that their opinions about the profession or about their preparation would be heard or honored.

Warren (1989) noted that in the 19th century and into the first part of the 20th century, the teacher workforce was basically transient in nature, underprepared, and immature; with these characteristics it was difficult to develop a strong professional identity or respected cultural presence. Instead, teachers were, even then, taken for granted in American society; they could be counted on to be present in the classroom and ready to teach (even if their qualifications were debatable). However, they were not paid very highly, their needs were not recognized, and, to make matters worse, they often left the profession as soon as possible, such as when a proposal of marriage was accepted. On the other hand, it is safe to say that there were two reasons for young women to enter the teaching profession in the early 20th century: either to prepare for marriage or to build a life for themselves outside of the confines of marriage. For young women who wanted to continue their education and postpone marriage and children, teaching was one of the few pathways available to them to have an independent life. From this perspective, young female teachers may have been among the most intellectually motivated of their gender.

Historically, the teaching profession has been marginalized for several possible reasons: It has been a primarily female occupation,[5] it has a tendency to attract middle- or working-class individuals who are sometimes more weakly prepared academically than are their upper-class counterparts, and it is often considered a transitory profession as male teachers advance to administrative jobs and women teachers often leave the profession, at least temporarily, to begin families. In the 18th century, men were the schoolmasters, and their reputation was that of disciplinarians who didn't hesitate to use the "cane" on a troublesome student. In the 19th century, the

[5]Warren (1989) noted that, in the 1980s, 70% of elementary and secondary teachers were women; according to the National Center for Educational Statistics, in 1999–2000, 75% of public school teachers were women.

feminization of teaching began because of growing professional opportunities for men and increasing numbers of students to be taught. With the increase in the number of factories and the rise of mechanization, more men began working away from the home and farm; women were more often relegated to the domestic arena, and motherhood and housewifery became their roles. Therefore, the cultural model of the male disciplinarian began to decline, in favor of the mother teacher. The woman was seen as the ideal teacher, because it was believed to be her biological nature to nurture and care for children. In a 1846 public address, Catherine Beecher argued, "women were natural-born teachers because they had the predisposition—the patience, the self-sacrifice, the moral superiority—to attend to the development of children" (Schell, 1997, p. 23).

It was not until the 1950s that the taboo against married teachers, enforced both formally and informally, was lifted, and teaching instead became a career that was consistent with marriage and motherhood. At least in part because of a lack of ample teachers to fill the need in growing schools, public opinion began to allow, and even favor, the married teacher, as long as the home was still her first priority. Clifford quoted an advocate of married teachers as saying, "The important task of educating the young should be entrusted to women who lead a *normal life*" (i.e., married, heterosexual women; my emphasis; Clifford, 1989, p. 314). Consequently, in the 1950s, the "spinster teacher" disappeared and married teachers became the norm.

The notion of teacher as "mother figure" or "nurturer" became more common by the middle of the 19th century, as the male schoolmaster of the 18th century was being displaced, and this trend was firmly established by the mid 20th century. According to the 1950 census figures, three quarters of American teachers in that year were women (Rury, 1989). One could say that the profession was beginning its "ghetto-ization" of women, who were consistently relegated to underpaid and undervalued teaching jobs. Their professional options were very limited, whereas men advanced to higher-status professional jobs or became administrators in the schools. The reader may note that all of the preservice teachers included in my study are women; this gender imbalance is reflective of the overall percentage of female students in the English education program at my institution. As of spring 2003, 73% of the English education students at Purdue University were female, and 99% were White.

The first teacher training institution in the United States was the Troy New York Female Seminary, created in 1821. The academy of Samuel R. Hall in 1823 in Concord, Vermont, soon followed (Ginsburg, 1988). State Normal schools for teacher education first sprang up in Massachusetts, when the legislature established four Normal schools in 1838, years after the first public high school for boys opened in Boston in 1821. The first high school admitting girls was not opened until 1855; however, Normal schools were primarily attended by young women. The goals of 19th century teacher education were the provision of a very basic general education and the guarantee that these teachers could provide a sort of moral guidance to the young. The schools were to offer instruction in "spelling, reading, writing, grammar, geography, arithmetic, and if time allowed rhetoric, logic, geometry, bookkeeping, navigation, surveying, history, physiology, mental and natural philosophy, and always 'the principles of piety and morality common to all sects of Christians'" (Herbst, 1989, p. 218). Academic requirements were kept low and students were admitted for a few weeks at a time during seasons when they couldn't work in farming or teaching. The Normal schools had little or no focus on pedagogical content knowledge or theories about teaching and learning.

Increasingly, women saw teaching as a compromise between society's demand that women stay in the home and their own desire to work and be present in society. Between 1820 and 1860, the United States experienced the opening of 200 female academies and seminaries, a handful of women's colleges, and the beginning of coeducation at Oberlin (Newcomer, 1959). By 1872, over 70 Normal schools were receiving some grant support, and by 1900 there were 345 in the United States (Pulliam, 1991). Most of the students in these Normal schools were women. In 1880, the percentage of women elementary and secondary teachers rose to 57%, and was up to 84% by 1918. Even though women worked for much less money than did their male counterparts, many still viewed teaching as a way to improve their lives and their social standing through the maintenance of a regular salary and a respected occupation.

The history of the African American teacher is a little different than for the white teacher, although this is not to say that gender discrimination did not occur. However, education and the profession of teaching were accorded a slightly higher status in 19th- and early 20th-century African American communities. Teaching was more often viewed as an honorable profession. After the Civil War and into Reconstruction, African Americans would become teachers not only for personal, social advancement, but also to "uplift" their race (Perkins, 1989, p. 345). Because very few slaves were legally allowed to become literate, African Americans understood the social and political power of education more clearly than did their White counterparts. However, African Americans were not always admitted into the first Normal schools, and many received their education at Oberlin College in Ohio, one of very few predominately White colleges in the late 1800s to admit African Americans and women on a regular basis. Additionally, in 1867, Howard University was incorporated as an institution for the training of African American teachers and preachers, and in 1875, Booker T. Washington founded and became a teacher in one of the first African American Normal schools at Tuskegee, Alabama (Pulliam, 1991). Although many northern universities began to be open to minorities between the Civil War and World War I, African American applicants were often screened out because of entrance requirements that eliminated graduates from the poorest public schools (Pulliam, 1991).

With the Civil Rights Movement of the 1950s and 1960s, doors of predominately White schools opened to African American students. The numbers of minorities attending college has been steadily increasing since statistics have been kept. In 1976, 17.4% of minorities (including African Americans, Hispanics, Asian or Pacific Islanders, American Indians, and Alaskan Natives) attended college, compared with 26.4% in 1995 (11% of this 26.4% were African American; U.S. Department of Education National Center for Education Statistics, 2000). However, at the present time, African Americans, both male and female, are sadly underrepresented in the teaching profession. A 1996 survey of public school teachers conducted by the National Education Association revealed that 90.7% of elementary and secondary public school teachers in the United States were White, the de facto prevailing cultural image of teacher. However, the Department of Education National Center for Education Statistics reported that, in the same year, 31.3% of all elementary and secondary students in the United States were either African American or Hispanic, and in urban areas the percentage jumped to 56.9% (U.S. Department of Education National Center for Education Statistics, 2000). It's clear that teacher educators have much work to do to recruit African American students into the teaching profession, as well as provide for their professional growth.

Some of the historical beliefs about public education and what it should do for American society have persisted until today, and they still affect the conditions under which teachers take on professional identities and work. In 1975, Dan Lortie wrote a much-cited ethnography of teachers working in a school in the Boston area, and he described their work as constrained by conservative cultural scripts of teaching and reasons for choosing the profession. He connected the history of education in the United States to the present state of education in our country, and he conducted a sociological study of the teacher. He wrote that teaching, unlike other professions, is constrained by perceptions of the job with which new teachers enter the field. For example, preservice teachers, unlike preservice lawyers or doctors, come to their teacher education with 12-plus years of experience interacting with and watching model teachers on a daily basis. Therefore, they think they have a notion of what a teacher's job is like and what a good teacher does. They have watched many teachers over the years, and they think they have developed a good sense of what distinguishes the successful from the not successful.

This is mixed news for the teacher educator. Positively, the education student's mind is not a blank slate, and there is plenty of prior knowledge on which to build; the negative flipside is that the student comes in with an entire set of internal narratives that define what, to him or her, a teacher is. And all of these are not positive images or consistent with what research and theory have demonstrated comprises good pedagogy. Therefore, the teacher educator must challenge these narratives, these cultural scripts, these ideologies, and build new ones in their place. Lortie called this the "apprenticeship of observation"—teaching based on imitation, not active construction of choices.

It is striking how the cultural script or model of the teacher has been fairly consistent for over a century now. Many of the characteristics I've been describing—of overwhelmingly White, young, female, middle-class, poorly paid, "mother" figures—are applicable today, and many of these qualities were cited by students in this study as included in their perception of the idealized secondary teacher. A prescient Pauline Annin Galvarro described the average teacher in America this way in her 1945 doctoral dissertation:

> The type, teacher, is traditionally so well established in this country that the pronoun *she* is universally used to refer to the teacher, and she is generally presumed to be single and serious—a young woman of "fine ideals." She no longer dresses queerly, and her hair and fingernails are carefully groomed, but she is expected to be above many things which other people do, and when she is invited to dinner, a rather dull evening is anticipated. Many superintendents carefully inquire before employing her whether she smokes, drinks, dances, or plays cards. There are employing superintendents who ask her whether she is sure she will not be married for two years, and there is at least one school board that forbids men and women teachers to have social relations. (p. 1)

This description of the secondary or elementary school teacher in the United States could be used to describe today's teacher, to a certain extent; change some of the anachronistic vocabulary, and the same criteria are, frighteningly enough, relatively applicable. The image of the teacher as a morally upright, serious woman remains today.

Media images of teachers have vacillated between binary poles symbolized either by the male schoolmaster or the female mother. Movies like *Stand and Deliver* and *American History X* depicted the teacher as disciplinarian and purveyor of "tough love" against incredible odds; films like *Dead Poets Society* envisioned the teacher as heroic nurturer, often at odds with the more discipline-minded administration. When teachers are characters in movies, television shows, and even books, they are often played as dim-witted, old-fashioned, unreasonable, ridiculous, and, at the very least, irrelevant. The TV show *Boston Public* might be an exception, as it featured younger, more hip teachers who were dealing with social problems in addition to teaching course content. However, the story lines "pulled from real life" were often violent or erotic, and followed the media tradition of exposing the extreme, both positive and negative. Images of teachers are ubiquitous in our society, and for the most part these images exist at binary poles, and often appear as distinct choices for the preservice teacher.

In this study, when I asked students to describe qualities of English teachers they had worked with or known, I received various answers consistent with these binary poles; furthermore, when I asked students to talk about the system or the structure of public schools, the expectations that exist within the system, and demands that are placed on the system by community and parents, the descriptions became more narrow and restraining. All of the students, at some point in the series of interviews, talked to me about how they believed they would be restrained or contained (the metaphor of a "box" was frequently used) by the characteristics of the system in which they would work. For example, they believed they would be restricted in their choices of texts to teach, would not be able to talk about certain issues in class because these issues would be deemed morally inappropriate and therefore not proper for a public school setting, and would have to dress or act a certain way for the benefit of those who may be judging their suitability for the job.

Reynolds (1996) wrote that as early as 1900, "the script for secondary school teachers and administrators at all levels called for white males of Judeo Christian beliefs, preferably mature and married, definitely heterosexual and supportive of the dominant political climate of the day" (p. 73). She also stated how shocked she was that stories collected from teachers in the 1900s described scripting and stereotyping similar to that experienced by today's teachers. Students in my study told stories about when they encountered such cultural scripts in their field placements and how they responded to the challenges these cultural scripts presented.

Although the quality and preparedness of teachers in our elementary and secondary schools have been an issue for nearly as long as teachers' existence, the fact that they need preparation of *some* kind seems to be universally accepted. Today's teacher education institutions try to teach disciplinary content, pedagogical content knowledge, the basics of educational research, and learning theories, all within a 4-year program. This is a tall order. However, because many of the teacher education students in our universities and colleges today still come from working- or middle-class backgrounds (Rury, 1989) they are eager to be on the job market in 4 years and making a salary soon after; therefore, lengthening a teacher education program is usually not a popular idea.

I attended one of these modern teacher education schools in the 1980s, at a large land grant university in the Midwest. I believe I received a good education in content, pedagogy, and learning theory; however, upon graduation, this education still wasn't enough for me to know how to be successful in my profession, and I believe such preparation is not enough for many other secondary school teachers. I struggled with how to become a teacher; I always felt as if I was simply playing a role, not taking on an identity, when I stepped in front of my class. I did not know at the time why I was having trouble thinking of myself as a teacher; I simply knew I was not succeeding in the classroom as I had hoped to. I now believe that being successful as a teacher means more than being able to keep classroom control, being able to present your content clearly, or being able to manage your classroom with confidence and organization. Success as a teacher is attached to a sense of professional identity that integrates the intellectual, the emotional, and the physical aspects of the teacher's life as well as taking on the subjectivities of "teacher." It means being able to combine what I call the core identity or personal beliefs and sense of self with a professional identity that in our culture is often very narrowly and rigidly defined. This transformative turn can be challenging for the preservice teacher.

DEFINING THE BORDERLAND

Borderland discourse is a central concept in this book, and, as such, it deserves a careful definition. However, such defining is difficult, in part because borderland discourse is not a singular, unitary type of discourse that can be identified easily based on linguistic features. Instead, it is complex discourse reflecting metacognition or critical reflection that seemed influential in the development of the preservice teachers' professional identities. As I analyzed the data from the participants for reccurring themes and concepts, I often saw evidence of contrasting identity positions creating a productive tension or cognitive dissonance. During qualitative coding of the interview transcripts and textual artifacts, I identified borderland discourse as discourse in which there is evidence of contact between disparate personal and professional subjectivities and in which this contact appears to be leading toward the ideological integration of multiple senses of self. I argue that such integration through discourse can lead to cognitive, emotional, and corporeal change, or identity growth.

I wish to make it clear that I was able to identify these examples as borderland discourse in part because I came to know the students so very well over the time of the study. It's a certainty that if I were to analyze the discourse of strangers, I could not identify such ideological tension. For example, I knew when Linda was struggling with the intersections of her home discourse, or narratives of family, and her narratives of teaching experience, because I came to know Linda as a person and a teacher. I knew that her mother was a teacher; I knew that Linda learned much about "school" from her mother's discourse, and I knew that her student teaching experience sometimes caused her to rethink these lessons she had learned at home. This knowledge allowed me to identify when Linda engaged in transformative discourse.

Another important point is that the result of borderland discourse was neither the repudiation of one discourse nor the subsuming of one discourse into another; instead, the result was a new discourse with characteristics of both of the earlier ones as well as new characteristics unique to the preservice teacher herself. I also have evidence that the expression of borderland discourse bears a relationship to the preservice teachers' decisions to stay in the profession: The more borderland discourse they expressed (through various genres), the greater their likelihood of becoming teachers.

The *borderland* is a term that I have borrowed from James Gee (1999), who used it in a study he conducted of urban middle and high school students from different ethnic groups who "came together" on the schoolyard. When they came together, they used borderland discourse to communicate, discourse that was "a mixture of the various neighborhood peer Discourses, with some emergent properties of its own" (1999, p. 22). It was at the borderlands of discourse, and by association at the borderlands of various identity positions, that the preservice teachers in my study began to discover how to move from being students to being teachers. There they learned to respect personal beliefs and passions while learning to embody a teacher identity. Examples of borderland discourse appear in future chapters. However, in its essence, it is discourse that allows preservice teachers to bring personal subjectivities or ideologies into the classroom and connect them to their developing professional selves. These connections were often in response to felt tensions among professional subjectivities or between personal and professional ideologies, and the expression of borderland discourse was synonymous with increased feelings of personal and professional power.

The borderland discourse was so named because it occurred on the borders of other types of discourse and associated subjectivities. In other words, there were several types of discourse in which the participants engaged during their education: for example, the discourse of the university, the discourse of their own experiences in school (e.g., their own narrative memories), the discourse from their personal, private lives, and the privileged discourse of the schools in which they student taught. All of these discourses might be said to reflect individual segments of the participants' identities and lives—they can be understood as "boxed off" into their own categories or compartments; at least, that's how the preservice teachers often seemed to view them. However, sometimes the students in the study displayed discursive evidence that the lines between the compartments were blurring or blending, and discourse and thinking occurred that was new, original, and transformative. In short, they were growing—they were becoming something new, and part of this new something was their teacher identity. When the participants discovered this borderland and engaged in these new discourses (usually due to new experiences and/or cognitive dissonance), they found that they could embrace viable subject positions as teachers. To put it into simple language: They began to feel like teachers.

Like sociolinguist James Gee, I believe that discourse analysis must have a point—it's not simply to "admire the intricacy of language" (Gee, 1999, p. 8), but its purpose is also to show how the understandings of discourse can be applied to real life and used to change reality for the better, such as with the education and preparation of teachers. Critical researchers engage in discourse analysis so that they can increase their understandings of interpersonal interactions, power relationships, and other real-life human problems in order to make a difference or promote change. This type of critical discourse analysis necessitates a specific definition of discourse that may not be among the most commonly expressed. When I talk about discourse in this book, I do not mean only conversation, or written language, or oral speeches—I am defining discourse in one of the broadest ways possible to emphasize its connection to identity.

As I mentioned in chapter 1, Gee (1999) discussed about two types of discourse: discourse with a small "d" and Discourse with a capital "D." Discourse with a small "d" refers to language activities (e.g., writing and speaking), whereas discourse with a capital "D" is "different ways in which we humans integrate language with non-language "stuff," such as different ways of thinking, acting, interacting, valuing, feeling, believing, and using symbols, tools, and objects in the right places and at the right times so as to enact and recognize different identities and activities ..." (p. 13).

Whenever I refer to discourse in this book, please keep in mind that I am always thinking of the type of discourse to which Gee assigned a capital "D." Even when I am talking about verbal or written language, I am thinking of these discourses as being part of the larger discourse of "teacher" that incorporates linguistic as well as other "non-language stuff" like thought, actions, feelings, notions of corporeality, and so on. Furthermore, to Gee, discourse is linked to identity; if you belong to a certain identity group, for example, you have been recognized as using a certain type of Discourse that is accepted by the community as the norm. Being a teacher means that an individual has mastered a certain set or kind of discourse—one that includes speaking, writing, dressing, acting, and even living within certain boundaries or in accordance with certain often unwritten rules that govern the discourse community. There have been many hours spent in student teaching seminars, methods courses, and one-on-one conferences with school-based mentor teachers discussing how successfully (or not) a particular student teacher is "living" the teacher discourse.

For example, just this past semester, I supervised a student teacher in our program whose spoken dialect, learning disability, dress, and appearance all placed her outside the accepted norm of an Indiana language arts teacher. She, her mentor teacher, and I had several conversations in which we tactfully tried to discuss these issues and how they were keeping her from true acceptance in the teacher community. However, it was difficult to discuss these identity characteristics *as discourse*, because the student teacher had never thought about being a teacher in these terms. It was difficult to keep the conversation from sounding like a personal attack. The student teacher had not engaged in much so-called borderland discourse as a result of her teacher education, and seemed only to see her "faults" as being inconsistent with what a good teacher is and does. As I was working on this book at the time of these conversations, I often asked myself how I might have taught my methods classes differently, or structured assignments in these courses differently, to have helped this student create a more successful professional identity without being forced to reject and vilify her working-class roots or disability status.

One way to consider this student and the type of education that may have assisted her identity development is to think about her education as the analysis and creation of "discourse maps." Gee wrote about the necessity of giving individuals "bigger and better Discourse maps" (1999, p. 23) so that they can shift discourses, be "bi-Discoursal" (1996, p. 136), and modify their discourse in ways that allow them to grow and participate successfully in various discourse communities or social milieus. Gee addressed transforming discourse as a way of transforming society: "Whatever [discourse] you have done must be similar enough to other performances to be recognizable. *However, if it is different enough from what has gone before, but still recognizable, it can simultaneously change and transform Discourses*" (1999, p. 18, emphasis added).

This space, where the discourse of the teacher is recognizable yet transformative (to both the individual teacher as well as the educational system), is what I call borderland discourse. This transformative space is the site of a delicate discursive balance that I hope to help preservice teachers inhabit. This discourse is at the borders between the established, status quo discourse and personal, seemingly conflicting discourses. Borderland discourse is integrative discourse that allows the preservice teacher to combine professional and personal selves and bring about positive transformations within themselves as teachers, and to get even loftier, to education as a whole. Let's face it; I am not educating students to simply go out and reproduce the status quo—to teach as they were taught and do as they are told. However, their change making must be located within the existing discursive system to some extent, so that they aren't ousted from the community (or choose to quit due to feelings of isolation) before they can do good work. The community affects their discourse, but their discourse also affects their community. James Gee stipulated:

> Language has a magical property: when we speak or write we craft what we have to say to *fit* the situation or context in which we are communicating. But, at the same time, how we speak or write *creates* that very situation or context. *It seems then, that we fit our language to a situation or context that our language, in turn, helped to create in the first place*. (1999, p. 11, emphasis added on last sentence)

The idea of discourse as not only representing or reflecting the reality of an individual but also playing a part in crafting that very reality is essential to my argument. This reciprocity is evident in the preservice teachers' development over time, and how their change was associated with particular genres of discourse. For example, students who engaged in many narratives with characteristics of borderland discourse in the interviews appeared to be more successful at beginning to integrate their personal and professional identities and university- and field-based ideologies. Jerome Bruner (2002) discussed the reflexive connection between identity and narrative, one genre of discourse in which the preservice teachers engaged: "I have argued that it is through narrative that we create and re-create selfhood, that self is a product of our telling and not some essence to be delved for in the recesses of subjectivity. There is now evidence that if we lacked the capacity to make stories about ourselves, there would be no such thing as selfhood" (pp. 85–86).

This stunning assertion supports the powerful influence of narrative borderland discourse in this study, or stories that allowed the participants to bring their personal and professional selves into contact. Like Bruner, Stanton Wortham (2001) also wrote about the power of narrative to transform as well as represent. He described how the telling of stories can position and reposition the teller in various subject locations that are dependent on the characteristics of the narrative. I cannot stress enough how this understanding of the reciprocity of discourse has amazing potential for educators whose primary mode of instruction is discourse. What else do we do in classes, except engage (and ask our students to engage) in various forms of discourse? If discourse has power to facilitate professional identity development, then we should be able to model it and encourage our students to use it in the classes we teach. However, the question about specifics remains: How can we capitalize on the power of discourse to help our students develop rich, professional identities? This question is one I attempt to answer by this book's end.

Let me say that I am not the first educational researcher to recognize the importance of teacher identity development. Richard P. Lipka and Thomas M. Brinkthaupt (1999) maintained that it is essential that teacher educators and mentors of new teachers help them balance their "personal development ... with their professional development" (p. 2). They explored why paying attention to the personal, in addition to the professional, is important for a workable teacher identity to result. Parker Palmer (1998) identified three paths to identity development, be it personal or professional: the intellectual, the emotional, and the spiritual. According to Palmer, an individual should address all three parts of this triadic identity. Palmer aptly called teaching "a daily exercise in vulnerability" (p. 29), as teachers attempt to find their "teacher within" and teach from a place of "integrity" (p. 13) that incorporates these three aspects of the self.

Deborah Britzman (1991) called becoming a teacher a type of identity "transformation," and argued through the case studies she presented that to become a teacher we often ask students to give up or suppress aspects of their personal selves that do not conform to the cultural model or "script" of the secondary teacher. We suggest to them though a discourse of objectivity that they should not reveal their personal ideologies or make pedagogical decisions based on their racial, ethnic, or gender subjectivities; on the contrary, and in order to be fair to all students, they should be intellectually neutral (and, of course, academically rigorous) as often as possible. However, this suppression of personal identity is only a sham, a facade, because personal subjectivities and ideologies do not disappear; they simply remain, and even fester, as sites of tension and discomfort. Britzman characterized this conflict or tension a type of "double consciousness," reminiscent of W. E. B DuBois' (1903) description of the double consciousness of the African American living in a White world and trying to remain a member of both communities (Britzman, 1998).

Although I agree that teacher educators should pay attention to and facilitate the identity development of preservice teachers, the understanding of such development is often oversimplified as bringing together the two conflicting identity positions of the personal and the professional. The idea is that once both aspects of the personality are attended to and nurtured, a holistic sense of professional self will result. I hope to complicate this binary understanding of professional identity. The six participants in my research study demonstrated that professional and personal identities are multiple and ever changing, rather than singular and consistently opposing. Therefore, a teacher's identity is a weaving together (Gee, 1999) of various subjectivities or understandings of self as expressed through genres of discourse and influenced by multiple life experiences. In this book, I identify some of these genres of discourse and discuss how they might be incorporated into a teacher education curriculum.

Postmodern or poststructuralist thinkers such as Derrida, Butler, and Foucault at times have emphasized and elucidated the power of discourse to create identity, sometimes at the expense of corporal and emotional ways of knowing. Although the preservice teachers in this study expressed discourse through oral and written language, I do not ignore the associated material, corporeal, and affective expressions of identity. In fact, chapter 5 is about bodily expressions of personal and professional identity. Teacher identity is "performed," similar to Judith Butler's (1993) later descriptions of gender identity. In *Bodies That Matter: On the Discursive Limits of "Sex,"* she explained that the discursive performance of an identity is closely connected to the materiality and corporeal existence of a human body; in fact, a linguistic expression of self can only occur when such expressions are linked to certain physical or material expectations or observable social norms. Likewise, Teresa Ebert (1996) valued the reality of the body and wrote that we cannot ignore material reality and the economic/physical reality of women's lives. Whereas the early postmodern tendency was to make gender constructions, class inequities, and other identity positions almost completely a result of discourse, feminist scholars such as Butler and Ebert, as well as Bronwyn Davies (2000), are among those who insist on the inherent relationship of the discursive to the material, and hence are consistent with Gee's broad definition of what constitutes discourse.

Despite many years of experience as a student and at least 2 years of college instruction specifically about teaching, once preservice teachers begin their new jobs, they often find that they do not know as much as they thought they knew; however, the choice then seems to become clear. Either they must choose the way of the teacher education program, or choose the apprenticeship of observation and teach as they perceive or remember they were taught. Unfortunately, there is seldom an opportunity to build a bridge between these two bodies of knowledge and experience. Instead, the student is compelled to choose one or the other. As shown in my study, the students who went on to become teachers more often selected the side of the "practical" or of the mentor teacher over their university education, and therefore sometimes sacrificed theories and ideologies associated with the university in order to become a functioning member of the teaching community. The power of practicing mentors who are dealing with the discipline, management, and bureaucratic overload of teaching in America's public schools prevails, because preservice teachers are in awe of the mentors' ability to manage a very difficult job. We need to find a way in teacher education to create a bridge or elucidate a borderland between the field or student-teaching experience and the university classroom. Such discourse, when it occurred in this study, resulted in the beginnings of the development of what I am calling a "personal pedagogy" that integrates and honors personal and professional subjectivities in their multiplicity.

Britzman (1994) rejected a binary notion of teacher identity development and recognized such complexities of professional identity formation:

> The notion of the unitary self, of a singular, cohesive and essential identity, is currently being "deconstructed" by poststructuralist theorists (Alcoff, 1988; Ellis, 1989; hooks, 1989; and Weedon, 1987). Under challenge is the idea that individuals have an authentic core or pure essence that has somehow been repressed by society .... *In this way, language—or more specifically discourse—becomes the site of the struggle, a place where the real is constructed, truth is produced, and power is effectuated.* (Britzman, 1994, p. 56, emphasis added)

Britzman was describing borderland discourse, the place where the "real is constructed" and "power is effectuated." Sometimes, the student teachers in my study were not able to experience or express borderland discourse and consequently felt a great deal of tension and discomfort in taking on the role of teacher. If the professional and personal identities and related subjectivities/ideologies seemed too distinct and even contradictory, the preservice teachers in this study could not always close the gap, and some of them opted out of the profession. Three of the six teachers in this study decided not to be teachers after their college graduation because of extreme tensions between their student and teacher subjec tivities or between their perceptions of the idealized (culturally accepted) professional identity and their personal beliefs or ideologies. The tension and discord were simply too powerful to negotiate.

In "Washing Dishes or Doing Schoolwork?: Reflective Action as Renewal" (2000), I told the story of a teacher called Kim who left her job after nearly 20 years in the classroom because she also could not negotiate the conflicts between her beliefs about what a school should provide for students and what her administrators valued; after years of tension and struggle, she left her job permanently. The example of Kim is powerful; although her teaching philosophy was consistent with many of the theories espoused by contemporary educators, her administration, perhaps representative of the governing bodies that control American education today, was more concerned with control, ensuring a lack of ideological debate, and keeping parents and other stakeholders (e.g., voters) content at all costs. Consequently, Kim's ideological stance was in conflict with that of the dominant voices within the school culture, reminiscent of Victor Villaneuva's concept of "cultural schizophrenia" (1993). Kim was experiencing ideological tension between her personal beliefs about education and the professionally sanctioned, and rewarded, priorities articulated by her administrators.

Successful secondary teachers know the importance of the search for professional identity, but the outside world, including teacher education institutions, does not always recognize it. Sometimes the teachers themselves cannot articulate how they do what they do so well, and teacher educators are often uncomfortable talking about aspects of self in a classroom that, according to the philosophy of academe, should be providing objective knowledge. Consequently, teacher educators teach skills, lesson-planning techniques, and discreet pedagogical and content knowledge that is relatively easy to provide and evaluate.

In *Teaching Selves: Identity, Pedagogy, and Teacher Education* (2001), Jane Danielewicz proposed "a pedagogy for identity development" and described "the qualities that must characterize our teaching in order for the students we encounter to become something other than students. Education is about growth and transformation, not only of culture, but of persons too" (p. 1). Her book was a series of case studies of six preservice English teachers, and it described how their life stories and initial teaching experiences influenced their developing professional identities. Danielewicz also recognized the power of discourse to affect identity. However, she did not focus on the discourse that the preservice teachers engaged in as they learned; instead she described the experiences the preservice students reported and what these experiences revealed. Her pedagogy for identity development was about structuring experiences for preservice teachers that can help them grow. Of course, teacher education programs almost always provide classroom experiences for students prior to graduation, and these experiences can and should be analyzed to be the most beneficial. However, one benefit of the discursive approach is that it can, I believe, facilitate the development of specific pedagogical strategies, approaches, and assignments to be used in the teacher education methods class.

Britzman ended her book *Practice Makes Practice: A Critical Study of Learning to Teach* (1991) by asking some questions that I think bear repeating here:

- What would a utopia of teacher education be like?
- What kinds of identities might be made available?
- Would there be a separation between learning to teach and teaching?
- How would knowledge be organized and understood?
- Would there be schools?
- How might we redefine the work of teachers and students?
- What kinds of knowledge, imagination, and ways of being would be desirable?
- How might theory and practice be recognized and understood? (p. 242)

I am going to address two of these questions that are foundational (yet still unanswered) for improving teacher education and the recruitment/retention of teachers: What kinds of identities might be made available to teachers? What kinds of knowledge, imagination, and ways of being would be desirable? I also add a third question that connects identity and knowledge: What kinds of discourse can be facilitated during preservice teacher education to help new teachers most effectively use their knowledge and develop a professional identity? These questions are central to the struggle experienced by new teachers who often wrestle more with issues of identity and "ways of being" in the classroom than with content knowledge, discipline, classroom management, or lesson planning.

Sociologist Richard Jenkins described identity as a "practical accomplishment, a process," the direct result of the "dialectical interplay of processes of internal and external definition" (1997, p. 25). In other words, identities occur; they are formed in a social, communicative context and for socially significant reasons. Through engaging in certain types of discourse during their education, preservice teachers might be able to avoid replaying the same old tapes and imitating the teachers of their youth, and might also be able to modify the often-stagnant cultural model in significant ways. Or, to call on Butler again, they can begin to recognize performances of discourse that they have been enacting all along, but that have gone unrecognized and unrewarded (and sometimes even punished) because they do not fit the social norm or the cultural model of teacher. This performance of teacher identity may eventually incorporate the intellectual, emotional, and physical aspects of discourse and reveal a holistic identity.

The most immediately and obviously "successful" teacher education students (defined as those who took secondary teaching jobs after graduation) in this study were those who were given the opportunity and the necessary guidance to begin to see complex connections among their educational memories, their university education, their practical school and teaching experiences, and their personal or core ideologies. This mixture does not necessarily mean the "loss" of one original discourse; instead, it means the creation of a new third discourse. One of our main goals as teacher educators is the creation of this borderland discourse that will enable preservice teachers to combine their core identities, their student identities, and others with their professional identities and create a new, albeit recognized, discourse or professional identity. Gee asserted:

> If your performance has been influenced, intentionally or not, by another one of your Discourses ..., and it gets recognized in the new capitalist management Discourse, then you have just, at least for here and now, "infected" one Discourse with another and widened what "counts" in the new capitalist management Discourse. You pushed the boundaries. In another time and place, they may get narrowed. (1999, p. 21)

The creation and expression of borderland discourse can be a political act, one of enriching and broadening the discursive and material identity of the teacher that is often perceived in the United States as being narrow and restrictive. The discourse used by some of the preservice teachers in this study to describe their identities, subjectivities, and associated ideologies assisted them in learning to occupy these borderlands between multiple identity strands that they expressed as various, context-specific subject positions, such as student, teacher, daughter, friend, mother, or feminist. The borderland is not the crossing of a simplistic boundary through easy identification with, or rejection of, the "other." It does not mean the elimination of any conflict or ideological tension. When a new teacher can rest in the borderland between multiple subjectivities and express him- or herself through various discourses, that teacher is beginning to understand how such multiplicity, such ambiguity, can be acceptable, comfortable, and even essential to his or her professional identity. It is at these discursive borderlands that the preservice teachers discovered how to move from being students to being teachers; they discovered how to honor personal beliefs and passions while also embodying a teacher identity that in our society, as Deborah Britzman (1991) noted, is so often overshadowed by simplified and stereotypical cultural models and media scripts.

METHODOLOGY OF THE STUDY

I began this study in January 2001, and it concluded in the spring of 2003. I began with the following goals:

1. Examine the philosophies of teaching English held by the participants and the modification of these beliefs over time.
2. Describe classroom practices (pedagogy) of the participants, its change over time, and how these changes are connected to the aforementioned beliefs.
3. Explore issues of self-confidence about teaching and participants' level of "comfort" in the classroom and how these change over time.
4. Describe changes in how the participants define their roles as English teachers over the time of the study.
5. Offer suggestions for mentoring preservice and beginning teachers and explore further research directions for understanding teacher development.

The study evolved to focus on teacher professional identity development through an emergent and grounded theory approach to analysis that allows meaning to evolve from the data collection rather than imposing thematic categories onto the research texts.

This study is, in part, an example of "narrative research" as defined and explored by D. Jean Clandinin and F. Michael Connelly (2000), among others. Amia Lieblich, Rivka Tuval-Mashiach, and Tamar Zilber (1998) stipulated:

> Narrative research refers to any study that uses or analyzes narrative materials. The data can be collected as a story or in a different manner. It can be the object of the research or a means for the study of another question. It may be used for comparison among groups, to learn about a social phenomenon or historical period, or to explore a personality. (pp. 2–3)

The preservice teachers expressed a great deal of the interview data as stories about experiences, memories, or tensions they felt as they became teachers. Therefore, the first part of this book is a discussion of my analysis of these narrative texts. The second part explores the genres of metaphor and philosophy statements.

After I taught my first methods course at the university where I am currently an assistant professor of English education, I asked for preservice teacher volunteers for this project. My goal was to recruit six to eight students. Originally, seven volunteered—six women and one man. After the male participant dropped out midway through the study when he moved to another state, the participants in my study were all White women, between the ages of 19 and 23. This gender and ethnicity is roughly representative of the English education program at my school. Keeping subjectivities of the participants at the fore, I describe the sample and events in depth, rather than quantifying and generalizing as might be done from a large sample.

Participants were drawn from one of two classes I taught: "Composition for Teachers" and "Teaching Literature in the Secondary Schools." They knew me as their teacher and in my professional subjectivity as a professor in the English education program at my university. During the many hours of interviews, we became friends as well as professional acquaintances. Linda and Janeen presented on a panel with me at a local teaching conference about their experiences during their first year of teaching, and I met regularly with Carrie and Karen for lunch on campus. All student names—as well as names of mentor teachers, family members of the participants, schools where the participants taught, and university instructors—are pseudonyms.

Although this was an interview-based, qualitative study, I also collected relevant artifacts such as lesson plans that the preservice teachers put together, philosophy statements and literacy autobiographies they wrote for methods classes, teaching metaphors they created, and notes I took when I observed them teaching. In order to establish "triangulation," multiple sources were analyzed before stating results (Denzin, 1978). The quality and purpose that I strove for in my interviews had been previously described by Irving Seidman (1998) quite well: "The purpose of in-depth interviewing is not to get answers to questions, nor to test hypotheses, and not to evaluate as the term is normally used. At the root of in-depth interviewing is an interest in understanding the experience of other people and the meaning they made of that experience" (p. 3).

I took a feminist approach to interviewing (Bloom, 1998; Kirsch, 1999) as I engaged in dialogues and conversations with my participants that intended, as much as possible, to break down the power differentials and authoritarian hierarchies inherent in our respective positions. During each of the five semesters of the study, I interviewed participants twice, for approximately an hour (sometimes the interviews ran as long as 2 hours), during which I asked them questions about their teaching beliefs, what they were learning in their methods courses and/or field experiences, how their beliefs and practices might be changing, and why they thought these changes were occurring. I began with semistructured interview protocols of a broad list of issues to discuss, but allowed the students to address other topics if they chose. Later, I had the audiotaped interviews transcribed. During the study, three research assistants helped me with the time-consuming work of transcription.

The process of analysis was conceptual qualitative discourse analysis focusing on the ideas, issues, experiences, and feelings described by the participants. I used the "categorical content" approach to data analysis, which is often called *content analysis*. In content analysis, categories are defined (coded), and examples from the text are placed into these identified categories or groups for analysis (Lieblich et al., 1998). The specific process of analysis of the interview transcripts and other artifacts included the following steps:

- Reading the artifact or transcript once and marking interesting concepts, ideas, etc.
- Reading the artifact or transcript a second time, again marking relevant or interesting concepts and ideas. During this reading, an attempt was made to consolidate or combine items of interest that seemed similar or connected.
- Comparing these themes or codes. Barney G. Glaser and Anselm L. Strauss (1967) called this process "constant comparison"; it allowed for the creation of the general characteristics of teacher identity discourse.
- Deciding on a final list of themes (codes) that commonly occurred throughout the research texts. These themes became (a) the list of the

various genres of discourse around which this book is organized, and (b) the generic subcategories or themes within each genre type.
- An outside analyst reviewed a sample of the data (10% of the total) and organized it within the thematic categories I provided, after a discussion of their definitions. The percentage of our interrater reliability was 99%.

Qualitative researchers define trustworthiness (vs. the quantitative concepts of reliability and validity) as possessing the following criteria, as described by Yvonna S. Lincoln and Egon G. Guba (1985):

- Credibility—Engagement in activities that increase the probability that credible findings would result, such as prolonged engagement in the research, persistent observation, and triangulation. (p. 301)
- Transferability—The use of thick description that allows the reader to decide if results are applicable to his or her context. (p. 316)
- Dependability—The use of triangulation and constant comparison. (p. 316)
- Confirmability—Availability of an "audit trail" of the research process, such as notes, journals, coded transcripts or field notes, and other records. (p. 318)

The data collection and analysis were thus conducted in ways that are credible, transferable, dependable, and confirmable. The knowledge that resulted from this study could only have been discovered through a qualitative, narrative approach. The depth of knowledge I gained about the teacher identity development of the six participants hinged on my knowledge of their personalities, concerns, worries, hopes, fears, and successes that was revealed to me through hours spent in interview conversation with each participant. The artifacts I collected were identified as significant through analysis of the interviews, and the "thick" field notes compiled during classroom observations allowed me to further triangulate records of observable behavior with the other data sources.

A total of 1,109 pages of interview transcripts and approximately 100 additional pages of supporting artifacts (e.g., observation notes and student-written lesson plans and reflective essays) were collected during this longitudinal study. Various theoretical and disciplinary frameworks were essential to analysis of the ample data I collected, including psychology, anthropology, sociology, literary studies, linguistics, and education. To locate myself in this study, as feminist researcher Gesa Kirsch recommended (1999), is to acknowledge all the background, knowledge, and life experience that I possess. First, without my own high school and middle school teaching experiences and subsequent experiences as a teacher educator, I would not have developed an interest in this project or devised the research questions that I did. Second, without my years of immersion in the culture of secondary school teaching and learning, I could not have been able to evaluate and analyze the data effectively and efficiently.

Chapter **3**

The Struggle of Subjectivities: Narratives of Tension

James and Tita French Baumlin (1994) claimed "mythos" as the fourth rhetorical proof, rounding out the Aristotelian trio of logos (logic, rationality), pathos (emotion and feeling), and ethos (the view of others toward the speaker; the speaker's credibility). Mythos is using language not to argue rationally, develop a persona, or express emotion, but rather to engage in imaginative or creative discourse that seeks and expresses a "truth" indirectly, but powerfully. One might call this Truth with a capital "T." Baumlin and Baumlin argued that "The mythic seeks ... to unite, to synthesize, to assert wholeness in multiple or contrasting choices and interpretations. Mythos thus offers a synthetic and analogical, as opposed to analytic, mode of proof, one that discovers—indeed celebrates—the diversity of truth" (p. 106).

They went on to note that mythos is a type of "healing story." Mythos is the Greek forerunner of our word *myth*, or *mythology*, a body of stories that are held to have some connection to a larger truth, at least for a certain group of people at a certain historical moment. Because much of the understanding of teacher identity discourse that I describe here resulted from an analysis of stories, narratives or stories are important in this book. Participants told simply scores of them during the interviews to describe and explain their teacher education experiences. Narrative was their genre of choice when discussing their developing professional identities.

Narrative offers one means of building ethos or justifying action. To return to Aristotle, he described the concept of ethos as the establishment of the trustworthiness of the speaker (or the modern writer) in relationship to his audience. The speaker or writer can establish such trustworthiness in a number of ways—one of which, Aristotle asserted, is through the telling of narratives, personal *or* impersonal, that demonstrate the speaker's wide knowledge of the issue about which he or she is speaking. Such narratives can serve as examples within an inductive argument. Aristotle discussed the concept of narration in Book II and Book III of *The Rhetoric*, and recommended that brief stories be scattered throughout a speech to back up specific features or qualities of the individuals or topics being described. Although qualitative researchers have taken up a variation of this idea about the ethos of narrative, they have broadened its significance to be evidence not only of researcher ethos but also the ethos of the very knowledge that a researcher claims to have discovered (Bizzell & Herzberg, 1990).

So what is a narrative? There are many ways that literary theorists, psychologists, sociologists, folklorists, and educational researchers have defined the word. Bruner (2002) wrote that in order for a text to be a story, a "peripeteia" (a term from Aristotle's *Poetics*) or a "sudden reversal in circumstances" has to occur (p. 7). He defined the whole narrative as containing a sequence of events, characters, a peripeteia, a statement of the significance of the story, and a "coda" or a return to the present. Michael J. Toolen (1998) maintained that narrative is a "report on some state and changes or change to that state" (p. 14). Mieke Bal (1999) viewed narratives as having two fundamental parts: the underlying story or "fabula" and the text that tells this story. In 1967, sociolinguists William Labov and Joshua Waletzky wrote a groundbreaking essay about narrative analysis. Labov (1972) went on to write more about narrative in specific social-cultural contexts. Labov and Waletzky identified formal linguistic properties and functions of narrative to assist in their conversational analysis. They came up with two broad functions when narrative is used by human beings (as described by Toolen): the referential function of narrative as a "means of recapitulating experience in an ordered set of clauses that matches the temporal sequence of the original experience," and the instrumental function for individuals that requires that a narrative have a point (Toolen, 1998, p. 147). Labov and Waletzky also identified a six-part structure for a "fully formed" narrative:

- Abstract—what the story is about;
- Orientation—answers, "who when where and what?";
- Complicating action—answers, "what happened?";
- Evaluation—answers, "why is this interesting?";
- Result or resolution; and
- Coda—communicates the story is finished and the teller is bridging back to the present. (Toolen, 1998, p. 152)

Labov and Waletzky also provided a shorter, less complex definition of narrative that I found useful when coding the data in this study. They stated that narratives are minimally comprised of "at least two necessarily sequenced clauses of which the second is consequential to the first" (quoted in Young, 1999, p. 197). This is how I defined narratives when I coded and analyzed them in the interview transcripts. I rarely asked the participants to "tell me a story" during an interview. The only time I specifically asked them to engage in narrative was when asking about early childhood or early school memories, and these narratives make up a small percentage of the total number of stories told by the participants. Participants told the remainder of the narratives spontaneously during our interview conversations.

Many psychologists, sociologists, and educators assert that personal narratives don't simply reflect identities, they *are* people's identities (Bruner & Weisser, 1991; Fischer-Rosenthal, 1995; Gergen, 1994; Gergen & Gergen, 1983; Hermans, Rijks, Harry, & Kempen, 1993; McAdams, 1993; Polkinghorne, 1991; Rosenthal, 1997). Consequently, analyzing narratives is one way of understanding identity development. This belief is reflected in the work of psychologists and psychiatrists who have long used the case study or life history narrative to understand people's lives. Jerome Bruner (1986) asserted that people lead "storied lives," and Bruner, along with Joseph Campbell, may be the preeminent scholar of narrative. He defined narratives as essential to the making of the self: "Self making is a narrative art, and though it is more constrained by memory than fiction is, it is uneasily constrained ... narrative acts of self making are usually guided by unspoken, implicit cultural models of what selfhood should be—and, of course, shouldn't be" (p. 65).

Bruner went so far as to say that if the human being wasn't able to make and tell stories that both identify the self as autonomous and link this self to a community in which he or she acts, the human being would lack a sense of "selfhood." Bruner actually identified a neurological disorder, "dysnarrativia," that occurs when a person doesn't have an understanding of story, and therefore cannot develop a coherent identity (p. 86). Similarly, Widdershoven (1993) noted:

> It is not concrete experiences that shape our sense of identity, but the stories we tell ourselves (and exchange with other people) about those experiences. Our stories become the means by which we make sense of our past, our present, and our future, even as the stories themselves gradually "fuse" with new stories, as new experiences occur. (quoted Lipka & Brinthaupt, 1999, p. 78)

D. Jean Clandinin and F. Michael Connelly's *Narrative Inquiry: Experience and Story in Qualitative Research* (2000) is a landmark text for those researchers in education and the social sciences conducting narrative research. Their book defines what narrative research is and gave specific ideas and guidelines for how to go about doing it. A more recent book, *Narrative In-*

quiry in Practice: Advancing the Knowledge of Teaching (Lyons & LaBoskey, 2002), is a collection of essays about "exemplars" or stellar examples of narrative research into teaching. Such narrative inquiry constitutes engagement in narratology, or the study of narratives and their meanings. Mieke Bal (1999) explained that "Narratology is the theory of narratives, narrative texts, images, spectacles, events; cultural artifacts that tell a story. Such a theory helps to understand, analyze, and evaluate narratives " (p. 3).

Narratology examines and describes all types of narratives with the goal of deciphering how a narrative is constructed and why it is constructed that way—for what social, cultural, or political purpose. Narratology explores theories of narrative creation and use (Bal, 1999), and is bigger than the genre of narrative alone—it is an organized and intellectual exploration of a cultural mode of expression that plays a significant role in human interaction.

Narratology as a field of study began in the late 1960s to early 1970s and relied heavily on theories of structuralism that neatly defined narratives and their function in texts. With the advent of deconstruction and poststructuralism, postclassical narratologists became less interested in defining the structure of stories and more interested in a socionarratological approach (or sociolinguistic approach) exploring the thematic content of stories and what function these stories play in particular communicative contexts (Jahn, 1999).

Since the 1980s, narratives have been commonly used in the field of education to organize data in action research projects and for the systematic sharing of pedagogical expertise. Recently, educators and researchers have written about how analyzing or interrogating narratives that teachers tell concerning their educational histories or memories can help new teachers overcome long-held and overly simplistic belief structures about what a teacher should be and what a classroom should look like (Bullough & Stokes, 1994; Knowles & Holt-Reynolds, 1991; Tillema, 1998). The goal is to help teachers overcome the temptation to simply teach as they were taught, no matter what research and theory tell them.

Such interrogation of narrative histories is especially important, because many studies (Crow, 1987a, 1987b; Holt-Reynolds, 1992; Knowles, 1992; Lortie, 1975) have shown that teachers tend to teach as they remember being taught, and that teachers aren't influenced that much by their teacher education programs. Gary Knowles acknowledged that "The results [of his research] suggest that early childhood experiences, early teacher role models, and previous teaching experiences are most important in the formation of an 'image of self as teacher'" (p. 126). Ivor Goodson, in *Studying Teachers' Lives* (1992), addressed life stories of teachers and how life story research can facilitate teacher identity development. Goodson and the authors in his edited collection advocated using teachers' stories to assist in their development of professional identity. Such research emphasizing the influence of narrative educational memories demonstrates the importance of the examination of narratives of experience during the education of a teacher.

THE EXPRESSION OF NARRATIVES OF TENSION BY THE PARTICIPANTS

During qualitative analysis, I thematically coded the narratives participants told, and identified five types of stories. These types are narratives of tension, narratives of experience, narratives of the embodiment of teacher identity, narratives about family and friends, and borderland narratives that describe the preservice teachers' initial attempts at connecting multiple subjectivities or understandings of self. Table 3.1 shows the types and numbers of narratives told by each student during the study. In this chapter and in the four chapters that follow, I examine each of the types of narratives that emerged from my analysis and describe how I believe it was important to the professional identity formation of selected participants. I begin here with narratives of tension.

An intriguing finding from my narrative analysis was that unresolved tension between discordant subjectivities and associated ideologies lessened the chance of the participants developing a satisfying professional identity or a sense of fulfillment as a teacher. In the analysis of the narratives, I saw three major kinds of tension: "student" versus "teacher" selves as preservice teachers moved from the role of university student to that of high school teacher, personal beliefs versus professional expectations, and university ideologies or educational methods versus the practical ones experienced in secondary field placements. Tension that was experienced by the preservice teachers concerned issues as diverse as classroom authority, professional confidence, opinions about pedagogical methods and curricular emphases, approaching classroom discipline, and negotiating their dual roles in family and career.

The three students who told the highest total number of narratives of tension decided not to take traditional teaching jobs after graduation and expressed some confusion as to their future professional lives. These students—Sandy, Carrie, and Karen—told a respective total of 34, 27, and 16 narratives of tension. Lois, Linda, and Janeen were able to either ignore these ideological tensions or negotiate them because of awareness of multiple subjectivities or because of engagement in borderland discourse and associated professional actions. Therefore, in the best-case scenario, students were able to begin to embody holistic professional identities. In these cases, the students' tension did not go away or become insignificant; instead, the students either found a way to honor and integrate the various subjectivities

TABLE 3.1

Types of Narrative Discourse Engaged in by Six Preservice Teachers

Narrative	*Linda*	*Janeen*	*Sandy*	*Lois*	*Carrie*	*Karen*	*Totals*
1. Tension							
Student vs. teacher	9	6	30	10	11	0	66
Personal vs. professional	0	0	0	0	12	15	27
University vs. practical	4	2	4	4	4	1	19
2. Experience							
As a student	7S*	8S	4S, 1F	10S	7S, 4F	4S, 2F	47
As a teacher	32S, 1F**	9S	13S, 5F	26S	2S, 2F	4S, 3F	97
3. Embodiment	5 (class, size, age, dress)	1 (age)	1 (class)	7 (age, appearance)	12 (class, gender/sexual orientation, dress, appearance)	8 (gender, class, race/ethnicity)	34
4. Family/friends	10	3	7	3	3	1	27
5. Borderland	12	7	2	15	0	1	37
Totals	80	36	67	75	57	39	354

*S = Success stories.
**F = Failure stories.

central to their lives or avoided ideological tension and opted for the acceptance of a less complex, culturally defined teacher identity.

The identity conflicts experienced by the students in the study seemed to occur when the students exhibited one of the following types of ideological tension: oversimplified binary tension in which perceptions of both personal (self) and professional (other) identity remained distinct from each other, yet relatively simple; tension in which the "other" was problematized, but the self was not; tension in which the self was problematized, but the "other" was not; and tension in which the student teacher problematized *both* the self and the other. This last type of dual, multiple tension was, ironically, the type that led to the most effective and productive professional identity development.

All of the tensions experienced by the participants in this study—tensions between student and teacher subjectivities, between personal ideologies and professional expectations and between university and real-world knowledge—were difficult for the preservice teachers to live with. Such ideological and discursive conflicts are never easy to experience, and the disease and discomfort caused by the tensions often led to failure to acquire or take on one or the other of the conflicting discourses. However, when the students were able to become, in Gee's sense, "bi-Discoursal" (1996, p. 136) or proficient users of multiple discourses simultaneously (professional/personal, student/teacher, academic/nonacademic), they were more successful in the early stages of their growth as teachers.

Linda exhibited the first kind of tension: simple, binary tension. She had an uncomplicated view of both her personal self and her professional life. She had known that she was going to be a teacher since she had been in high school, and was a "cadet teacher" or teacher's aide in her mother's fifth-grade classroom. Because both her mother and grandmother are teachers, she is comfortable and familiar with the teacher life and with her understanding of teacher discourse; she seems to know what kind of teacher she wants to be and is confident she can become that teacher. Similarly, she also seems to have clear plans for her future personal life, which include marriage and a family.

Although Linda engaged in a comparatively large amount of borderland discourse, it was primarily negotiation between various pedagogical approaches and practices advocated by different mentors or instructors; she never expressed any discourses of tension between personal subjectivities and professional expectations. During an early interview, she described to me how she felt about the philosophies and approaches of her mentor teacher during student teaching and how they intersected with her own. In the following excerpt, you can see how her assessment of their relationship as well as her awareness of transformative discourse emerging from their relationship primarily revolved around the professional:

> I think we'll [she and her mentor teacher] have somewhat of the same expectations. I don't know philosophically I would say in the long run, yes, but now maybe in our approaches. If I were going into the classroom not having her as my mentor teacher but in my own classroom, I probably will go about it a little differently, but at the same time I think the expectations are very similar. I don't think she is too rigorous, but I certainly don't think she is too easy either. She seems to have a good feel; she has been teaching this class for a long time. Over time she has learned, so it's nice for me to go in and see those things that I wouldn't have had any clue about necessarily. But I think for the most part we are on the same page. (September 11, 2001)[6]

Linda seemed to realize that at this point in her career her transformative discourse was primarily professional and practical in orientation (she said, "I don't know philosophically," implying that perhaps someday she would be able to tell if she and her mentor, Ms. Vanderholt, were ideologically compatible).

Sandy exhibited the second type of tension, when the professional life of "teacher" is problematized, but not the personal. In other words, she saw the professional life she was about to enter as very difficult and complex, and sometimes contrary to what she thought she believed about education. Sandy appeared to know what she wanted in her personal life, or if she didn't have these answers she seemed comfortable with the ambiguity. However, her professional life seemed very difficult, as she couldn't completely make the transition from a student to a teacher identity by the end of the study.

Carrie exemplified the third kind of tension, which consists of problematizing the personal but not the professional. She had difficulty with understanding her personal subjectivities and ideologies and making decisions about her personal life. She was struggling to understand her sexual identity and how it could mesh with a relatively uncomplicated, yet hard to embrace, professional identity. The same was true of Karen, who had trouble understanding how to integrate her family with her career. However, she did not question her understanding of the life of a teacher. Her problem was not with understanding what this professional identity entails, but rather with accepting it and making it work with her personal identity. Such personally oriented confrontation between the personal and the professional seemed the most difficult type of tension to negotiate, because only one borderland narrative directly addressed it; students who engaged in the most such discourse ended up choosing not to teach.

---

[6]I did conduct interviews on September 11 and September 12, the day of the attacks on the World Trade Center and the Pentagon and the day following. Although the participants and I discussed the attacks during the interviews on September 11, the events were still unfolding and we were unaware of the extent of the damage and loss of life. Therefore, the discussions about education and teaching were able to occur relatively normally. On September 12 the participants and I, while engaging in interviews, also mourned with the rest of the nation.

The fourth kind of tension occurred when both the personal and the professional were problematized. Lois experienced this kind of dual tension. She understood her personal identity as multiple and sometimes contradictory, but she also understood the professional identity of teacher as being complex and many faceted. Therefore, this dual tension allowed for multiple opportunities for intersection, or increased opportunities to engage in borderland discourse. As Britzman maintained, "Reading for alterity begins with acknowledgment of difference as the precondition for the self" (1998, p. 92). In other words, one must understand and accept one's own multiple subjectivities before accepting those of others. Lois understood her own multiple subjectivities as well as the nonunitary subjectivity of the "teacher." Ironically, and perhaps even counterintuitively, this increased acceptance of multiplicity and awareness of many possible sites of ideological tension led Lois to experience more productive professional identity development.

Although Lois' borderland discourse primarily concerned professional decisions, her open-minded understanding of her own identity as an apprentice teacher helped her entertain multiple possibilities as well as cognitive dissonance. The majority of Lois' tensions were between her competing student and teacher identities, and she confided this tension, this concern, to her mentor. Perhaps her large number of stories about successful school experiences (see chap. 4) increased her confidence when admitting problems. Lois confided her fears and insecurities to her mentor teacher so that they could confront them head on—together. Lois told me several stories with characteristics of transformative discourse about her mentor teacher assisting in dealing effectively with her tensions:

> It's been really good [teaching the composition course during student teaching]. We've kind of team taught it. You know, that's what we decided we want to do, because she wanted me to have as much of it as I wanted to, but it's so important for the kids. Like if they miss one thing—it's so important for their grades that—I was scared, and she was scared to have me in there by myself. So it's kind of like, she'll leave me in there, I'll teach a lesson or something, and then sit with the—she's in and out. So it's been really good. (December 4, 2001)

And from the same interview:

> I see it with Mark and Carol [two fellow student teachers in the same building]. I'll walk past their classrooms and one of their teachers is teaching or I see them [the teachers] sitting there grading, and I'm like, "Hmm. I grade my own papers." My mentor teacher is so cool with that, too, she's like, "You know, this is your assignment, you need to grade it."

These stories expressed Lois' awareness that her mentor was not only teaching her, but was also helping her to develop a teacher identity. It's not simply that her mentor was giving her jobs to do or telling her what she was doing right and wrong—she was working with Lois, paying attention to her strengths and weaknesses, and giving her duties that would increase her confidence and abilities, even if they were harder or required more work. Because Lois knew that these jobs, such as grading, were helping her learn, she didn't see them as busy work. I discuss Lois' borderland narratives, as well as those told by Linda, Janeen, and Karen, in more depth in chapter 7.

In the sections that follow, I describe in detail the three main types of narratives of tension (teacher vs. student, personal vs. professional, and university vs. the practical), and I provide several examples from stories narrated by Carrie, Karen, Lois, Sandy, Janeen, and Linda. To refresh your memory about the lives of the participants, see the brief sketches in chapter 1.

Am I a Student or a Teacher? Finding a New Place in School

Not surprisingly, the tension between feeling like a student and feeling like a teacher was relatively common in the study. As new teachers move from being students to being teachers, a certain amount of identity confusion and tension is expected. Of the three kinds of tension evidenced in the study, this type was among the most easily smoothed, as the new teacher gained classroom experience and began to generate narratives of teaching. In other words, for some of the participants, borderland discourse was more common as it related to tensions between the identity positions of university student and secondary school teacher.

The student with the most of these narratives was Sandy, who told a total of 30 stories narrating tension between her student and teacher selves. Remember that Sandy was one of the three students who chose not to take a traditional secondary school teaching job after graduation. However, she did choose to stay in the field of education, becoming an administrator with a local branch of an educational support and tutoring service. Carrie, who also decided not to take a traditional teaching job after graduation, told a total of 11 narratives of tension between student and teacher subjectivities. Karen, the third student who chose not to teach, surprisingly told none of these narratives. However, her lack of narrated tension in this area can be attributed to her decision in her junior year to not pursue a teaching license; therefore, Karen never student taught or took part in any long-term field experiences. It was during such field experiences and student teaching that narratives of tension between student and teacher subjectivities were the most prevalent.

While Sandy was at the university she was also a tutor in the writing lab, and she loved this job. She was a very good tutor, and she could describe her tutoring process vividly and explicitly. Sandy often compared her feelings about being a tutor with those of being a teacher. She found tutoring more comfortable than teaching because, in part, she did not have the final call on students' grades, nor did she have to prepare daily lessons to teach in class. She described being able to tutor students almost automatically after a year or so of experience; she knew the kinds of questions to ask and the kinds of feedback to give in certain situations. She had developed internal scripts for initiating and sustaining various types of one-on-one conferences. However, she did not feel as if this comfort and instructional identity as a tutor transferred into or assisted her identity development as a classroom teacher.

Sandy described ideological tension between her student and teacher selves in the context of tutoring. In our first interview conversation on January 30, 2001, Sandy addressed the feeling of being in limbo between student and teacher:

> It's just weird because as much as we've talked about grading and stuff, it's kind of weird how she [the teacher of the course for which she was tutoring] would look at it [a paper written by a tutee] and give it a C, and maybe I could look at it and say it's a B, so it's just kind of weird how it's so subjective. If they [students] didn't like something in class, then they wouldn't tell her, but they'd tell me about it instead, so when we have our meetings where I communicate [to the teacher] that they didn't really like that or whatever—it's weird being that kind of middle man. I was exposed more to being the middleman as opposed to being the teacher or just being the student, you know?

Later, on February 1, 2002, in the fifth of our interviews, I asked Sandy if she would rather be a teacher or a tutor. She replied, "Oh, if I were doing my choice, I would rather tutor somebody. As long as you can connect to the student, and learn, and try to talk to them in terms they understand—then you don't have to worry about whether 25 other people understand."

Sandy's tension between her student and teacher subjectivities centered around her experiences as a tutor and trying to move from the perceived middle ground of authority occupied by a tutor to the full authority and responsibility of the teacher. As I've already mentioned, it was interesting that, after graduation, Sandy took a job with an educational company that provides tutoring to young people who have reading problems. At this point in her professional and personal identity development, Sandy found tutoring more comfortable, perhaps because it necessitated a less complete teacher identity. Being a tutor may have allowed her to vacillate between the role of the student and the role of the teacher. As a tutor, Sandy could act as both a knowledgeable peer providing advice and an authority figure consulting with a classroom teacher. Both scenarios are one-on-one communicative contexts, allowing for a less formal enactment of the teacher role.

During her student teaching in the fall of 2001, Sandy experimented with a more traditional teacher identity, and she was overwhelmed with the daily paperwork and bureaucracy that fills the teacher's life. On November 9, 2001, she said to me:

> She [Sandy's mentor teacher] has a filing cabinet in her room, right by her desk that just has papers. I went in there one day during my teacher's study hall. So I went up there to talk to her to see if I could come observe, and students would come up and say, "Oh, I missed this assignment, can I get this worksheet?" And she had a filing cabinet *full* of worksheets she had given, and I was thinking, "Oh, no, I won't be able to keep up with this!"

Over time, Sandy became more comfortable in front of the classroom and with the daily bureaucracy of teaching, but she never really quite felt like a teacher. She didn't feel integrated or welcomed into the professional community by her mentor teacher. At the end of her student teaching experience, she told me she felt she had not received a lot of positive feedback or support. In short, she did not engage in much borderland discourse. I was able to identify only two borderland narratives in Sandy's interviews despite her large number of student-versus-teacher narratives of tension, which for some other participants made borderland discourse more likely. Sandy's few borderland narratives did reflect the beginnings of a deeper understanding of the teaching life and increased empathy for the difficulties of the professional transition from student to teacher. However, they didn't resolve her difficulties with moving into a teacher role.

Like Sandy, Carrie struggled with tension between her student and teacher identities. She had the second-highest number of such narratives of tension, with 11. She came to Purdue to study computer engineering, but once here she decided to become a secondary English teacher, primarily because of positive high school memories. In our third interview, which took place on September 19, 2002, she told me the story of the exact moment when she made this decision: "I seriously laid staring at the bunk bed above me going through occupations and asking myself, are any of these giving me at least a spark of interest? And this is the one—the only one—that gave me a spark. I'm afraid of not having passion in my life. I'm afraid of having a job that I'm not going to want to go to every morning."

Ironically, Carrie ended up deciding not to be a teacher for similar reasons—she didn't feel that she would be happy in the profession. During her field experiences in secondary schools, she never felt comfortable and confident as a teacher. In her last year, she had an extended field experience in a high school English class, and this experience was not positive. On December 13, 2002, she told me:

> I had a hard time viewing myself as a teacher, and as I'm getting closer to graduation I'm having a hard time viewing myself as an adult. Because it's like I'm expected to go out there and get a job and they're going to give me responsibility, and I just want to look at them and say, look, I'm just a kid!

> What am I doing here? I can't do this stuff! So when I was in the classroom, I felt a whole lot more like a student than I did a teacher. I identified with the students more and even in my relationship with Mrs. Cave [field experience mentor teacher], and I don't know if it's reflective at all of how she viewed or treated me, but I felt more like a student than a peer. I just don't feel like I'm necessarily that prepared to go into a classroom at this point.

Carrie had initially decided to be a teacher because of inspirational English teachers she had in high school, and how their classes made her think and feel. However, in her field experiences during her university education, she never re-experienced these positive feelings, and therefore couldn't regain her excitement for the profession. Perhaps her memories of heroic teachers became daunting role models, because she never felt like a teacher herself and never engaged in transformative discourse in her interview conversations with me.

Neither Carrie nor Sandy could negotiate the transition from student to teacher by the time of their graduation. Interestingly, they both experienced tensions that problematized either the professional or the personal, but not both. Therefore, Sandy and Carrie felt restricted as they tried to make connections between personal and professional subjectivities and identity positions. For Sandy, her understandings of self seemed too straightforward and simplistic to accommodate the complex professional identity of teacher. For Carrie, her complex understanding of self seemed inconsistent with her perception of the culturally defined teacher life and ideal teacher.

The Personal Confronts the Professional: Negotiating Conceptions of "Normalcy" for Teachers

There is a myth of normalcy (Britzman, 1998) in education, and it goes something like this: The teaching life is relatively uncomplicated, and those who select it are "average" citizens (usually female) who wish to maintain their "regular" (married, heterosexual, conservative) lives in well-adjusted, middle-class contexts. In fact, students sometimes choose to be teachers for that reason—they think that teaching will allow them to concentrate more easily on other parts of their lives, such as family. Some think that teaching is a culturally and socially uncontroversial professional choice, especially for young women from middle- or working-class backgrounds. Additionally, in schools of education, the promise of normalcy is often implied, if not stated directly. In education classes, teaching can be depicted as a body of knowledge that can be learned, and teacher educators suggest that their teacher education students will also be successful teachers, *if* they learn and implement the preferred pedagogies appropriately.

However, this study reveals that this myth of normalcy is not always accurate. Britzman (1998) quoted Freud as saying, "In sending the young out into life with … a false psychological orientation, education is behaving as though one were to equip young people starting on a Polar expedition with summer clothing and maps to the Italian Lakes" (p. 79).

Are we sending new teachers out into the cold with only summer clothing? Britzman (1998) went on to suggest that "one might read Freud as saying that there is a problem with narratives that promise the normalcy of life, that presume a life without difference, without a divided self" (p. 80). This promise of normalcy is a dangerous oversimplification. The problem arises when a culture's definition of normality is inconsistent with the personal beliefs or values of the individual seeking to become a teacher. When tensions arise, preservice teachers recognize the difficulty of the professional role, yet often do not have the license or the language to discuss the problem and figure out the source of their frustration. Typically, neither the culture of the school of education nor the secondary school provides space for such discourse; it is simply smothered by the myth of normalcy.

Several students in this study struggled with tensions between their personal belief structures and their perceptions of professional expectations. Like the narratives of tension between teacher and student subjectivities, the students who experienced the greatest number of these tensions decided not to become teachers (at least immediately after graduation). Of the three who chose not to be teachers—Sandy, Carrie, and Karen—two of them told a large number of these types of narratives of tension: Carrie told 12 of these narratives and Karen told 15. Sandy did not tell any narratives of tension between personal and professional subjectivities, because her tension primarily concerned conflicts between student and teacher selves as described in the previous section. The three students who chose to teach, Linda, Janeen, and Lois, did not tell any such narratives.

The kinds of tension experienced in this category included conflict about educational philosophies, curricular emphases, pedagogical approaches, political and familial loyalties, sexual orientation, and epistemology. Discourses of tension between personal and professional subjectivities were the most difficult to navigate, because little transformative discourse was generated in response to them. A look at Table 3.1 demonstrates that the students who expressed the most borderland discourse didn't express any narratives of personal/professional tension. Why were personal/professional tensions so difficult to manage? Possibly because the personal beliefs brought to the fore in these identity conflicts were those central to the preservice teachers' core identities—these tensions touched on emotional or even spiritual understandings to which the preservice teachers were deeply committed.

Carrie experienced a great deal of tension between personal and professional subjectivities, namely about curricular focus and the extent to which her personal life could be visible in a professional context. Her academic interests lay in the areas of women's literature and feminist theory, and the classes she enjoyed the most as a university student tackled issues of gender, sexual orientation, and the cultural constructs related to them. Through Carrie's experiences in local secondary schools, she became convinced that such topics would not be accepted as a part of secondary school curricula. In my third interview with Carrie, in September 2002, she said:

> I'm realizing that the environment I loved so much and that I wanted to recreate is going to be very rarely recreated [in the secondary school] ... since a big aspect [of mine] is wanting to get into my areas of interest that have developed more into the feminist and queer theory and wanting to approach those and being restricted [in high schools] with what books I can show to my classes, what topics I can talk about—even if I'm not doing an entire unit on homosexuality, am I going to get yelled at or whatever for having it come up in the classroom? I'm like, why the hell am I going to even be there?

This quote was an expression of tension, one that Carrie could not resolve by the end of the study. Carrie identified herself as a lesbian, and therefore she also struggled with the idea of her marked body being accepted in the secondary school classroom. She described herself as looking "butch"—short hair, androgynous clothing, and no makeup. She told me one time she was referred to as a "young man" by a school secretary, and although she said that this didn't bother her, she seemed hurt by the mistake. She was afraid the other teachers and administrators, who did fit the stereotypical image of teacher, would not accept her appearance. Kozik-Rosabal (2001) wrote about how keeping closeted as a teacher can be devastating to the individual *and* to the educational process:

> For a person entering the teaching profession, the weight of these lies keeps them closeted for many years and saps the glorious energy and passion for teaching they could instead direct toward their work. I have known wonderful teachers, gay, lesbian, and bisexual, who have gotten ulcers, had nervous breakdowns, and experienced all kinds of stress-related illnesses, which they believe were the direct result of living two lives: one public and one private. (p. 109)

Carrie told me in interviews that she did not want to "be in a situation where I have to censor myself" (April 23, 2002). She told stories of several of her high school teachers who had been gay, and how they seemed to negotiate any professional problems it caused:

Carrie: Well, it was really frustrating growing up. The little town right next to me, Harristown, was basically, like, a suburb of Millsburg, right? You blink and you're through both towns. They had a GSA—Gay-Straight Alliance—in their high school.

They have graduating classes of 40 people, and they had a GSA. Our high school, you know, a thousand students, fairly good diversity, whatever, we tried to get a GSA in there, and the most that we could do was get a diversity club. It was frustrating. I knew of gay teachers. I knew that Miss Martin our teacher was dating Miss Thomas, the Spanish teacher. And, of course, you know, the gym teacher.

Janet: Did the other teachers know it?

Carrie: Well, I'm trying to think. It's like, how did I know this? I'm trying to remember how I knew this. And, you know, I would swear up and down that it's true, but I can't think off the top my head how it is that I knew this. And, you know, how open were they about it? Because I can't—she was a gym teacher. I remember when I had her as a freshman—I mean, as an elementary school [student], she first entered the Millsburg school system. And then I remember in high school she was around again. She was a coach, and she was a part-time physical educator. Then my sophomore or junior year she left because she went to Vermont to get a civil union with her partner. And so I know for certain about that one. (Laughing)

Janet: So you may have had insight or knowledge—

Carrie: Yeah.

Janet: That maybe other students didn't know.

Carrie: That other students didn't know. And so, it's like, I knew but I—

Janet: Did they know that you knew? I mean, did you actually talk about it?

Carrie: I definitely went and talked to Miss Thomas about it. She was the Spanish teacher. She was the first person that ever gave me a C; I didn't like her. (Laughing) We had issues with each other. I talked to Miss Martin a lot, but I don't think that we necessarily ever openly talked about her orientation. And I knew about other gay teachers, too.

Janet: So when you decided to be a teacher, it wasn't something at first that you were worried about.

Carrie: Was I like, "I can't do this because I'm gay?"

Janet: Right.

Carrie: Um, no. It wasn't until after I decided to be a teacher that I went to see a lesbian comedian, Suzanne Westenhoffer, and her partner is a teacher. I think she's an elementary school teacher, or junior high or something. And Westenhoffer uses that as part of her act. She talks about it. And, you know, part of the big thing that she talks about is how closeted they have

> to be about their relationship, and how closeted her partner is, because since she's a teacher, she can't come out. And that made me start thinking. That was one of the first times that I started thinking about it. It was like, wait a second. Can I not be out if I'm a teacher? And I was like, okay, we've got some issues. Because I don't want to live a closeted life. I've been out since I was 16, and I've fought long and hard to be comfortable about it—and I don't want to get into this adult professional life and suddenly be back in the closet again. I think that it probably has influenced my decision to stay at the university level instead of going into the public education system and working on my graduate degree while teaching, or something. I also have the mindset, though, that by the time students get here [the university], this isn't when we should start working on it. You know? (Laughing) Maybe we should squirt some liberal people down into the elementary school system and start discussing things then.

Calling herself an "alternative teaching figure" (September 19, 2002), Carrie recognized that her liberal views about education and what should be included in a secondary curriculum caused her tension when she was taking her methods classes. During a lesson plan that was taught by her peers in an advanced methods course the semester before her scheduled student teaching, Carrie struggled with how her peers approached the concept of "gayness" through literature. The students teaching in class had the best of intentions: They wanted to practice how they might address the issue of homosexuality in a secondary classroom and place it on an equal plane with other issues of difference and discrimination, such as racism, classism, and sexism. The students began the lesson with a brainstorming session about gay males before playing a Jewel song, "Pieces of You," containing antihomophobic lyrics.[7] Their intent was to make students aware of the discrimination often directed toward homosexuals and help them to empathize with others unlike themselves. Carrie described this lesson on September 19, 2002:

> They [the students doing the teaching] kind of prompted a discussion by asking, "What's a stereotypical gay male like?" They said, "Think *Will and Grace*. How does the TV sitcom *Will and Grace* present gay males?" And the

[7]The relevant lyrics from "Pieces of You" by Jewel are as follows

You say he's a faggot, does it make you want to hurt him?
You say he's a faggot, do you want to bash in his brain?
You say he's a faggot, does he make you sick to your stomach?
You say he's a faggot, are you afraid you're just the same?
Faggot, Faggot, do you hate him
Cause he's pieces of you? (Kilcher, 1995)

> class kind of produced "emotional," "feminine," things like that. And they said, "Your friend is out in the hall and he's crying, and you ask him 'Why are you upset?' and he says, 'Well, I didn't get a date to the prom.' How do you react to him?" Well, the answers were, "He's a wuss and blah blah blah." So kind of making the point that guys are afraid to express emotion because they might be targeted as gay. When I was writing a response to the teaching, I said I thought they did a pretty good job of introducing the homosexual aspect, but I kind of felt that we stereotyped gay males as emotional, and we didn't really talk about how is that stereotype created. What is good or bad about that stereotype? We just kind of said, okay, gay guys are emotional, now your straight friend is crying and he doesn't want to do that because he might be considered gay. It was presenting this negative thing and having everybody accept this as the stereotype, this negative aspect, and we're going to use this to talk about a heterosexual male who doesn't want to express his feelings. You can't talk about this prejudice [homophobia]. Parents are going to get upset if you talk about this one. But there's only a small number of schools that are primarily White that will get upset if you talk about prejudice against African Americans. But talk about homosexuality in the classroom, that's a big no-no.

Although the students teaching the sample lesson were trying to make their lesson as liberatory as possible, they failed to address some central concerns that Carrie noticed immediately. She told me that she hesitated to be too critical of them in her response, because she did not know if she was being too "personal," or too "social commentaryish," as she put it. However, she was frustrated. On April 23, 2002, she told me that she didn't think she could be a secondary teacher because of such frustrations and the feeling that she would be metaphorically "crushed" by the profession:

> I think there are so many problems, and there's so much room for reform. And I just don't think I'm the person to do it. You know, I think by being in the environment [secondary schools], I'd get crushed. I just don't think that I could live in that environment without being hurt by it almost constantly. But I don't think that I can change it, either. And if I try to change it, I think that I'd get crushed even faster.

Teresa Ebert (1996) commented that, during modern times, homosexuality has become more common and socially accepted (in certain cultural milieus) because, in advanced capitalism, heterosexuality and the resultant labor force are no longer required for economic stability. Therefore, because economic conditions no longer require compulsory procreation or divisions of labor-based on preestablished gender roles, open homosexuality becomes possible. In secondary education, however, compulsory heterosexuality still exists. As Carrie's stories demonstrate, the "environment" of the public school almost always demands a heterosexual, "normal" lifestyle, and this demand seems linked to economic conditions of schooling. In order to secure and maintain taxpayer support of education, public schools must maintain and exude a conservative identity that does as little as possible to offend or alienate stakeholders. Therefore, objectivity and lack of ideological debate are often the desired characteristics of a public school culture.

Such resistance to open homosexuality in public schools is evidenced by the recent controversy over the Harvey Milk School in Manhattan. An Associated Press article published on the CNN Student News Web site explained that New York City spent $3.2 million to expand the school into a "full-fledged public high school for gay, lesbian, bisexual and transgender students" (Ferguson, 2003). The reaction to the school ranged from anger about perceived segregation to outrage over the open admission of homosexuality by gay adolescents. However, supporters of the school cite its necessity to ensure the safety of gay students. The article cited a 2001 survey in which "83% of gay students reported being harassed at school because of their sexual orientation and nearly 70% felt unsafe." In a hostile school climate, being a gay or lesbian teacher might be almost as difficult as being a homosexual student.

Karen also articulated tension between her personal and professional subjectivities. Her tension focused on balancing her family and career: How could she be an attentive mother and also be a secondary teacher? Nearly every time I met with Karen, she had a new idea for how she would integrate these two worlds; in fact, during the writing of this chapter, she e-mailed an update of these plans to me. At various times she told me she would be a high school teacher, a bookstore owner, a graduate student in American Studies, a creative writer, and an adult educator. In our fourth interview, on November 13, 2001, when talking about her idea of opening a bookstore—which she had already named "Worm's Books"—she said:

> I don't really know why I just decided—it was just one day I woke up and I was like, I don't know if I really want to teach anymore. I kind of want to do this business, I think, because I want my family to be a part of it. Because I want James [her husband] to be a part of it, and I want my kids to have a place that they can come after school if I can't be there.

Karen told me in later interviews that she wanted the bookstore to be educational and offer learning experiences and readings for kids. She intended it to be small and community oriented. In a professional writing class she took at the university, Karen developed a Web site for this hypothetical store in which she included a floor plan and a detailed description of purpose.

In addition to her struggles with the logistics of being a teacher (e.g., seeing her children regularly, being able to "connect" with them), Karen also struggled with her beliefs about what schools should be teaching kids. Throughout our interviews, she expressed conservative moral sentiments about the place of politics in education. She supported President Bush and the war in Iraq, for example, and she was a fan of Rush Limbaugh. Being a new mother, she felt very strongly about young people and the kind of education they should be provided. She talked about how becoming a mother had changed her views on education. During our fifth interview conversation, on January 23, 2002, she described two substitute-teaching experiences, one at an alternative school and another at a suburban public high school:

> It's [the alternative school] really small. What it actually used to be was the prison, and you can tell. So they got these kids locked in a prison. Okay. There are two teachers in there, in case something happens. And so, I was talking to one teacher, and she's like, "Yeah, all these kids, their parents—both parents—are either in jail or dead—except for one, and his mom is a prostitute." Okay, so I felt really bad for these kids. They're good kids, beside the fact that they really have problems. You can tell that it stems from their parents' lifestyles. So then the very next day I go to teach at Washington High in the class for the "Tiger-ettes." Tiger-ettes is like this dance club they have, where they wear next to nothing and do half-time shows. The class is a time for them to practice, and it's offered during all 7 periods each day. So I'm thinking, you know, we can fund these things, but we can't take care of these other kids? So yeah, I think about teaching a lot. I think about what I *don't* want to be a part of. And that's what I don't want to be a part of.

This excerpt demonstrated Karen's frustration with budgetary inequities in public education and how such unfair allocation can hurt real students. In our last interview, on April 5, 2002, Karen summarized to me why she had decided not to become a teacher:

Karen: I think it had a lot to do with the fact that I was taken away from teaching classes for a little while and able to see what really was going on with me. And I think a lot of it had to do with Emily [her daughter] and James and the uncertainty of knowing that I was going to graduate without a degree—or a teaching degree—and trying to fit myself into somewhere else, and then saying, well, I just don't want to go back there [to teaching], you know?

Janet: It seems like there were a lot of things in your life taking you in the direction that you've ended up going, but could a little part of it have been your rejection of "the box"?

Karen: I'm not a box person. Yeah, that had a lot to do with it .... You don't have to do that with other professions. There are a lot of things you can and cannot do when you're a teacher just because you're a teacher.

Karen struggled with a job definition that would require her to exhibit and even teach some kind of morality, but simultaneously take religion out of the classroom. During the study, Karen was not able to create and express the necessary borderland discourse to grapple with her tensions. A year after graduating from the university with a degree in English, Karen began the process of applying to graduate school at another university, where she hoped to learn about adult literacy education. Perhaps she just needed more time to figure out how to negotiate the multiple identity positions necessary to becoming an educator. Like Carrie, she saw ideological contradictions between her personal and professional selves that she didn't immediately know how to negotiate. While coaching basketball at a middle school after her graduation, Karen sent a letter to me via e-mail on December 16, 2002. In part of the letter she wrote, "A couple of questions that I'm trying to figure out are: Are there certain types of people who belong in certain schools as teachers? Do I belong in this school as a teacher? Am I helping these kids or hurting them? Do I belong in teaching?"

These sound like questions Carrie might also have asked, but for very different reasons. Teacher educators could welcome, or even encourage, such questions in methods courses where they could be explored through discussions or writings. Such explorations might assist preservice teachers in the difficult negotiation of their personal and professional selves and eventually in undermining the myth of normalcy.

The University versus the "Real World": Integrating Secondary and Post-secondary Knowledge

All six students struggled with tensions between what they learned about teaching in university methods courses and what their mentor teachers in secondary school classrooms taught them. These conflicts often went unresolved, because the student either sided with the university and hence could not respect many of the mentor's experience-based practices, or alternatively sided with mentor praxes that challenged many ideas and theories taught at the university. Those who sided with the university had a more difficult time transitioning into the profession, because they struggled to develop collegial relationships with other teachers. In the face of a lack of respect for their mentors, the new teachers sometimes isolated themselves emotionally and intellectually.

Borderland discourse can allow new teachers to build bridges or find connections between their university education and their field-based education. However, when the students did not clearly engage in much borderland discourse, these ideological connections were not made as easily. Moving from their university education into student teaching and/or field experiences made it inevitable that they would compare the two learning environments and what was valued and enacted in each. Two of the three students who became teachers—Linda and Janeen—ended up identifying more strongly with their practical, field-based education and chose to emulate their mentor teachers, whom they found to be successful, effective instructors. Although Linda did engage in borderland discourse, it did not overcome her tendency to disregard the university-based knowledge. Her home discourse about teaching, coupled with her field experiences, left little room for it. The third student who became a teacher, Lois, expressed various borderland discourses that helped her to connect the two experiences fairly consistently, and I did not get the sense that either university or real-world discourses were privileged.

The three students who did not choose to teach—Sandy, Carrie, and Karen—identified primarily with their university education and seemed to believe that what they learned in their methods courses was not being appropriately or adequately enacted in secondary school classrooms. They engaged in little borderland discourse and made few attempts to integrate the two ideologies. Because they thought they were in the right, it may have seemed hypocritical to these preservice teachers to consider opposing pedagogical approaches.

Linda knew a lot about the teaching life from growing up and hearing her mother's discourse about being a middle school teacher. Many times, Linda talked to me about issues such as salary contracts, unions, discipline, and curriculum; she often sounded like a teaching veteran, and in a sense she was. She knew a lot about the "culture" of the secondary school from her mother. This knowledge benefited her as she student taught and became integrated into the profession. She felt she was, in a sense, already acclimated into the profession through this in-home apprenticeship of observation. Linda believed that the methods classes she took were a little unrealistic, when compared to her other teaching knowledge:

> Well, when you go out in the school, I feel like some of the methods classes I had last semester were, you know, very student oriented. Which is true, I totally believe that and that you should do lots of group work and stuff. But yet, when you go out in the schools you see this style where it's not so much that way. And it's hard to get a feel for like, is there a happy medium? Because that is what I would like. I want plenty of group work and stuff, but there is still, like the Nancie Atwell book [*In the Middle*] .... I'm not sure I could pull that off unless I was an incredibly veteran teacher. I think I would have problems with it myself, actually. (Interview #3, September 11, 2001)

Linda was recognizing the importance of borderland discourse (a type of a happy medium), but she was not yet able to engage in such professional integration. In addition to doubting how realistic her university instruction was, Linda also felt torn between the differing perspectives of her mentor teacher and her university supervisor. She worked hard to please both, but she believed that the mentor teacher (representing field-based knowledge), the teacher with the most recent hands-on practical experience, was the more knowledgeable and dependable source—even though her supervising teacher (representing university-based knowledge) had been in the high school classroom for 17 years prior to attending graduate school:

> You have to juggle the mentor teacher's expectations, then your supervising teacher, and then of course your students who would be there anyway. And that's been stressful because my mentor teacher's thoughts are so much different than my supervisor's thoughts. Mandy [supervisor] wanted me to move two people, and Mrs. Vanderholt [mentor] didn't. And so I didn't [move the students] because I figured it was her classroom and I just can't move them. I think Mrs. Vanderholt has been teaching for so long that she sees everything. And I think in a lot of ways it's good. I mean I really do. At first, because I've been in college so long, when I first went in there I thought, this seems so structured and stuff, but she knows what doesn't work. She really, I think, judging from all her lesson plans, she has really tried everything over the years. And I think sometimes the university supervisors see things from a more philosophical standpoint. (Interview #4, November 12, 2001)

Linda entered her student teaching experience thinking she really didn't agree completely with the methods of Mrs. Vanderholt, her mentor teacher. However, after spending some time in her classroom, she rejected some of the university instruction and came to believe that the mentor had the correct approach. She even got angry with her classmates who described Mrs. Vanderholt as too traditional and "structured":

> Really, it almost frustrates me in some methods classes, some people will talk about my mentor teacher, who was one of the field experience teachers last year, and they would say things in class like, "Oh, she's so structured," and things like that, and it would bug me because she *is* very structured. But at the same time you know, I'd like to see them go in and make it better because I'm not sure that [they could] ... she's been doing it a long time. (Interview #3, September 11, 2001)

There are two things I found interesting about this comment: One is that Linda and her classmates initially thought that structure was inherently bad, and they seemed to have gotten this idea from their methods classes, and second, Linda was defending her mentor teacher's "structured" approach because it had stood the test of time. Why does it seem appropriate to teach students that structure is a negative classroom quality? Structure seems to be equated with conservatism, traditionalism, and authoritarianism. However, a high amount of consistently applied structure can be a very positive and useful quality in a classroom, especially at the middle school level. In the four narratives in which Linda spoke about feelings of tension between the university courses and secondary school mentorship, she privileged the so-called practical over the university coursework in three of the stories. However, Linda was making attempts at being proficient in two discourses: the discourse of the university and that of the real-world classroom in which she was working. She was aware that the binaries existed. Consequently, her attempt at living in two discursive worlds at the same time was sometimes frustrating for her, and she seemed to feel like she was being pulled in two opposing directions. From her interviews, it appeared that Linda believed she had to choose one side or the other in order to avoid hypocrisy or inconsistency. My hope is that she resisted such a simplistic choice in favor of more complex integration.

The perception of the necessity of juggling others' opinions when making classroom decisions was a common theme among the study's participants. Similar to Linda, Janeen and Sandy also experienced such tension when they tried to make pedagogical choices. It seemed as if their enactments of professional identity were filtered through various points of view before they could be realized, and then they were often enacted in a modified form. Linda, Janeen, and Sandy all told stories about changing their classroom practices based on what their mentor or their supervisor expected, despite what their own beliefs and opinions were. The viewpoints they enacted were refracted through the lenses of the people who evaluated their performance and eventually assigned their student teaching grades.

Janeen, who like Linda tended to identify with the practical ideologies, described a lesson that she and a peer taught in a methods class because they thought it was practical—even though it didn't seem to be as entertaining as many lessons taught by their peers:

> A lesson that we did in class was just on literary devices, and it was very basic, and the response that we got from a lot of the students was that it was more boring than some of the other lessons; but one person wrote down that it seemed like something that you would actually have to do in a real classroom. We had to do so many lesson plans in that class, or we had to watch so many lessons, that it got to the point where people were just trying to outdo each other. For us, we didn't want to do an entertaining lesson. We could have cared less whether we entertained them, but we actually wanted to do a lesson that you would really use. (Interview #3, September 10, 2001)

Janeen noticed a difference between the typical sample lessons taught by her peers in methods classes and the *real* types of lessons a teacher would teach on a daily basis. She seemed to see two categories of lessons: those that are entertaining and fun or those that would be really necessary. Janeen told two narratives of tension between practical and university ideologies and approaches, and she took a teaching job after graduation at a large, urban high school in northeastern Indiana. She appeared to be successfully beginning her career in this setting.

Carrie told the same number of narratives of tension between university and practical experience as Linda did (a total of four), but, conversely, she privileged the university ideology in each narrative and chose not to teach after graduation. In fact, she decided not even to student teach. Many times in our conversations, Carrie talked with frustration about the methods employed by a field experience mentor with whom she worked. She found the class boring and repetitive, and she was disappointed with the quality of the work she saw students completing. As she said on September 19, 2002, in our third interview conversation:

> But the excitement's gone away, too. My first visit was interesting because it's an 11th-grade English class, and I don't know what the tracking is at McCallister High School, but it's pretty much just an average level 11th-grade class. It's American literature, and my first day in there I realized that their textbook is an anthology, and I started to think back to my own history, and I don't remember having anthologies when I was in high school. So immediately that just didn't mesh with my idea of what high school English should be like. And then they were doing the Declaration of Independence; they were reading that, and it was very odd. They have this workbook that goes along with it and that has text in it, but that has questions in the margins, and I thought the questions were very simplistic. The way she [mentor teacher] led the class—not to criticize her at all—but I mean it just seemed that what the university teacher education program has been teaching me and preparing me to do when I get in the classroom is like 20 feet over the head[s] of the students I am going to encounter in the classroom.

Carrie believed that little of what she had learned in her methods classes would actually work in the secondary classroom she was observing, and she was startled by the discrepancies between the classroom, her own memories of high school, and the portrayal of high school classes in methods courses. She said that it was hard for her to accept this contradictory reality because, as she was observing the class, her education had "been kicking in" and making her increasingly critical of what she was seeing. In the end, she felt that there were not very many ways she could apply what she was learning at the university in the secondary classrooms in which she worked. Again, she confronted the opposition of the personal and the professional, and her passion to teach dwindled.

Although it is true that Linda, Janeen, and Carrie struggled with tensions between what they learned in their university courses and what they saw happening in real secondary classrooms, it is more relevant that they could not completely integrate the two or see how what they learned in the university might be modified and successfully implemented in the secondary classroom. Linda and Janeen, who chose to become teachers, dismissed some of their university education in favor of the practical knowledge bestowed by their mentor teachers during their student teaching experiences. Linda, more than Janeen, engaged in increasing amounts of borderland discourse in our last two interviews, which I describe in detail in chapter 7. Carrie, who chose not to be a teacher because of a variety of tensions she experienced, decided that her university education would probably not make sense in a secondary context. Consequently, she was frustrated and disillusioned. Lois, alone among the six participants, seemed to be able to use borderland discourse to understand connections between university coursework and real-life teaching and begin to become, in Gee's (1996) words, "bi-Discoursal." I also describe her discourse in more depth in chapter 7.

A final way of understanding the tension between university and real world education is to think of it in terms of defining the field. In July 2003, at the International Federation of Teachers of English conference in Melbourne, Australia, Allan Luke (2003) described in his keynote address how English teachers have a problem because we don't know what our field is anymore—we don't know what it means to be a teacher of English. Are we literature teachers? Writing teachers? Cultural studies teachers? Media teachers? Or all of the above? Our field seems potentially broader than some disciplines may be. We often don't see ourselves as simply teachers of skills or competencies related to reading and writing. Making the problem more confusing is that others also have their definitions of what an English teacher should be and do, and these conceptions are often very different from what the teachers themselves value. In part, what the students in this study were experiencing when they moved from their university classes to their field experiences were discursive expressions of varying definitions of the field and, by association, of the teacher's place within it.

Chapter 4

Memories and Enactments: Experiential Narratives of Teaching and Learning

As John Dewey (1938/1963) argued, experience is a vital aspect of an effective education. Through experiencing various intellectual, hands-on activities, students can deepen their understanding of the topic at hand. In order for an experience to lead to learning, it must connect to and positively influence future experiences as well as encourage interaction with the material, social world. Dewey emphasized that experience by itself is not inherently educative; experiences must exhibit the qualities of continuity and interaction in order to lead to human growth:

> Different situations succeed one another. But because of the principle of continuity something is carried over from the earlier to the later ones. As an individual passes from one situation to another, his [sic] world, his environment, expands or contracts. He does not find himself living in another world but in a different part or aspect of one and the same world. What he has learned in the way of knowledge and skill in one situation becomes an instrument of understanding and dealing effectively with the situations which follow. (1938/1963, p. 42)

This continuity, this connection between past and present experience, is consistent with borderland discourse through which the preservice teacher connects personal ideologies and subjectivities to professional ones. Random experiences without such connection do not lead to professional identity development, and sometimes disjointed experiences can lead to the rejection of the idea, concept, or issue under consideration, such as when a new teacher rejects a particular teaching method because of a failure to see its long-term classroom potential. Conversely, continuous experiences provide opportunities for the preservice teacher to enact the behaviors and embody the physical presence of a professionalized, successful teacher. Daily experience is how identities are translated into real-world action, and such action affects the lives of others, namely students. Dewey discussed this material and social component of experience in *Experience and Education* (1938/1963):

> The statement that individuals live in a world means, in the concrete, that they live in a series of situations. And when it is said that they live *in* these situations, the meaning of the word "in" is different from its meaning when it is said that pennies are "in" a pocket or paint is "in" a can. It means, once more, that interaction is going on between an individual and objects and other persons. (p. 41)

Similar to learning concepts or mastering ideas, identity construction not only affects experience, it also depends on experience—or the bodily enactment of ideological positions—in order to come to fruition. This chapter lays the groundwork for this discussion of experience by analyzing narratives told by the six participants about educational events they remembered both as a student and as a teacher. The experience itself, when it is happening in the present moment, is the enactment, the embodiment (or attempt at embodiment) of a particular identity position; the narrative told after the experience represents each preservice teacher's attempt to understand the experience and reflects how the preservice teachers fit this experience into their developing personal and professional selves.

The experiential narrative is a genre of discourse that, when engaged in by the preservice teachers, was influential in the development of teacher identity. Sometimes these experiential narratives helped the participants make connections and become more confident and effective secondary teachers; other times, the narratives led to frustration and the decision to leave the profession. Regardless, it is safe to say that experience is a powerful factor when learning to teach. Researchers J. Gary Knowles and Diane Holt-Reynolds (1991) wrote up their discovery that experiences as a student and as a teacher tended to have the most powerful influence on how new teachers chose to teach; therefore, Knowles and Holt-Reynolds tried to structure their methods classes around a series of *experiences* rather than the description of discreet facts or the passing on of discreet bits of knowledge. They maintained, "Preservice teachers use their experiences as students as if these were prototypical" (p. 104). In other words: Preservice teachers remember what made them feel good or bad when they were students, and then they try to reproduce the pedagogies they associate with these feelings when deemed necessary.

The students in my study reacted similarly to their educational experiences. Along with Knowles and Holt-Reynolds, I believe that the teacher educator must provide opportunities for these experiences to be reflected on, reinterpreted, and reorganized "as an internalized vision of self" (1991, p. 103). The students who were given opportunities to do such reflection and reinterpretation, or who were able to engage in such activities on their own, began the more successful development of a professional identity. Such reflexivity was reflected in their borderland discourse—the discourse that makes connections or establishes continuity and takes into consideration knowledge provided by others, such as university instructors, peers, and mentors.

THE EXPRESSION OF EXPERIENTIAL NARRATIVES BY THE PARTICIPANTS

The students told many stories about their experiences of being a student and, more recently, of teaching in field placements, substitute teaching assignments, practice teaching in methods classes, or student teaching internships. I categorized these stories as serving one of two general purposes: describing positive memories and successes ("success" stories) and describing negative memories ("failure" stories). Some stories began as failure stories and by the end turned into success stories (the preservice teacher found a way to correct or improve the situation). I coded these stories "success stories" because their overall function seemed to be to describe a success.

When analyzing experiential stories about student experiences, few failure stories were told. There were only seven student failure stories across all six participants. The lack of such negative stories about school experiences may demonstrate that students who become teachers tend to have had positive experiences as students and retain mostly good memories of middle and high school life. In contrast, there were a total of 40 student success stories told across all six participants. The number of success stories alone did not predict whether the preservice teacher chose to teach after graduation. There were other important variables—such as the amount and nature of narratives of tension and narratives of failure as a teacher—that were also significant in this decision. However, there are indications that the students chose teacher education to eventually relive the positive feelings they had had as students and create similar positive memories for others. For example, Carrie, Karen, and Linda told specific stories about positive or life-changing experiences with teachers and school, and linked these memories to their initial decisions to become teachers. However, when real teaching experiences didn't match these memories of secondary school life, tension resulted, as I described in chapter 3. Such disjuncture seemed to make Dewey's intellectual "continuity" between experiences less likely.

The students who told the greatest number of success stories about classroom teaching (as opposed to experiences as students) during their student teaching experiences or secondary field placements were often more likely to become teachers after graduation. Linda told 32 such teacher success stories, Lois shared 26, and Janeen told 9. Additionally, these same students told fewer failure stories about teaching than did their peers who chose not to become teachers: Linda told one failure story about teaching, and Lois and Janeen told none. Sandy, Carrie, and Karen—who decided not to teach—told five, two, and three teacher failure stories, respectively. As can be seen in the narrative chart (Table 3.1), Sandy actually told more teaching success stories than did Janeen; however, Sandy's stories were primarily about her tutoring experiences or practice teaching in methods courses (5 of the 13 total success stories were about tutoring; 3 were about teaching in methods classes). Sandy told only five teacher success stories about her student teaching or other field experiences in which she worked with secondary students; as I've indicated previously, she chose not to take a secondary school teaching job upon graduation.

It can be argued that the telling of positive stories about teaching not only reflected but also affected the quality of participants' early teaching lives. Although I cannot demonstrate that the telling of positive stories *caused* positive experiences, the students who told the most positive stories about teaching in the secondary school decided to stay in the profession, as well as expressed more good feelings about their student teaching internships and excitement about their future teaching lives. Bruner (2002), Wortham (2001), and Gee (1990/1996) all wrote about the reciprocal relationships between discourse and identity, and the data demonstrates that the students in this study whose discourse about teaching was positive tended to have more successful experiences in student teaching internships as measured through grades, supervisor and mentor teacher responses, and self-reports. Linda, Janeen, and Lois all earned an A in student teaching; Sandy earned a B, and Carrie and Karen chose not to student teach at all, changing their professional goals prior to the start of the internship semester.

Stories of Learning

All six participants told positive stories about being a middle school, high school, or university student, and had positive memories of this time of life. The telling of positive stories about educational memories was a common feature of the preservice teachers' discourse. The preservice teachers told these positive stories when they explained why they decided to become teachers in the first place. They linked their decision to specific memories about classes, teachers, and school experiences that made them feel good about themselves. Following are examples of student success stories told by Lois, Linda, and Janeen.

Lois told the following story on January 25, 2001:

> I came as a pharmacy major and hated all my pharmacy classes, and then I took an English class and I absolutely loved it. I was getting great grades, and in my other classes I wasn't getting, you know, so good of grades, and then it was so weird because I was like, I've always loved this, and I knew that I wanted to be in English. And then I took half professional writing courses and half English education courses. I took one of each. And then I decided that I would enjoy teaching because I could not only study the subject matter, but also I thought it would be fun.

Likewise, Linda told a positive student experience story explaining why she chose to become a teacher. Unlike Lois' college story, Linda's story was from high school, and she narrated it at the beginning of the study on January 18, 2001:

> It started in high school. My freshman year, English was okay. You know, I've always liked to read. In fact, I had a really great sixth-grade teacher so that kind of balanced out the [negative] eighth-grade experience. I had a great sixth-grade teacher, and I started getting interested in teaching, well, administration was my first thing. I wanted to be an administrator really bad. I didn't want to be a teacher, and that was an issue because my mom was like, you know, you really probably can't do one without the other. So then I was trying to think, well, what could I teach? And my first thing was Spanish, because I was pretty good at Spanish, and then I decided that I just couldn't deal with that every day. But my junior year I had a great English teacher that I just loved, and I had two great English teachers my senior year, and after that I slowly started to want to teach English. I really wanted to teach at the secondary level, and then I kind of wanted to teach Spanish and then I got into English. And then it just clicked, because I had, for my junior year and my senior year in high school, I just had incredible English teachers. I loved them, and so I made this decision probably my junior year and since then, I don't know if I want to be an administrator anymore. I thought I did, but now I really want to teach English.

Janeen told success stories of her life as a high school student. She connected these positive feelings about herself to her decision to become a teacher, despite the fact that these stories were not always glowing reports about her teachers. In fact, she thought she was smarter and more qualified than most of her teachers. She told me during our first interview, on January 23, 2001:

> But I wasn't really prepared for the kind of writing that I needed to do in college. So then I thought, well there's obviously a lot lacking in high school, and I took advanced placement classes so I thought I could be a better advanced placement teacher for English [than her teacher had been], and I thought

> about things like that and how I could do better than my teachers had done. I always was—if not the best student, one of the best students. I always had my homework done, things were always perfect, I always got hundreds. A lot of things moved too slowly, and, I really could've done them on my own faster. When I was in the seventh grade, I was in a gifted program. I had two friends, and myself, and another girl, and we were on a future problem-solving team, and it was run through that gifted program, so she [her English teacher] would give us the English assignment, and just say, "Go out of the room, do it," and we would sit down and do it in 3 minutes, where the rest of the class would take the whole hour to do it.

Because, like Janeen, all six of the participants narrated positive student memories, I began to wonder why only half of them decided to become teachers after graduation. What was the difference between the discourse and experiences of the three students who chose to teach and began to establish professional identities, and the three who did not? Why were success stories validated and reproduced in some students' teaching lives, and not others?

One difference seemed to be related to the number and type of failure stories the participants told, about both teaching and learning. In addition to telling their success stories, those preservice teachers who chose not to become teachers told failure stories about being students. Sandy told one failure story and four success stories, Carrie told four failure stories and seven success stories, and Karen told two failure stories and four success stories. Linda, Janeen, and Lois told *no* student failure stories. Additionally, the students who did not become teachers told more teacher failure stories than did their counterparts.

The following story from Carrie is an example of a student success story about her high school experience that she told me during our third interview, on September 19, 2002:

> I pretty much loved my college-level literature classes. Reading these texts and really getting into them and talking about issues and all sorts of different things about them. And in my AP lit and comm class in high school we did do that. I don't remember us hitting a lot of controversial issues. We read *Beloved* by Toni Morrison, and we read that gangster city book that you and I searched for last year and never found. And so that was an inner-city heroin-gang-related autobiography. That was the riskiest that we got and that's "safe-risky." The structure of it, though, was literary analysis. It was really getting in and picking apart what these books are about, what are their messages. A critical approach, and I really like that, and I think that's what led me into teaching—I'd really enjoy basically getting into Mr. McCallum's shoes—my senior high school teacher—and that was such an awesome class for everybody who was in it.

Despite such positive experiences in high school, Carrie had a difficult time as a *college* student, struggling with persistent depression and feelings of confusion and inadequacy. She had a poor class attendance rate, and had to take several incompletes or retake classes before eventually graduating. She told this student failure story during our second interview, on April 23, 2002:

> I came here, went into engineering. Engineering didn't have a foreign language requirement. Yeah for me! So freshman year I didn't have to worry about it. Then over the summer when I switched majors and I switched schools, I took Spanish 103, which counts as 101 and 102, over the summer, and I got an A. It was all right. Then I took 201, which is Spanish 3, and struggled with it, but got by with a B or something. And then Spanish 4, which satisfies my requirement for the School of Liberal Arts. I've taken it twice now, and the first time I got a D, second time I decided I was going to take it over again to improve my grade, because I knew that I could do it and it was just a matter of me going to class and being on top of it, blah, blah, blah—well, I failed it. And so now I have to take it a *third* time to satisfy my requirement. And it's just like—it's the thorn in my side. This is a class that I dislike, that I fear to a certain extent, you know? I have all these psychological impediments concerning this.

Carrie's success stories about being a student existed simultaneously with failure stories about other student experiences. Perhaps memories of the negative experiences acted as roadblocks or counterweights to possessing complete confidence in herself as a student and as a member of the academic community, especially because her failure stories narrated more recent school events.

In conclusion, the preservice teachers all told positive stories about being students in middle school, high school, or college, and these positive stories often doubled as reasons for entering the profession. However, when participants also engaged in discourse that narrated failures as students or teachers, they were less likely to develop successful professional identities and become secondary school teachers.

Stories of Teaching

The six preservice teachers also told several stories about being teachers or enacting the role of secondary school teacher in field placements or in assignments for methods courses. The greater the number of teacher success stories the participants told, the greater was the likelihood that they would take teaching jobs after graduation. The two students with the highest number of teacher success stories went on to take secondary teaching jobs after graduation—Linda told a total of 32, and Lois told 26 teacher success stories about student teaching and field experiences in secondary classrooms. Janeen, who also went on to teach, told a total of nine teacher success stories. Sandy, who chose not to teach secondary school, told 13 teacher success stories, but only five of these had to do with experiences in real secondary classrooms; the rest of her stories were about methods classes or tutoring experiences. Carrie and Karen told two and four teacher success stories, respectively. In contrast, the three students who did not pursue teaching careers told the most teacher failure stories: Sandy told five, Carrie told two, and Karen three; whereas Linda, Janeen, and Lois told one, zero, and zero, respectively.

Linda and Lois told the greatest number of teacher success stories, and the telling of these stories seems related to the beginning of a successful teaching career. Linda's discourse about herself as a teacher was very confident, and she spoke *as* a teacher often; she seemed to have adopted the teacher persona or role. When talking about teaching during her student teaching internship, she often spoke of her mentor teacher and herself in the first person plural, as "we." She saw the two of them working together, as teaching colleagues. When I asked her during our sixth interview, on April 9, 2002, what she saw when she closed her eyes and remembered back to her student teaching experience, Linda said:

> I see me in front of the classroom behind the podium, probably just talking with the kids, and them being pretty open and talking back. Like, just, you know, conversational. If it were world lit, we'd be reading a story or talking about a story. And they might be writing something. If it were honors, we'd be talking about *The Scarlet Letter*. Or doing an activity with *The Scarlet Letter*. Academic 12 could be a free-for-all. (Laughing) Could've been anything. I always think of academic 12 when I think of student teaching because I taught them the entire time, I think. They were more my class. I think about them a lot. But world lit also, because I loved world lit. I loved teaching that class. When I go back, when I went back yesterday and I saw some of those kids in the hallway, they're the ones who are really excited to see me. Honestly, when I think of student teaching, I didn't have a lot of real problems, and so I think that's why I remember only the good kids, for the most part. I don't think too much about my stressful ones.

Linda actually had a hard time remembering anything negative from her student teaching. She told me that she mostly remembered positive, successful teaching experiences, and she looked forward to having her own classroom where she could continue having such positive experiences. It wasn't as if Linda didn't experience challenges and difficult days—they were just not what she chose to remember after the fact.

Likewise, Lois told many positive stories about her young life as a teacher. I relate only a couple of the 26 teacher success stories that Lois narrated over the 2½ years of the study:

> I had problems with a student I couldn't get to turn in her research project. She was one of my best students last semester. Got a B. Helped me out,

helped me keep the class quiet. You know, one of those kind of classroom-governor types. Helped me keep the class quiet, knew the answers, volunteered to read, and then all of a sudden she just went in this slump. And she ended up arguing with Miss Holmes [mentor teacher], and I just talked to her because I had a really good relationship with her. I help coach the cheerleaders. So I took Becky to cheerleading practice with me one day, and she helped me with the bulletin board, and I said, "Look, I don't know if there's something going on, you know, but," I said, "Becky, you were up here," I said, "and I just watched you come down. This is not the work that you're capable of." I said, "You went from a B to an F right now. Your dilemma should be whether you're getting an A or a B, not whether you're getting a D or an F." And I said, "Why haven't you turned in this big project?" We sat and talked for a while, and I said, "You know, I don't know if there's something going on outside here, but if you need to talk, you know you can come to me." She's like, "I know." She turned in her project the day after that, and it was almost a month late. I can't pass her, but I gave her half credit, which will help her grade immensely. (December 4, 2001)

Lois' story is a perfect example of a teacher success story. She spoke about how she helped a failing, unmotivated student refind her motivation and begin to pass the class. This narrative indicates that Lois was, at this point in her professional development, interested in helping, motivating, and challenging students in her classes; furthermore, she realized that the personal lives and concerns of her students must be recognized and taken into consideration when planning lessons and making assignments. This realization is evidence of an increased awareness of the multiple, fluid subjectivities or perspectives of an effective teacher who must strike a delicate balance between varying the mode and content of her instruction in response to individual student needs and interests, while not foregoing her own goals for instruction. Here is another, similar teaching success story from Lois:

I write really big [on a student paper] "TELL ME MORE, JAMES. TELL ME MORE." He'll just give me a little bit, and I'm like, "Oh! James!" But in class, he's just so good. He makes comments, and I say, "I never thought of it that way," or "Wow," you know. He's so good that way, but he's just not going to go that extra level [on written work]. I've talked to him about it, and he's just like, "Well, you know, this is just what I'm going to do." I stopped him after class [on a day when James did good written work], and I said, "You did such a good job today. Please continue it. I don't know if it was the assignment, or you just decided to work today, but you did really, really well." And he improved for about three days. (December 4, 2001)

Amazingly, Lois was the only participant who did not tell even one negative or failure story about either teaching or learning throughout the entire study. Lois was also the preservice teacher who engaged in the greatest number of examples of borderland discourse during the study, and she eventually became a successful secondary teacher who, as reported in follow-up conversations and e-mail messages, seemed to enjoy her teaching and her students. One could certainly say that the power of the positive story was very great in Lois's teaching life. Among the students in the study, there appeared to be some value in focusing on the positive and creating one's reality (and fledgling professional self) through positive narratives of teaching and learning. Such narratives built much-needed confidence and sustained enthusiasm.

The number of teacher failure stories also seemed important, because the three preservice teachers who chose not to take teaching jobs told the most of this type of story: Sandy told five, Carrie two, and Karen three. Although these numbers are not huge, they are greater than the number of teacher failure stories told by those participants who took teaching jobs: Linda told one such story, and Janeen and Lois told none. As noted in the previous "stories about learning" section, one difference between the preservice teachers, who all told positive stories of being a student, was that some of them also told negative stories of learning and also negative stories of teaching; the students who chose not to take secondary jobs, and, it can be argued, also did not successfully develop strong, initial professional identities, engaged in more discourse that was negative or that told of experiences they viewed as exemplifying failure. For example, Carrie related the following story about a field experience in which she participated during her final methods course. This field experience could have been the final straw in terms of making her decision not to become a secondary school teacher. Carrie told this story during our fourth interview, on December 13, 2002:

> I had one bad experience in there and I'll take full responsibility for it. The first time she [mentor teacher] had me lead the discussion over *The Crucible*, I looked over the study guide questions the night before, and there were actually questions on the back [of the sheet] and I didn't notice that. So I wrote answers to the first page briefly, and it was pretty apparent, plot-based things. So I didn't put a lot of thought into what I was going to do the next day. And then being up there in front of the class and getting to the end of it and at that point realizing I need to flip the page over and seeing there were more questions. The last question was actually more of a conceptual question. And when I got to it, I read it out loud, and I read it wrong because in *The Crucible* you have Reverend Proctor—no John Proctor and Reverend Hale. And Reverend Hale's first name is John. This is setting up my mistake. And throughout the play he is referred to as Reverend Hale and then there is John Proctor. And reading the question it said John Hale blah, blah, blah. And I think I probably read it correctly, but in my mind John equaled Proctor, so on the fly, based on what I read off in the class, I tried to supplement the answer and explain the question a bit, only I'm applying it to Proctor instead of Hale, so I'm confusing the class because most of them realized it was Reverend Hale and not John Proctor. I started getting really nervous and body heat was exuding, palms

> were sweating, going oh, well this is going really badly, and Mrs. Cavanaugh stepped up and took over and actually one of the students asked her a question and she said, "Are you talking about Reverend Hale or John Proctor?" and I looked at the question and said, "Okay, we're talking about Reverend Hale. Ignore everything I just said for the last 3 or 4 minutes as I was rambling trying to explain this," and then she stepped up and kind of took over. That was a bad experience for me. All my confidence was stripped. And I don't feel comfortable being in front of the class, and I don't feel prepared; I don't feel confident; I don't feel ready; I don't feel anything.

Carrie's confidence did not return, and she never felt comfortable in the role of a secondary teacher during the time of the study.

The students in the study told many experiential stories of teaching and learning that began to connect past and present academic experiences. Telling the stories allowed some amount of reflection on these experiences and how they might affect their developing teaching lives and future pedagogical decisions. Many researchers have found that past memories, biographies, and life histories affect teaching performance in both positive and negative ways (Britzman, 1991/1994; Connelly & Clandinin, 1988; Knowles, 1992; Lortie, 1975). As Schon (1983) argued, meaningful classroom experiences can work in tandem with pedagogical knowledge to create truly effective teaching. On the other hand, experiential narratives can become internally held narrative scripts that, without interrogation or reflection, are reproduced materially as classroom pedagogies, whether they are effective or not. Therefore, experience by itself is not inherently useful; it is helpful only if it is subject to critical reflection. Hence, teacher educators can ask students to tell experiential narratives and then examine them, exploring how these narratives affect their current educational philosophies and pedagogical choices. In the next chapter, I discuss a genre of discourse closely related to the experiential narratives: narratives about the embodiment of teacher identity, which also are important to the formation of a holistic teacher self.

Chapter **5**

Denying the Mind/Body Split: Narratives About the Embodiment of Teacher Identity

A third type of narrative that emerged from the data set was the narrative about the embodiment of teacher identity. In addition to mastering the language of the teacher and having the necessary pedagogical and theoretical knowledge, a new teacher must learn how to physically embody the identity of teacher. Embodiment narratives in this book are connected to experiential narratives because memories, of course, have a sensory, corporeal component. Many readers are likely to be familiar with the theories of Donald Schon (1983, 1990) who, like Dewey, has explored the centrality of experience in the education of a teacher. Schon noted, "Once we put aside the model of Technical Rationality, which leads us to think of intelligent practice as an *application* of knowledge to instrumental decisions, there is nothing strange about the idea that a kind of knowing is inherent in intelligent action" (1983, p. 50).

Schon discussed "reflection-in-action" and its counterpart, "knowledge-in-action," as ways the teacher can connect thinking with doing, or act within a meaningful context to develop specific strategies that are applicable to the situation at hand. In other words, the pedagogical decisions a teacher makes are the result of a combination of intellectualizing *and* doing. Knowledge-in-action does not separate mind from body, or the internal from the experiential; therefore, Schon's work validates the experiences of teachers as important to pedagogical expertise. As teachers pursue their professional lives and commit more and more successful classroom experiences to memory, their expertise grows. James Gee expressed similar ideas when he wrote, "Discourses are related to specific acts carried out by individuals .... The relationship between secondary Discourses and their 'acting outs' (performances) establishes through space and time *social institutions* (schools, businesses, churches, governments, street gangs, and their sub-institutions)" (1990, p. 178).

Those interested in philosophy and psychology have been debating the veracity of the mind–body split since ancient times. Bakhtin believed that personal meanings are only dialogical when they are embodied (Hermans, 1993, p. 74). These meanings occur when a human voice narrates or expresses utterances that position the speaker in various ways, sometimes in a dialogic relationship with other speakers. Rhetoricians and philosophers Aristotle and Plato argued about whether the mind acts independently of, or in concert with, the body (Plato came down in favor of the independent mind; Aristotle in favor of empirical investigation). Baruch Spinoza, writing in the 17th century, believed that the mind and body were intimately related. Gilles Deleuze, a 20th-century French philosopher, and Robert Hurley (1988) described Spinoza's philosophy this way: "The body is a mode of extension; the mind, a mode of thinking. Since the individual has an essence, the individual mind is constituted first of all by what is primary in the modes of thinking, that is by an idea. The mind is therefore the idea of the corresponding body. Each thing is at once body and mind, thing and idea" (p. 86).

Contemporary postmodern thinkers, particularly feminist theorists, agree with Spinoza and caution those who want to understand identity as a linguistic construction and ignore the material conditions of life. Bronwyn Davies, bell hooks, Teresa Ebert, and Judith Butler have addressed the importance of recognizing the embodiment of identity when describing the lives of women. Because it can be argued that much of women's oppression has been related to discrimination on account of material realities and bodily exigencies—namely, childbirth and childrearing—the recognition of how living in a female body affects a woman's life is essential. These theorists have also pointed to other oppressive realities of women's lives (economic, social, familial) and how these realities are often the result of patriarchy and misogyny.

George Lakoff and Mark Johnson (1999) argued against the traditional Western philosophic thought that the mind is separate from and superior to the body and that, through self-reflection and concentration, reason (or the intellect) can transcend the physical. They asserted, "Reason is not disembodied, as the tradition has largely held, but arises from the nature of our brains, bodies, and bodily experience. This is not just the innocuous and obvious claim that we need a body to reason; rather, it is the striking claim that the very structure of reason itself comes from the details of our embodiment" (p. 4). To put it another way, thought or reason cannot exist without their embodiment—both in the obvious way (in order to think, one has to have a brain and a head to keep it in) and also in a more complex way:

The physical experiences and material and discursive realities of a person during a lifetime create certain brain patterns, neural connections, and synaptic threads that make reasoning possible. These biological realities make certain understandings more likely and possible for a particular individual. In short, according to Lakoff and Johnson, one's biological or physical makeup and corporeal experiences exist in a reciprocal relationship with thinking, reasoning, and decision making.

Likewise, the life of the teacher is constructed, in part, through and because of the material realities of a teaching life. As I described at length in chapter 2, the life of a teacher in the United States is constrained by political ideologies that seek to further various and sometimes contradictory agendas, often with little actual attention paid to the preferences or expert knowledge of teachers. Since their inception, public schools have served a cultural function in addition to an intellectual one. Schools have been sites for the promulgation of rules for "good citizenship" and proper social behavior for children and young adults. Therefore, bells ring, school desks are hard and unforgiving, and teachers enforce rules that regulate the bodies of students in addition to their minds: for example, seating charts; dress codes; eating and drinking; going to the bathroom; and when, where, and how to talk. Teachers are also subject to such regulations; although their rules may be less explicitly communicated, they are no less real.

The preservice teachers in this study came to realize the difficulties in embodying the teacher identity during the time I knew them. For some of the students this embodiment was much harder than it was for others. The ease or difficulty of embodying a teacher identity was dependent on the amount of similarity between the preservice teacher's body and that preferred in the discourse community of secondary school teachers. The greater the perceived difference between the personal and the professional, the less likely it was that the preservice teacher would choose to teach upon graduation.

When I refer to teacher identity and the discourse used to facilitate it (i.e., borderland discourse), I am talking about discourse as a way to bridge the gap, not only between various internal states—such as what I'm calling subjectivities, situated identities, or ideologies—but also between these internal states and the physical enactment of "teacher." Discourse can be seen as an attempt at embodiment because it seeks, in part, to close the gap between the outer, material world of sensory input and the internal, intellectual, or emotional world. Through self-expression, an individual can both respond to and initiate physical activity or concrete action. Much of a teacher's classroom life involves decision making and acting in response to student needs; therefore, the teacher must be able to enact her identity, beliefs, or philosophy on a regular basis. However, stereotypical, culturally scripted notions of the teacher's body complicate the situation by providing rigid guidelines for appropriate action and teacher embodiment. The new teacher has to figure out how to place herself in the body of the teacher, a body that is often culturally defined as White, female, middle aged, politically conservative, and heterosexual.

In the October 2004 issue of the journal *English Education*, Tara Star Johnson wrote about a research project she conducted examining the bodily, or "erotic," aspects of teaching. Using bell hooks' definition of pedagogical "eros," Johnson discussed how the preservice teacher participants in her study were concerned about their physical appearance. Her student participants worried about how they dressed, if they looked "old" and professional enough, and if they looked too sexually attractive. Johnson asserted:

> The underlying assumption here is that it's not okay for female teachers to draw attention to their bodies in ways that could be interpreted as "slutty" ... anything outside of the typical female teacher's appearance is grounds for students' noticing and remarking upon the teacher's body. It is impossible to escape the students' gaze. (p. 16)

Similar to the students in Johnson's study, the students in my study struggled with the physical aspect of establishing or creating a professional identity. For these preservice teachers, attention to the bodily component of teaching, or the "performance" of teaching, was essential for effecting a successful transition from life as a student to that of a teacher. Various genres of discourse assisted in this embodiment, including the narratives describing the embodiment process itself, which are the subject of this chapter. Later in the chapter I also include details from selected observations I conducted of one of the preservice teachers teaching in a secondary classroom. (In my research, I conducted observations of four of the six participants.) These descriptions both provide documentation of how she enacted with her teacher identity and supplement the self-reports of such embodiment.

Traditionally in teacher education, the Cartesian separation of body/mind creates disembodiment and a sense that teaching is a purely intellectual act. However, those who have written about identity development (Erickson, Maslow, Freud, Belenky et al., Gilligan, etc.) have known that the material body, the physical enactment of identity positions, is important. What all of these thinkers have in common when they discussed identity was the belief that an individual's sense of self is formed, in part, through interaction with the world and with other human beings. Although these theorists had different ideas about the progression of identity development and what its key "stages" are, none of them understood human identity as a completely internalized process. Whether it's Maslow's "hierarchy of needs" or Gilligan's "ethic of care," all of the theories incorporated an individual's physical interaction in and with the world in some fashion. In Maslow's hierarchy (1962), one must have basic material needs met, such as food and shelter, before turning to more abstract processes of growth. In Gilligan's (1982) and Belenky, Clinchy, Goldberger, and Tarule's (1986) feminist schemes of identity development, women were shown to form their identities, at least in part, based on connections with others. Belenky et al. called this "constructed knowing." It is logical that such theories of personal identity construction would apply to the construction of professional identity as well.

To develop a critical pedagogy for teacher education that takes into consideration professional identity development processes, teacher educators must address the difficulties of the embodiment of a teacher identity. A critical pedagogy is not simply intellectual; as Paulo Freire (1970/1993) described it, it is also potentially freeing from societal constraints. Critical pedagogue Peter McLaren (1995) termed embodiment "enfleshment" in which unequal relations of power are manifested through our bodies and embedded in our experiences (quoted in Hocking, Haskell, & Linds, 2001, p. 146). Hocking, Haskell, and Linds wrote about embodiment as transformative:

> Often we take the notion of transformational pedagogy to involve simply changing minds—changing ideas. It may be concerned with issues of societal change at an ideological or structural level. In this context there is overlap with critical pedagogy. Adding elements of embodiment moves us towards a holistic approach; our idea of consciousness moves us from something exclusively rational and in the mind, and broadens it to include feelings, emotions, desires, and our bodies. Transformation begins through our embodied interactions with/in the world. (p. 77)

In general, teacher educators are not comfortable discussing the emotional lives of students. I often talk to teachers who would really rather not know about anything too personal concerning their students, nor do they really want to talk about their students' personal, bodily, or emotional responses to texts or experiences. This hesitance may, in part, explain the difficulty negotiating personal versus professional tensions discussed in chapter 3. As academics, we are used to living lives in our heads, because we prefer intellectualizing above all other ways of knowing. However, a teacher stands up in front of students every day—his or her body is the object of their gaze. Learning takes place not only in the mind or even in the emotional, internal life of the student, but also in the body where thoughts and feelings are housed.

The belief in embodiment and the necessity to pay attention to and nurture the mind, body, and spirit is often referred to as holistic education (Miller, 1997). Memories, emotions, and beliefs are, in part, understood through the body, and attention to bodily responses to various experiences is important to holistic learning and identity formation. Preservice teachers could be asked to reflect on their bodily responses and feelings before, during, and after teaching a lesson, for example, or interacting one on one with students, parents, administrators, or colleagues. Bodily responses such as tension, aches and pains, nervousness, or fear are not only thought about, they are felt.

Cultivating an awareness of these corporeal responses can help preservice teachers better understand their development as teachers and assist them in becoming more comfortable and effective in the role of teacher. Denying or ignoring the bodily component of teaching and insisting, explicitly or implicitly, that teaching is an art that can be learned completely through intellectual study and critical thought is essentially unfair to the new teacher who must place his or her bodily self in front of 120-plus students every day to enact the role of teacher. Teachers stand, sit, move around the room, talk, smile, point, yell, sigh, dramatize, and laugh as they feel necessary or compelled. Teaching, although of course an intellectual act, is also dependent on a human body. Otherwise, distance learning would be overwhelmingly privileged as an educational method, and that is not the case, regardless of the benefits of computerized instruction. Janet Emig (2001) argued in "Embodied Learning":

> Foremost, I believe that this shift [to technological learning] requires us to make powerfully and ineluctably the case for what I and others call *embodied learning*, the learning that can take place only through transactions with literal others in authentic communities of inquiry. Embodied learning is unique. We must make the case for what embodied learning represents and achieves over cyber learning. Otherwise, our grounded, subtle, and complex knowledge will not, I believe prevail—politically and economically—against the seductive simplicities of technological models that confuse the acquisition of information with the comprehension and creation of concepts. (p. 273)

Some of the preservice teachers in this study could not embrace the stereotypical body of the teacher as their own. In addition to the compulsory age, race, ethnicity, and sexual orientation (at least in more conservative areas of the United States, such as where my university is located), the clothing of female teachers often situates them as less professional than their administrative or postsecondary colleagues and even innocent or childlike (e.g., sweaters with apples or other brightly colored, cartoonlike designs; holiday-oriented clothing or jewelry; and book bags with pictures or teacher-friendly slogans). This discourse of clothing and appearance is more suited to the child than to the adult professional, and it is relatively asexual. In Ginsburg's study of the teacher education program at the University of Houston in 1985, he wrote about the importance of "professional" clothing, and how faculty advisors and mentors often stressed to students the significance of a certain kind of attire. He viewed this emphasis on "socially constructing an image of professionalism" through clothing as being inherently connected to issues of social class stratification. He maintained:

> In a culture in which white collars and blue collars serve well as symbols of a complexity of differences in lifestyle and life chances as well as economic and political power, it would be difficult for references to clothing to be understood otherwise. The point is that students were not only being advised on how to get a job, but on how to symbolize their aspired to class position with clothing. (Ginsburg, 1989, p. 137)

There is a certain kind of material, physical orientation to the world that is preferred in various communities of discourse, and the discourse of the secondary school teacher is no exception.

Heightened awareness of the present moment is essential to creating a satisfying professional identity that honors material and bodily experiences. I agree with Kozik-Rosabal (2001) when she asserted that teacher education students must become aware of their feelings, thoughts, and physical responses to pedagogical or classroom events. I remember a story I once heard about a Buddhist monk who often spent time receiving visitors seeking his advice and assistance. These people would come to him with all manner of ailments, and although he didn't claim to be a "healer," the people flocked to him daily. When asked how he could deal with such persistent and consistent pleas for help, he answered that it was easy: He simply listened to the person in front of him at the time and interacted with him or her as if only that moment existed; he didn't worry about all of the other people in line with different problems.

I find this story useful when we think about teaching.[8] Secondary school teachers are overwhelmed with the number of decisions they must make in a single day, or even in a single hour. There are constant demands from students, and every student has an issue or a problem that, to him or her, is the most important problem or issue in the world. It is easy to feel overwhelmed with all of these demands to the point that a teacher is continually thinking about what is to be done next instead of living in the present moment. With heightened awareness of the embodiment of teacher identity, perhaps teachers can find enough peace and focus to calm their bodies and nerves and listen to a student's request or truly engage with a student's comment during a class discussion—rather than thinking what they should say or do next. This is not to say that teachers should ignore pressing needs of students who might not be engaged in the present discussion; however, I think that too often teachers are overwhelmed by the constant stimulation and demands of the school day. They go about their duties in a state of keyed-up

---

[8]Much of what I refer to in the chapter about embodiment is consistent with Buddhist philosophies. Concepts such as mindfulness, holistic awareness, and concentration are basic tenets of Zen Buddhism. Vapassana meditation practices ask the practitioner to focus on the corporeal and how emotions and thoughts "feel" or reside in the physical body. The Buddha reportedly said that humans are composed of "five aggregates": form, sensations and feelings, consciousness, perceptions, and intentionality. To read more about how Zen Buddhism and English teaching intersect, see Robert Tremmel's *Zen and the Practice of Teaching English* (1999).

nervousness or agitation. Such a mental and physical state does not foster effective interactions with students or emotional health.

So how can teacher educators help their students achieve such embodied peace or calm purpose? One way that has been used frequently in methods classes, although for a slightly different purpose, is oral or written reflection on practice. Reflection, as it is normally done in such courses, allows only the intellect—not the body or emotions—to speak up. We ask students to write about their process of creating or teaching a lesson plan, for example, and we are referring to their *intellectual* process. We ask students to evaluate the lesson based on how it addresses state educational standards or the alignment between objectives, activities, and assessment. These things are important, but they ignore the bodily and the affective. In order to achieve a truly liberatory or holistic education, we must pay attention to the mind, body, and spirit of student teachers. To do this, we might ask them to write or talk about their identity positions or subjectivities in addition to examining and seeking to accept those of others, and to pay attention to the "moment" when they are teaching—be aware of not only their intellectual responses to teaching but also their affective and bodily responses. Then, students can reflect on these responses because their awareness has created the necessary amount of distance from them. Without such attention to the bodily, without admitting that the core identity is not only intellectual or ideological but also corporeal, the new teacher will have a difficult time developing a self-actualized professional identity.

THE EXPRESSION OF EMBODIMENT NARRATIVES BY THE PARTICIPANTS

The narratives of embodiment told by the participants concerned issues of gender, body size, age, class, sexuality, and race and ethnicity. Much like the narratives of tension, if the narratives of embodiment of teacher identity expressed an overwhelming concern about the disconnections between the student teacher's perception of self and the perceived cultural script or model of the teacher body, then the student often did not choose to become a secondary teacher upon graduation. The issues of gender, body size, and age were more common and less difficult to resolve—the issues of sexuality and race/class were more difficult to overcome.

The students who told the most narratives about confusion or frustration concerning embodiment issues had the most difficult time integrating into the profession immediately after graduation. Carrie told 12 such stories, and Karen told 8. Carrie's stories were predominately about sexual orientation and related issues of appearance. Karen's stories were primarily about race and ethnicity, although she also told stories about gender and class. The remaining participants all told stories of embodiment, and there didn't seem to be a connection between the number of stories they told and whether they elected to take a teaching job upon graduation. However, the stories of Linda, Janeen, Sandy, and Lois were all about less difficult, although still relevant, issues of class, body size, age, and dress. In the rest of this chapter, I give several examples from the narratives of Carrie and Karen. Also, I share some of Linda's stories along with some notes about my observations of Linda's teaching during her student teaching experience.

Karen had difficulty with the notion of diversity and multiculturalism as it was discussed in her education classes. Often, the notions of multiculturalism include the idea of a kind of color blindness or rhetoric of sameness. Although notions of "multiculturalism" have become more complex in recent years, and educational researchers and university professors rarely see multiculturalism as offering a type of cultural "buffet," it's unclear to me whether students understand the complexity of the diversity issue. I can think of no student in my program who would argue that all students, regardless of racial, ethnic, gender, or class markers, should not be treated fairly and equitably. However, I'm not sure they know how to enact pedagogies that value diversity. In short, it's one thing to learn the "diversity mantra"; it's another to value and respect diversity in day-to-day practice.

Vivian Paley, in *White Teacher* (1979/2000), frankly discussed how she learned to work effectively with African American students in her kindergarten classes. Paley, who at the time was a 60-ish, White, Jewish elementary school teacher with a middle-class background, initially found herself awkward and uncomfortable with the notion of difference in her classroom. Therefore, she avoided the topic (even when her students brought it up) and simply refused to discuss differences among the children, as if the acknowledgment of difference constituted tacit discrimination. Paley's response to diversity in her classroom is a classic example of the enactment of the "rhetoric of sameness" that multiculturalism often produces, despite the best intentions of its practitioners. In the preface to the 2000 edition of *White Teacher*, Paley told the story of a faculty meeting in 1973 that prompted reflection on her interactions with African American children. I recount the story here because Karen's story echoed Paley's early revelations:

> The year is 1973. A unique event is taking place at our bimonthly faculty meeting. Six African American parents have come to talk about their children's experiences in our school. I don't recall how the invitation came about. The faculty is known for its liberal ideas and there is a long tradition of rational discourse in our community. That we happen also, with the exception of two teachers, to be white in a predominantly white school hardly seems to matter. We expect to be told, by this panel of black men and women, how well we are doing.
>
> The story that emerges is entirely different. "If six boys are running in the hall," says one father, "the black boy will be singled out." Another parent is

> even more specific: "I have watched teachers make so much of what a white child says, then barely acknowledge the opinion of a black child. It has happened to my own daughter." And so it goes around the table, each speaker declaring the existence of prejudice and unfairness in our school.
>
> We are caught by surprise, as though none of us has a clue about the things we are hearing. "You're wrong," a teacher says. "There's absolutely no color line here. All the children are treated the same."
>
> My colleagues and I become silent .... Later it is discovered that someone neglected to turn on the tape recorder. The meeting is never referred to again at school. (Paley, 1979/2000, pp. xiii–xiv)

The teachers' defensiveness spurred Paley to begin keeping a journal detailing her interactions with her students, and eventually to confront her tendency to ignore and suppress differences between White children and children of color. I think this anger, this defensiveness, was similar to Karen's attitude that was revealed in her interviews with me. Like the teachers at Paley's school, her intentions were good—however, I believe she was in denial, a denial based on a logical, intellectual commitment to "multiculturalism" that is rooted in no embodied or emotional understanding of diversity.

An emphasis on false objectivity or a rhetoric of sameness can make preservice teachers less likely to think about and interrogate their own subject positions. Their own race or ethnicity is not the issue; rather, the issue is a tolerance of the race and ethnicity of others, namely their future students. Karen's narratives made it clear that perhaps a lack of attention to the preservice teacher's racial and ethnic subjectivities is not the most effective way to educate a new teacher, especially one with little experience with people unlike him- or herself. Britzman (1998) wrote about how examining one's own "otherness" can affect one's response to difference in others:

> But such efforts involve thinking through an implication that can tolerate a curiosity toward one's own otherness, one's own unconscious desires and wishes, one's own negations. My interest is to provoke conditions of learning that might allow for an exploration that unsettles the sediments of what one imagines when one imagines normalcy, what one imagines when one images difference. (p. 95)

By examining one's own various and particular subjectivities, a person might recognize that he or she does not define "normalcy" and that there are a variety of types of people in the world with whom he or she will be asked to interact. In contrast, Karen, a White, working-class student from Indiana, felt that much of the discourse about diversity during her college education was nothing more than "politically correct" identity politics. In fact, she often used the phrase "political correctness" when discussing her teacher education or the policies that guide public schools. She seemed to believe schools were fearful of lawsuits and other societal retribution if teachers and administrators didn't engage in so-called politically correct language or behavior. Like many other conservative Americans, Karen had difficulty with these notions and seemed to feel censored in her discussions of difference—it was as if she couldn't talk about certain things because she was a White person, and she resented the feelings of White guilt that such politically correct attitudes made her experience.

For example, Karen was deeply unsettled by a "literature of Black America" class that engaged in a discussion of whether White teachers should be able to teach African American literature. She was angered and confused when her African American teacher suggested that this should not be allowed. She described the incident this way in interview #3, conducted on September 10, 2001:

> So then I do my presentation, because you have to do presentations in that class. I did the first one, and I read an article about what does it mean to respect African American Literature? I did my report on that, but in the article, it was talking about how there were not a lot of African American Ph.D. students. It was talking about those statistics and stuff. And the author was talking about so, if you don't have a lot of those African American people to teach the literature, who teaches the literature? Well, obviously White people are going to teach the literature. So then in class, during my presentation, we get into this discussion about "can a White person teach African American literature?" having no background being an African American. And some people said, well, yeah, they can if they learn about the African American culture, and other people said, no, because they really don't know anything about being African American. So this put me in a place like, hold on! In my [education] classes, we're being taught, you know, be multicultural, be this, be that—and—but I have no basis for being anything else than what I am.

Karen was experiencing some direct conflicts between her "multicultural" education about teaching and her education about diverse literature at the college level. She felt as if her own racial and ethnic identity was relatively static and easily definable (White); she seemed to think it was unfair to assume that only African Americans can teach African American literature—after all, she would always be White, and what could she do about it? Whiteness is the default race—it's the nonrace, if you will. Karen was the norm, the majority. She simply couldn't help being what she was. Karen's response got dangerously close to accusations of reverse discrimination, although Karen never described herself as a victim of oppression because of her race. She did tell me that she thought her own cultural heritage was being disregarded, even though she didn't seem to have a very strong idea of what exactly this heritage was.

This tension between her working-class, White upbringing and the diverse discourse of the university was consistently expressed throughout our conversations. Only toward the end of our time together, when Karen took a job coaching middle school basketball at a school with primarily African American students, did she begin to work through these ideological tensions. In fact, she wrote me a long letter in which she tackled them. In December 2002, she wrote, in part, "I have told you that I was called racist every day. But the situation was that from the moment some of the parents came into our first practice or when they came into the parent meeting I held, they judged the fact that I was [W]hite."

Karen was beginning to understand that she also had a race, and that her race might be an obstacle to communication in certain contexts; she was beginning to understand that race was not something that she only thought about in terms of the "other"—it was also something she had to apply to and understand about herself. In other words, she was starting to figure out how to live in her own skin (her White skin) and in her own body, as a teacher.

I'm not sure exactly what went on in those parent meetings, but I do know that for the first time in her life Karen was interacting with people different from herself, different from those in her hometown. And she didn't quite know how to deal with them. She had to remove several students from the basketball team because of disciplinary problems, and when those students were also the African American students on the team, dissension resulted. In response, she defended her own actions and her commitment to fair and equal treatment. She appeared to be trying in good faith to enact a multicultural pedagogy, but the theories she had learned at the university didn't provide her with the tools to enact them in the real world. She had little idea about how to translate a multicultural philosophy into pedagogical action. Unfortunately, Karen had no mentor while she was coaching who could assist her with this phase of her identity development. One course in "multiculturalism" and frequent admonitions to respect diversity were not enough to help her embody an effective and well-rounded teacher identity.

Carrie similarly struggled with issues of embodying a teacher identity, although her frustrations were most often connected to her sexual orientation, not her race. Carrie was a self-defined lesbian, who came out in high school. She was worried about how her "butch" or masculine appearance would be accepted in the secondary English teaching community, especially by her colleagues, students' parents, and administrators. This concern about fitting into the culture created anxiety about teaching, and seemed to increase Carrie's worry, which exacerbated her lack of self-confidence in the classroom. Forming a sexual identity is a discursive act (if one accepts the definition of discourse as including embodiment); therefore, like other various subjectivities and identity positions, sexual orientation is a part of a whole human being and, therefore, must be compatible with one's professional identity and the discourse that creates and reflects this identity. In secondary teaching, such compatibility is very difficult unless a teacher fits into the standard identity model, which is, of course, heterosexual, and usually also married with children.

A new teacher who is lesbian or gay might struggle with the notion of the compulsory heterosexuality of the American teacher and attempt to hide his or her lifestyle. Carrie did not want to live a closeted life. She wanted a professional life in which she could freely express her personal subjectivities when and if appropriate. As I discussed in chapter 3, Carrie experienced tension between her personal and professional subjectivities—for example, concerning her desire to teach feminist and queer theories and texts to her future secondary school students. To Carrie, suppressing these ideas and goals was paramount to personal hypocrisy, in addition to constituting the elimination of much of her passion to teach. Carrie described her frustrations and struggles with assuming a teacher body in the following excerpt from our first interview, conducted on January 23, 2002:

> Coming from where I'm coming from, and looking to the future, I feel like when I start teaching, I'm going to have to change my appearance. Because I don't feel like I'm going to be accepted in a classroom with the way that I look right now. I've always kind of had this thought in my head that when I grow up I'm going to look a certain way, it's just going to naturally happen. It's like I'm just going to naturally metamorphose into the way that I see these adults look, you know what I mean? And this started when I was young. When I was in elementary school and early junior high, I'd look at some people—some of the girls who were just a few years older than me, and in high school, they'd wear makeup. And I'd be like, "Well, when I'm that age, I'll wear makeup too." Yeah. I'll just, you know, naturally, that'll just happen, because that's what happens. And then suddenly I was in high school. I still wasn't wearing makeup. I was like, hey, why didn't that happen? (Laughing) You know? What's going on? I personally—appearance-wise, for myself, I think that I could change my appearance, to a certain extent, without feeling like I was giving up part of my identity. Because my hair is very short right now. I just got it cut. But when it was longer than it is now, still not long, but you know when it was a little longer than it is now, I still felt pretty comfortable with myself. I can be kind of flexible in that respect without really feeling like I'm really losing too much of my identity. If they expect me to go in to work every day wearing a skirt or a dress, and having my bangs teased out, or whatever, I'm sorry but—you know, I just—I couldn't—I mean, I think about my experience in high school and I can remember female teachers wearing skirts and dresses, but I do feel as if I could be a professional- looking educator without totally going against my identity. But I still foresee issues. I think you still have to be really careful about being in the education field.

Although Carrie said that she would be willing and able to modify her appearance to a certain extent in order to teach in a secondary school, she was not willing to "wear a skirt or dress" everyday or "tease out" her bangs. These details were perhaps overstatements about codes of appearance for secondary teachers, but Carrie clearly felt as if she would have trouble fitting in and that her bodily discourse was not the clearly accepted norm in the classroom.

Although Carrie related stories about high school teachers she had who were able to negotiate personal lives as lesbians and professional teaching lives (see chap. 3), she told of more recent experiences in which friends or acquaintances had trouble embodying a teacher identity:

> There's a friend of mine, she's 37. She graduated from this university with an education degree. Secondary education degree. She substituted for a little while. She hasn't been teaching for probably about 6 or 7 years, and the main reason why she left teaching was because she didn't feel like she socially fit in. And it was largely due to her appearance. She just never—you know, she's not a classically feminine, I guess—I don't really—because I wouldn't really consider her to be masculine either, but I would say that typically you would consider her to dress a lot younger than her age, and not conservatively or whatever, and she's got a lot of issues with her physical appearance. And one part of her says, this is how she's comfortable, this is her independence; another part feels like she can't be an educator because she can't fit into it, and there's too much pressure for her to fit in physically that she can't live up to. And now she's trying to get back into it [teaching]. And she's facing the same issues again, and she's like, well, if I start substituting, I have to go out and buy a whole new wardrobe. See, she loves working with kids, and if that's all there was to it, I think she would feel very comfortable. But she has to consider dealing with her peers and the other teachers, then she feels like she's giving up part of her identity, and she doesn't fit in—that she'll never be accepted. (Interview #1, January 23, 2002)

This knowledge of the experience of her friend reinforced Carrie's belief that the physical embodiment of a teacher is very rigid and culturally defined as conservative. Although Carrie's understanding was rooted in an unfortunate truth, I believed there were ways for Carrie to integrate her personal identity discourses with the professional ones that might ideally stretch societal definitions of "teacher." Unfortunately, Carrie experienced no borderland discourse at all—she worked with no mentor who was able to help her make linkages or find connections between these various and contrasting identity positions or spaces. Carrie's situation was very difficult; the connections she needed to form were between very diverse identity positions that often seemed irreconcilable. Without strong mentorship at both the university and the secondary school levels (and perhaps even at home or with personal relationships), it was almost unrealistic to expect that Carrie would be able to create and express appropriate and helpful borderland discourse. To complicate matters further, Carrie came from a lower-middle-class background that valued vocational training and getting a job that paid a living wage after graduation. Carrie wanted and needed to explore her personal subjectivities and how they may have intersected with various professional choices; however, this contemplation seemed to necessitate leisure that she couldn't have:

> I grew up in a lower-middle-class family, and I very much understood money and happiness as being together. And now over this past year, I've had such a complete transformation. What I told myself is, when I graduate, I can do whatever the hell I want. It doesn't matter, you know? It's like I can do whatever I want. I have no responsibilities to anybody at that point. If I want to go to the boat—to the coast and work the boats, which, you know, has been this lifelong kind of battered-down dream—I've had an obsession with boats my entire life—then I can do that. But then what I had to realize was that I'm going to be graduating with somewhere like $25,000 worth of student loans. Twenty-something, last year, I think—last year it was around $16,000 and by the time I graduate I'm estimating probably around $25,000. But with that there I need a source of income that at least is going to let me pay $300 a month to student loans. You know, and that got me down again. (Laughing) I started to get depressed again. But then I talked to my brother, and going out to Nevada seems to be kind of a compromise between the two things. He's a foreman [in construction] out there, and he can probably get me a job. (Interview #2, April 23, 2002)

Class issues were another embodiment concern for Carrie. Economic realities affected her professional choices in a number of ways. Although she would have liked to take some time to explore personal and professional options, this option was an economic impossibility for her. In the discipline of English education, many of our students are from similar working-class or lower-middle-class backgrounds and families that value a vocational component to education. The earning of a "straight" English degree is not encouraged. I can hear the parental chiding from my own adolescence: "And what exactly would you *do* with such a degree?" Carrie told me several times that she would like to go to graduate school and pursue advanced degrees in women's studies. However, at the time of this book's writing, she was working for a moving company, with no definite plans to further her education.

I include some of Linda's narratives of embodiment tension because she was one student who chose to take a teaching job upon graduation and who seemed to negotiate some bodily tensions fairly easily. However, Linda's tensions were primarily about issues such as age and body size, and their relationship to classroom and professional authority. As I said earlier, such embodiment tensions seemed to be easier to deal with than were the more complex and personal issues of sexual identity, race, or ethnicity. Linda described the following embodiment tensions, all in our third interview, conducted on September 11, 2001:

> They're [male students] very, you know, they're just so much taller than I am. But really everybody is. But they're just big guys, and that just intimidates me

> because how am I supposed to control a student who is twice my size? But at the same time my mentor teacher does it and she is not going to totally throw them to the wall either, which is good. And she [mentor teacher] did tell me, which I appreciated, that it helps especially when you're younger to look more professional because the more professional you dress, the more the students will see you with respect. Because, especially the fact that I'm short, too. You can blend in pretty easily, but if you're pretty dressed up they're going to be paying attention. We had a girl in one of our methods classes who was wanting to know if she had to dress up for an interview and we were all wondering, what do you plan to wear when you are teaching? And she's like "I just figure the kids will respond better if I just wear regular clothes." And we're all kind of like, oh my goodness! Because I never even thought about that because I was always thinking that you have to dress up. My mom when she started teaching was very, very dressed up—they wore business suits and stuff. And since then, over the years, she's gotten to where she is wearing khakis with Keds. But you can tell her apart, you know, you can still tell that she is teacher, but a part of that might be that she can do that because she is older now. That might help.

As you can see, Linda's embodiment issues seemed more easily negotiated and less personal or emotional. It is significant that Linda wanted very much to achieve the teacher body, to assume the culturally accepted appearance of the secondary teacher. She appreciated advice about "dressing up" and looking professional. She worried about the relationship between her small size and discipline, but the model of her mentor teacher calmed her fears. Carrie, on the other hand, did not value or strive to express the culturally accepted bodily discourse of teacher. The nature of this rigidly defined teacher body was in conflict with her core identity and ideologies. Resisting such discourse is much more difficult than striving to assume it; although neither Carrie and Linda completely embodied a teacher identity, Linda *wanted* to assume it and did not feel that it presented a fundamental contradiction with other parts of her self.

I observed each of the students who student taught (four of the six students) during their experience. Because I've discussed embodiment narratives from Carrie, Karen, and Linda, I now discuss my observations of Linda's teaching, because she was the only one of the three who actually saw her degree program through to this culminating field experience. Linda, as I just described, worried about issues of embodiment that connected with authority and disciplinary issues. In my observations of Linda, she seemed very confident and in control of the classroom. Although not loud or overtly aggressive in her command of the class, Linda exuded a calm self-assurance that seemed to create an atmosphere of peaceful productivity. In other words, I did not see evidence during the two times I visited Linda's classes that she was having any problems concerning control or authority. Here are some excerpts from my field notes taken during each visit:

Observation #1 on November 6, 2001, during first period, 7:30 A.M.: Linda takes roll and writes passes for a while. Two kids leave—where to I don't know. Soon after roll is finished, Linda says that they will take a quiz "if you were here yesterday" and she tells them to "pull out their notes." She stands at front behind the podium. The teacher's desk is at the back right corner of the room. She seems confident and well-organized when giving instructions. The students do what she asks, and she has a strong, confident voice and manner. She doesn't seem nervous at all.

When students finish the quiz, they put it in the "basket" at the back of the room, the place where they have been instructed to put all work when it's finished, apparently. They do it without asking permission, so it seems like a normal part of the class. Linda tells them that when they are done they can get a British world literature book off the back shelf to use today. Apparently they don't take the books out of the room. Students get the books, and overall, I am struck by how quiet and well behaved they are. They do what they are told in a very routine fashion. The students are dressed in typical teen ways, at least for this area. There is one White boy with dreadlocks and a Marilyn Manson t-shirt, and there are several girls wearing hip-hugger jeans and tight sweaters that allow their midriffs to show. There are one or two kids with "funky" hair—green or long—but not too many. They all wear school ID badges around their necks on black cords.

Observation #2 on December 6, 2001, also during first period at 7:30 A.M.: Before the bell rings, Linda is asking students who don't have their IDs on where their IDs are and asking them to get them out. She gives a tardy slip to a student. It is hot in the room today because of the unusually warm weather, so there is a box fan on the floor, running. Linda has a couple of announcements and reminders about an assignment due tomorrow which is to bring in the address of someone to send a Christmas card to. The mentor teacher is typing up a worksheet on her computer, and Linda looks to her and asks if there is anything else that needs to be mentioned. She says no. Linda says, "Turn to page 253 in your texts." She writes, "Dramatic Irony, Situational Irony, and Verbal Irony" on the board and says that they are all types of irony in the play they are going to read today. She asks, "Does anybody remember what dramatic irony is?" A student answers, too quiet for me to hear but supposedly answers correctly. She asks students about each type of irony, and then she says that they will need to know these terms for the quiz after they read the play today. There are 21 students in class. She asks for volunteers to read the different parts in the play and some students do volunteer. She tells them they are going to take a quiz after reading. A student comes in late. Linda reads the narrator part. They are reading a Nigerian play called *The Jewels of the Shrine,* by James Henshaw. Students read their parts and keep up fairly well. Linda interrupts occasionally and asks them comprehension questions about what's going on—maybe 3–5 times over the course of the hour. There are *Scarlet Letter* mobiles hanging from the ceiling and they are very visually appealing and seem very well done. There are images and quotes from the text hanging from the hangers. For example, one student has attached a real tree limb from the hanger, one a foam sun, one fake roses, and another the silhouette of a man, and these images are surrounded by typed up quotes that I assume explain the symbols, although I can't read them from my seat. The play they are reading is about a grandfather whom

> his grandsons treat poorly and who fools them into treating him well until his death. After they finish reading, Linda asks them what they think—do they think we should respect our parents and grandparents? One student says "yes." She [Linda] hands out a worksheet and the students begin filling it out. They are also asked by Linda to give one example of each kind of irony from the story on the back of the sheet. Linda writes the full definitions of each kind of irony on the board for their reference. Class ends. Most students have turned in the worksheet in the box at the back of the room.

Both of these excerpts show a classroom that was fairly tightly managed and controlled. During my visits, I observed no disciplinary problems or even hints of them. Whereas the first excerpt contained more of my personal reflections than descriptive evidence, the second excerpt provided empirical support for the assertion that Linda did not seem to be having problems managing her class—even if the class might have seemed to be engaging in pretty routinized, predictable activities. However, it's interesting that Linda appeared concerned about her authority and issues of control, as stated in the interview excerpts. Perhaps her level of concern actually resulted in a more tightly organized and traditionally structured class than would have been necessary or even optimal for student learning (e.g., worksheets, and question/answer versus discussion). It's only a hypothesis, but it's possible that with more attention paid to her embodiment of teacher identity, including critical reflection on how both her experiences and sense of corporeal self affected her classroom discourse, Linda may have been less worried about control issues and more likely to take curricular and pedagogical risks.

The embodiment of a teacher identity is an important part of learning to be a teacher, and I believe it is the component of teacher identity that is most often overlooked. Talking to students about their "teacher bodies" and how they can negotiate the transition to a professional identity that is too often associated with stereotypical and conservative physical traits or behaviors is not easy; however, such attention to material and physical issues is important in the teacher education class. This attention cannot stop where it traditionally does—with a simplistic and often patronizing discussion of "professional dress" and appearance. My theory is that most teacher education students know they are supposed to "dress up" when they engage in field experiences. What they don't know is how they can negotiate the divide they often feel between their bodies and material lives and the body and life of the teacher as it has been conveyed to them through books, movies, classes, and other cultural texts. This is where the teacher educator must step in with assignments and classroom activities that assist in the creation of a fully embodied teacher identity.

Chapter **6**

The Influence of Others: Narratives About Family and Friends

It should be no surprise that in many of the participants' stories, significant others (family, friends, partners, or peers) were often mentioned. Human beings are inherently social, and we often handle stress and celebrate success by sharing experiences with others who care enough to listen. We also tend to evaluate ourselves by comparisons with others who are engaged in similar activities. The six women in this study were no exception: They talked to me about family and friends who were important to them. Although these people often had personal, family connections to the participants, they also played significant roles in the participants' professional development.

Clearly, people who comprise the home discourse community to which students return at the day's end, during the summertime, and during school holidays affect how they think and feel about teaching. The professional self does not exist in isolation from the personal self and associated relationships, even if the teacher does not consciously acknowledge the connection. In fact, many of the foundational narratives and images of teachers that a student brings to a teacher education program are formed in the home discourse community, during childhood and adolescence. Gary Knowles (1992) noted, "The results [of his research] suggest that early childhood experiences, early teacher role models, and previous teaching experiences are most important in the formation of an 'image of self as teacher'" (p. 126). Our parents and other close family members are our earliest teachers and educational models, whether for good or bad, and the lessons we learn from them remain with us and often affect our actions without our conscious awareness, until we subject them to critical reflection. Additionally, there is a connection between family and professional embodiment. The family and community into which individuals are born determine their social class, ethnicity, race, and ideological frameworks or foundational beliefs. These biological and material realities result in ideologies and discourses that constitute an individual's identity. As Brent Hocking suggested, "Family members, lovers, and twins often seem to orient themselves to the world in very similar ways. Their biologies as well as their manners of living have become embedded in particular network of relationships—ecological niches—that bind them together" (Hockin et al., 2001, p. 227).

The home discourses or "ecological niches" formed by the family and friends of the participants sometimes created bridges for students as they moved from being students to being teachers, helping them integrate more easily into the teaching life. However, at other times these home discourses provided only transitory assistance as the preservice teachers either simply imitated the educational discourse of family and friends or found themselves taking opposite ideological positions for the sake of individual differentiation without a great deal of reflection. Occasionally, home discourses actually impeded a preservice teacher's access to the educational community because social class positions or family responsibilities alienated them from the "normal" cultural definition of a teacher.

When analyzing the data, I noticed something interesting about the six participants: Half of them came from "teacher families"—they had mothers, aunts, uncles, brothers, grandmothers, and so on who were currently teachers or had been in the past. These students' beliefs about teaching were powerfully influenced by these role models. Linda's mother, as I've mentioned, was a teacher whom Linda often consulted for advice during her education, and her grandmother, an uncle, and an aunt were also teachers; Janeen's brother was an English and social studies teacher, and her boyfriend was studying to be a physical education (PE) teacher; and Sandy's brother was a practicing English teacher, and her mother was a former school board member.

When I discovered the prevalence of these multigenerational teacher families, I began wondering why this phenomenon seemed to happen so often and if it was unique to teachers. I discovered one research study that addressed this issue, conducted by Alice Duffy Rinehart (1983), who explored the issue from a feminist perspective. She found that "Occupational inheritance was progressively more likely among women teachers, with daughters following their mothers, sisters, or other female relatives into teaching" (p. 302). Over half of the teachers in her study who were all women had direct relations with people who were teachers, reaching back at least one generation. Rinehart's study did not include men, so there was no way to compare genders. However, anecdotally, my experience has been that male preservice students also often come from teacher families. Rinehart's findings remind us of the primarily female cultural definition of teacher that I discussed in chapter 2. Historically, teaching is a "woman's" profession, and many of the problems faced by teachers, including low wages and lack of cultural status, can be traced to early misogynistic responses to female educators. In fact, Mark B. Ginsburg (1988) posited that the hierarchal structure of a typical career in public education is modeled on a traditional patriarchal family system, with the men (administrators) at the top organizing and supervising those doing the day-to-day labor (female teachers). In 2003, an AP news story stated, "only two out of ten teachers in America are men, the lowest figure in 40 years, according to a National Education Association survey" (Feller, 2003, p. 1).

So why would having teachers in their families make the participants also want to become teachers? Teaching is an incredibly difficult occupation, and the low wages, low status, and increasing governmental control often make teaching seem like a profession to be avoided rather than pursued. Knowing more about the profession because of family members' discourse may seem to increase the likelihood of one *not* becoming a teacher instead of the reverse. However, because that didn't seem to be the case for my participants, the rewarding aspects and positive potential of a teaching life must also be communicated very convincingly through these home discourses. Another possibility is that increased comfort or familiarity with educational discourse might lead young people to choose teaching as a career—they feel that they know the good and the bad, and there will be few surprises. This theory seems particularly accurate to describe Linda's experience. Additional research concerning these multigenerational trends could be very enlightening for teacher educators who are interested in broadening the demographic characteristics of those who choose teaching as a career.

THE EXPRESSION OF FAMILY AND FRIENDS NARRATIVES BY THE PARTICIPANTS

To summarize, two of the students who chose to continue to teach, Janeen and Linda, came from families of teachers. Two of the three who chose *not* to teach, Karen and Carrie, did not. The remaining two students, Lois and Sandy, did not fit this pattern of teachers' children becoming teachers themselves, because Lois had no immediate family members who were teachers but still chose to teach, and Sandy had a brother who was a teacher and still chose not to be a classroom teacher. Therefore, in this group of participants there was not a one-to-one correspondence between having family who belonged to the professional discourse community of teacher and becoming a teacher, although the majority of the students who became teachers did come from teacher families.

Linda demonstrated the highest occurrence of narratives about her family and friends in connection with her teaching life, with a total of 10. Linda spent her childhood hearing her mother's teaching stories and learning to assume the discourse of teacher. One might guess that Linda herself was often the subject of her mother's teacher discourse as she instructed Linda in various life and literacy skills. Linda's mother helped her to define the teaching profession and understand what she saw, as an adult, as the limits and boundaries of its discourse. Surely, conversations were had at the dinner table, phone conversations with colleagues were overheard, and Linda was a student in classrooms down the hall from her mother's.

In her case, this apprenticeship seems to have had both positive and negative repercussions. Initially, Linda was enabled and assisted by her mother's life as a teacher, as she felt more comfortable and confident entering the profession. However, her imitation of her mother's discourse, from language to lesson planning and from work habits to dress, initially may have limited critical questioning that could have lead to creative, innovative approaches and ideas. As described in chapter 3, Linda's ideological tensions were limited to those I call "simple, binary" tensions between university and real-world pedagogies and student versus teacher subjectivities.

Although Linda did engage in a relatively large amount of borderland discourse during which she attempted to negotiate these binaries, in many ways she continued to imitate her mother's teacher discourse and pragmatically apply it to her own experiences and education as a teacher. Hence, most of the time she chose the real-world pedagogies exemplified by her mother and mentor teacher over the university-sponsored ones. Linda did not express any tension concerning her ideological beliefs about education or educational concerns that may be termed personal or political, such as race, class, and gender. Remember that, in chapter 3, all of her narratives of tension were experienced as conflicts between student and teacher identities and university and practical pedagogies; she told no stories about conflicts between personal and professional ideologies or expectations. This evidence suggests that Linda believed her ideological positions were stable and not in direct conflict with those of the educational system. The borderland discourse in which she engaged (and that I describe in depth in the next chapter) was discourse that problematized pedagogical decision making on a "micro" (classroom) level, not on a "macro" or sociocultural level.

Linda's lack of personal versus professional tension made sense considering the environment in which she grew up. She had been exposed to so much educational discourse that she might have felt she had had the time and opportunity to establish her personal beliefs, and to admit that she still had questions would be suggesting that either she was not as prepared as she had thought she was or that her mother's modeling was not up to the task. It can take time for a new teacher to begin to integrate her personal self with her professional life and embrace tensions that can lead to positive change. Admitting the existence of contradiction and ideological conflict is a huge risk, especially for a student like Linda who believed she was very knowledgeable about the profession. Such a cognitive move would result in vulnerability and admitting the imperfection of her most revered model. Eventually, however, based on the experiences of other preservice teachers with whom I have worked, I believe Linda will begin to problematize both her professional and personal subjectivities and recognize how she is different from her mother as well as similar to her. I hope she will allow herself to experience some cognitive dissonance related to her identity as a teacher. In this way, Linda will be able to move from imitation to enactment of teacher identity discourse leading to professional (and personal) identity growth.

Sandy and Janeen's stories were similar, because both of their older brothers are teachers. Their brothers' experiences affected them similarly to how Linda's mother affected her teacher development. Like Linda, Sandy and Janeen engaged in no narratives of personal versus professional tension as described in chapter 3. Sandy and Janeen looked up to and liked their brothers, and they respected their career choices. They both described having professional conversations with their brothers, and these conversations seem to have been arenas for practicing educational discourse.

Sandy had the second-largest number of narratives about family and friends, with seven. Although she chose not to teach in a secondary school, she did decide to work for an educational tutoring company that assisted adolescents struggling in school. Sandy, however, had a very low number of borderland narratives (two), and her narratives of tension revealed that she tended to problematize her professional subjectivities and ideologies, but not her personal ones. Because of her tendency to avoid critical reflection concerning her personal identity and its intersection with a teaching life, her stories about her brother didn't provide her with fodder for true dialogue (either internal or with her brother) about teaching; instead, her brother's teaching stories became (a) inspiration for her own entrance into the profession and (b) models for how she might deal with classroom problems in the future. Although such roles for the narratives might have been helpful at the time of the study, I argue they didn't provide adequate intellectual stimuli for identity growth.

Janeen told fewer narratives about family and friends, with a total of three. Like Sandy, she told stories of her brother who was a teacher and also about a grandmother who used to teach. Like Sandy, Janeen struggled with problematizing her personal subjectivities along with her professional ones; however, she exhibited seven examples of borderland discourse that helped her begin to make the jump from student to teacher. Her examples of transformative discourse demonstrated the beginnings of true critical reflection, as I discuss in the next chapter.

The other three participants—Lois, Carrie, and Karen—did not have primary family members who were teachers, although they could all identify significant others in their lives who were teachers. Additionally, if they traced their family trees, they could usually find someone with an education background in their ancestry. These students told few stories about family and friends when they were learning to be teachers (Lois told three, Carrie told three, and Karen told one), and the stories they did tell were about seeking support from others during high-stress times or concerned positive memories of childhood experiences that had influenced their desire to become a teacher.

In this chapter, the types of narratives about family and friends are categorized as follows: stories about families and friends modeling the discourse of teacher; stories about how families and friends helped participants during times of tension as described in chapter 3; stories about how families and friends, and interactions with them, helped to craft teacher beliefs and philosophies; stories about how families and friends determined or modified issues of embodiment, such as class, gender identity, and sexuality; and stories about how families and friends became an audience for the expression of professional voice.

Family and Friends as Discursive Models

The narratives told that fit into this category were about family and friends who were models for professional educational discourse and hence assisted the preservice teachers in joining the educational discourse community. The educational discourse modeled by selected family and friends introduced the preservice teachers to ways of acting and being that they could imitate in their future careers, provided examples of difficulties of which they needed to be wary and the goals and objectives of a "good" teacher, and encouraged the participants to pursue a teaching career. Linda, Sandy, and Janeen all told stories about how family or friends acted as models of educational or teacher discourse. Sometimes these discursive models were long-term aids for the students as they developed teacher identities; other times, they served as only temporary assistance during specified periods of time in the new teachers' development.

In every interview session I had with Linda, her mother came up. Linda respected her mother as a teacher and valued her advice. However, Linda's mother's experiences as a teacher were, of course, not always positive, and Linda had also heard discourse in the home that expressed her mother's stress and frustration about teaching. In our first interview, on January 18, 2001, Linda said:

> Believe me, when I was in school there were plenty of times I kind of second-guessed [teaching]. Yeah, second-guessed it because we always have dinner together at my house and, she'd [her mother] come home every day, and be like, you know, "Oh, James did this today, and I'm so mad!" and you know she'd bitch to us, well, especially me, and I'd be like "Oh, no, I can't do this." Through high school and even in college, when I'm home over breaks or even now over e-mail, I hear the frustrations, and I have second-guessed it more than once. You know, can I really deal with this type of thing?

Even though Linda heard negative stories about teaching growing up, she still decided to be a teacher. The positive role model of her mother outweighed the negative stories. She worked with her mother as a teacher's aide in the mother's fifth-grade class, and this positive experience solidified Linda's decision to teach.

Also through her mother's discursive modeling, Linda learned about the teacher body and what is and is not appropriate clothing to wear when teaching. As I mentioned in chapter 5, in our third interview Linda told me about her mother's transition in clothing choices over the course of her career and how her mother's decisions had affected her own beliefs about teachers' appearance. Other examples of discursive modeling that helped Linda decide what she should be like as a teacher provided information about useful work patterns and time management strategies. Linda explained that by watching her mother's work habits, she learned how to work effectively as a teacher and still have a personal life. She told me during our fifth interview, on February 23, 2002, "She [her mother] does almost all her work at school. Like she'll put in long hours there to try to avoid bringing work home. I mean she still brings things home occasionally or looks over her lesson plans at home. But she would rather work 10-hour days than bring it home with her."

Linda liked this idea, and she planned to work this way herself once she was a full-time teacher. Linda imitated much of her mother's educational discourse: words, appearance, actions, values, and so on. At this point in her teaching life, I believe Linda was engaging more in an uncritical apprenticeship of observation rather than identity development that would require an awareness of and grappling with ideological tensions and contradictions. By watching her mother, Linda learned a lot about the externals of teacher identity that facilitated her initial move into the profession; however, eventually, Linda will work to integrate personal and professional subjectivities by engaging in borderland discourses, instead of simply imitating the discourse of another. As Lortie (1975) argued about the teachers in his study, "Neither the apprenticeship of observation nor their formal training prepared them for the *inner world of teaching*" (p. 65, my emphasis). They needed to engage in transformational discourse in order to begin to develop holistic professional identities.

Sandy's decision to study to be a teacher was influenced by her brother's current status as a junior high English teacher and football coach. When he decided to teach, Sandy also chose to follow that professional path:

Janet: So does your brother being a teacher have any effect on you wanting to become one?

Sandy: I think partially it does just because my brother and I are really close. My first semester I was undecided, and then I knew I wanted to be a teacher but I didn't know if people would think I was too stupid—there's that doubt, but then my brother decided that's what he wanted to do. He changed his major to education, I forget what it was before, so when he decided to do it I was like, "Well, if he can do it, I can do it," you know? (January 30, 2001)

Sandy believed that if her brother, who existed on a similar experiential and societal plane, could succeed as a teacher, then she could, too. Perhaps no other role model could have so effectively encouraged Sandy to challenge her insecurities and pursue a teaching career. Although Sandy's brother didn't provide many physical or material discourses for her to imitate because they didn't see each other regularly at the time of the study, Sandy's decision to be a teacher was based, at least in part, on her brother's decision to do the same. She and her brother often talked about education during holidays and family get-togethers:

Janet: But do you have conversations about teaching?

Sandy: Mmm hmm. It was his first teaching experience and his own class. He had mentors to talk to, but he still had problems with students just sort of failing. They'd come up to him and be like, "You know you gave me an F?" and he didn't really understand. You always hear other people talk about these things, but when you hear your brother or your mom talk about it, it kind of puts it more into perspective. (January 30, 2001)

Sandy's brother talked about problems he had in the classroom enacting a pedagogy with which students could be successful. Hearing his problems and talking about them with him helped Sandy understand and become more confident about living a teacher's life.

Janeen didn't have any immediate family members who were teachers, but her boyfriend was a PE major and a future PE teacher, and her best friend, Linda (who was also a participant in this study), shared many stories with Janeen about her student teaching experience the semester before Janeen was scheduled to do her internship. Hearing Linda's discourse helped to prepare Janeen for her own student teaching:

Janet: So, how has that been, like, hearing her stories? Has it made you feel better, or more scared?

Janeen: I don't know, because we're so much alike that we're carbon copies, so I know exactly what she's saying is exactly what I'm going to have. You know, when I ask, "Well, how much work do you have?" That's how much I will have because we work the same way. When she says, "I'm tired at this time of night," I know that I'll be the same way. Because we used to be on the same schedule, and we work the same, we put forth the same amount of effort, so I just know that that's how it'll be. So, I don't know if it's making me more scared, but I know exactly what to expect. Sometimes I try to get her to tell me, like, she'll say that a kid was misbehaving, and I'll ask, "Well, what did you say, exactly?" (Laughing) "Well, what were your exact words?" (November 12, 2001)

Janeen saw Linda as a role model for future classroom discourse, almost to the letter. Perhaps she even exaggerated their similarities just a bit. In a later interview, Janeen discussed how she actually didn't experience some of the "low" points of student teaching like Linda did. As it turned out, their experiences weren't identical, and Janeen later recognized this difference. In our last interview, Janeen described both how Linda's discourse had provided accurate preparation for her own student teaching and also how it had turned out to be different from her own personal experience as a new teacher:

> The time [spent on teaching] she [Linda] was right about. Talking about it prepared me for it. It's not as bad actually doing it as thinking about it. I had the same rut [that she had] about last week. I had a rut, and it really started to drag a little bit. But I never had—she said she had a point at Week 6 where she was like, why do I want to do this? I haven't ever had that. (April 4, 2002)

This recognition of personal difference is evidence that Janeen wasn't simply imitating Linda's discourse, but was merging it with her own personal responses. There's a difference between using another's discourse as a model for creating one's own discursive space in a new community and appropriating such discourse as your own. The second seems only a precursor to reflective identity formation. As Lortie (1975) asserted:

> The apprenticeship of observation undergone for all who enter teaching begins the process of socialization in a particular way; it acquaints students with the tasks of the teacher and fosters the development of identifications with teachers. It does not, however, lay the basis for informed assessment of teaching technique or encourage the development of analytic orientations toward the world. (p. 67)

When learning a new body of discourse it seems perfectly natural and helpful to imitate proficient others at the beginning; however, eventually an individual must create his or her own discursive space in order to be a happy and fully functioning member of a community.

Family and Friends Resolving Tensions

The second major category of narratives about friends and family address those that are about how others help ease stress or tension related to teaching. In this section, I describe narratives told by Linda, the most obvious example of a participant relying on family members to assist her integration into the professional discourse community. The two stories that Linda told in this category narrated how her mother helped her decide when to do her student teaching and how her parents supported her during a difficult middle school experience that influenced her future decision to teach. On January 18, 2001, Linda told me:

> I struggled with the decision of whether to do my student teaching in the fall or in the spring. I knew I'd be ready in the fall, as far as having my classes done. So I really struggled with it, but then I decided that I really felt like I needed that semester after I student teach to prepare myself for interviews and get a job. That decision came, also, kind of from my mom.

During the same interview, Linda described how her mother and father supported her during a difficult experience when she was in middle school and how their support made it possible for her to consider teaching middle school English:

> I had an awful middle school experience in English. I hated English when I left middle school. I despised it because I had a really bad teacher. I told my parents about all the things that were happening. They had always taken the teacher's side, because my mom's a teacher, I think, she naturally gravitates towards the teacher aspect of it. Which I understand, and I think that's good. Most parents don't. So at first I think they were a little [skeptical], but eventually they started realizing that I wasn't just embellishing things, that it was really happening, and they were very angry.

Linda went on to say that working with her mom as a cadet teacher, in concert with the support they provided for her during the difficult time in middle school, made it possible for her to consider, and eventually act on, becoming a secondary school English teacher.

In general, Linda talked to her mother for moral support whenever she felt frustrated or depressed about her experiences teaching. Her mother, as a teacher, could understand her emotions. Linda told me:

> I call her [her mother] with my bad days it seems like. Bad days, like that day when my supervisor came. I think I cried on the phone. I can't be a teacher; it was too awful. I'm going to get a bad grade in student teaching. I'll never get a job. That sort of thing. When I'm tired I get a little more emotional. So they came after a football game, and she could tell. She was just like, "Okay what's wrong?" And so I'm just like, "I can't do this." She listens to me. And it's nice. (November 12, 2001)

Such support is needed for anyone moving into a new profession as emotionally and intellectually demanding as secondary school teaching. Conversations like this helped Linda successfully complete her student teaching and begin her move from student to teacher.

Family and Friends Affecting Beliefs and Philosophies

The third type of family/friends narrative told by participants concerns how family and friends affected the developing teaching philosophies or personal pedagogies of the participants. Linda, Sandy, and Janeen told stories of how family members' discourse, including language, attitude, actions, and appearance, affected how they thought about education as well as how they defined good teaching. On February 23, 2002, Linda related to me:

> So, when I was a senior in high school I did the cadet teaching [being a teacher's aide] in fifth grade with her [her mother]. And I just loved that, but I knew those kids were very mature. She just had a great class that year. And they were a lot more mature than your average fifth graders. And that's when I started thinking well these kids probably have the mentality of a seventh grader, so that's when really started thinking well maybe that's where I might want to be [teaching seventh or eighth grade]. Because we got along really well. They were not quite to the point where they didn't care or were totally apathetic, and they liked creative things a lot.

This story demonstrated that Linda had made a decision, with the help of an experience in her mother's class, to teach junior high or high school because those ages are capable of intellectual work that she found interesting as an educator. Linda also narrated how seeing her mother make mistakes as a teacher helped her decide what she didn't want to do as a teacher. For example, Linda told me during the same interview:

> She used to yell. I remember when I was in elementary school I could hear her yell down the hall. And I would be so embarrassed. But now she doesn't yell at all with her kids. And she says that's much better that way because they don't get as upset. I mean they know they've done something wrong; they know if they're written up that that's bad.

From examples of her mother's ineffective teacher discourse, Linda continued to form a mental perception of the good teacher and an ideal classroom environment.

Like Linda, Sandy's mother had an influence on her beliefs about good teaching, although to a lesser extent. Sandy's mother had been on the school board of her school district for a while, and Sandy remembered her mother's opinions of certain teachers she knew while she served in this position. These memories of her mother's opinions and attitudes stayed with her: "My mom was on the school board a long time ago, and she would say, 'You know this teacher has taught the same exact way for 20 years?' and it was just kind of bad" (January 30, 2001). The message was one of condemnation of a teacher who was resistant to change and growth.

Interestingly, Sandy also saw her peers and friends in English education methods courses as important models for development as a teacher. She told me during our third interview, "When I'm in class I feel more confident just because I see where everybody else is as far as lesson planning and stuff like that, and you can feed off everybody else in class, so you can kind of gauge yourself, too, as far as what you believe in, and things like that. You can kind of judge where you are" (September 11, 2001). I found this an interesting comment and an expression of a sentiment that I also heard from other students during the study. Working with peers in classes is important for the students to sustain their motivation and confidence concerning themselves as teachers. Without their peers and friends as role models and points of comparison concerning educational discourse, the participants sometimes found themselves floundering in terms of crafting their teaching identities. Karen expressed a similar feeling when she told me that she lost her desire to be a teacher, in part, when she took a semester off from taking English education courses and was no longer in an environment with peers and teachers talking about teaching. Apparently, excited and positive models of educational discourse are important to sustaining and nurturing preservice teachers and helping them be reflective about their developing identities.

Janeen's grandmother, like Linda's and Sandy's mothers, provided Janeen with a model concerning what a teacher should strive to be. In an autobiographical essay for a methods course in January 2001, Janeen wrote:

> Once I officially became a secondary English education major, I began to contemplate how I had gotten to this point in my life. The answer to this question

> laid largely in the influence of one single teacher. Although at the time, I was not sure that I would ever become a teacher myself, I knew that, if I did, I wanted to model my career, and more specifically, my teaching methods after hers. Her name was Mrs. Parker, and she just happened to be my grandmother, in addition to the teacher who coordinated the gifted opportunities program at my grade school. Mrs. Parker had two credos that both pervaded her learning space, and she encouraged us to function by them: Every idea is a good idea and no put-downs. As simple as they might sound, their effect was quite complex. Learning in such an open environment made me want to teach other students how to read and write in such an environment because it focuses on the students' creation of ideas. By using Mrs. Parker as a model, I hope to teach students how to think about what they read.

Despite Janeen's own negative experiences with "busy work" during her grade school years, she remembers her teacher-grandmother as an exemplary educator who helped her make her career decision. Clearly, Janeen's grandmother affected her early teaching philosophies, which stressed fairness and intellectual exploration.

Family and Friends Affecting Embodiment

A fourth type of family/friend narrative concerns how family and friends and the associated home discourse communities have a direct effect on the embodiment of a teacher identity. As I wrote in chapter 5, all identities are embodied, as are intellectual reason and decision making. Educating a new teacher and ignoring the material realities and corporeal aspects of a teaching life shortchange the student's teacher education and leave him or her only partially prepared to enter the classroom. In chapter 5, I discussed how issues of race, ethnicity, gender, sexuality, age, appearance, and social class affected the professional identity development of the participants. When discussing the material realities of their lives that often affected the ease or difficulty of their embodiment of professional identity, the preservice teachers told stories about their families and friends and where they "came from." Carrie, who was from a lower-middle-class background and had difficulty paying for college, described her family situation to me on January 21, 2002:

> My dad stayed in our lives for a little while. We had visitations with him for a certain amount of time, and then it slowly trailed off. I saw him once when I was 12; I saw him once when I was 14. I haven't seen him since I was 14. And Jason is 7 years older than I am, and so his teenage years were when we were visiting, but it was starting to trail off, and it just seems to have had a big effect on him. He's back with my mom, and my grandparents live in Massachusetts in a different part of the state. Jason sometimes lives at home, sometimes he doesn't. I decided to, you know, get away from home when I came out to school.

Carrie's mother raised her family alone, and she was funding Carrie's education with a certain amount of sacrifice, of which Carrie was well aware. This financial hardship increased Carrie's desire to graduate on time, and it exaggerated her guilt when she decided not to pursue the career for which her education prepared her. Carrie's difficulty resolving tensions between her personal subjectivities and her perceptions of professional expectations stemmed in part from her childhood and adolescence, spent in a lower- or working-class family for whom, perhaps, the stereotypical teacher identity was somewhat foreign. Additionally, Carrie learned in her family the importance of independence, knowing your own mind, and acting on what you believe is right. Perhaps because of these ethics Carrie found it more difficult to give up or repress her belief in critical and feminist pedagogies in the secondary classroom. Additionally, I think this class background added to Carrie's struggles with assuming a personal identity in a world that didn't value her upbringing and lack of financial capital. She was working to find a place for herself in the world, and the additional difficulties posed by assuming a teaching life were more than she could grapple with for the time being.

The material realities of Karen's life involved her status as a wife and a mother. Because of this role, which Karen freely chose and seemed to relish most of the time, she made very different educational and career decisions than she might have if she had been single and a "traditional" student. Her husband and daughter determined, to some extent, the educational discourse in which she was willing and able to participate, just as they contributed to some ideological tensions described in chapter 3. Karen described to me how her husband's job search took precedence over her own educational plans: "If we don't find a job, then we'll probably move to Cooperstown, [and I'll] go to grad school. So I won't be far away. I don't know. Our plan last year was over spring break to find out where we're going by then, and we'd find a house, or somewhere to live" (January 23, 2002).

Karen decided to finish her degree in English at my university and postpone getting her teaching license until after this uncertain move, at which point she intended to go to graduate school. In my last conversation with Karen, she had been accepted to a master's program in education at a university close to the town in which her husband found a job, but she decided to focus on adult, rather than secondary, education. As I discussed in chapter 5, Karen also struggled with issues of race and her own Whiteness while she was in college and also later when coaching in a predominantly African American school. In these ways, Karen's corporeal reality, decided by the family and community into which she was born, affected the progression of her development of professional identity.

Family and Friends as Audience for the Expression of Teacher Voice

The last category of narratives concerning family and friends and their impact on professional identity development is comprised of stories about how such significant others served as an audience for participants when they discussed their teaching experiences. Having a voice and feeling like it was heard were very important to the students, and many feminist theorists have argued that finding one's voice is essential for healthy identity development in general (for example, Belenky, Clinchy, Goldberger, Tarule, Gilligan, hooks, Tompkins).

So, what actually is voice? Is it simply verbalizing an idea or opinion? The before-mentioned feminist scholars defined the term more broadly, as I do here. Voice can be meant literally, as verbalizing ideas to another; it can also mean speaking out or expressing oneself and one's beliefs through writing, through actions or behaviors, or even through appearance. *Voice,* like *discourse,* is a term that in postmodern theory is often understood as plural or multiple. Voice(s) is a sincere expression of ideological belief coming from an individual within a particular subject position. Voice has become a metaphor for individuality and acceptance in our culture, a perception often stemming from talk shows and new-age self-help books. To be "given voice" instead of "silenced" means that others want to hear what you say and respect what you say (or do, or think).

The concept of voice appears frequently in the disciplines of feminist studies and composition studies. The term, much like *classroom community,* is one that is often under scrutiny or is the subject of debate. Many postmodern thinkers see the idea of voice as expressivist and essentialist, assuming an independent, isolated, and relatively stable view of self that simply doesn't exist. How can writers, for example, find their voices in writing when these voices are many and context-dependent? Much of this book has been built on the premise that identities, subjectivities, and ideologies are multiple, shifting, changing, and sometimes contradictory, so I agree that there isn't one essential voice inside us all fighting to escape and make us whole through its expression. However, I think expressing oneself through discourse and having this expression heard and respected is important in order for an individual to develop a healthy identity. Preservice teachers need to voice their developing professional identities so as to continue to make decisions about the identity positions they will choose to adopt.

In composition studies, voice has been applied to the teaching of writing and is often associated with so-called expressivist theorists like Peter Elbow, Donald Stewart, and Donald Murray. Peter Vandenberg (1996) defined how voice is understood in composition studies this way:

> The term voice in composition theory and pedagogy marks a profoundly wide intersection of meaning. It has been variously deployed as a rallying cry for expressivism (Stewart), a symbol for the stage of maturity in a schema of women's intellectual development (Belenky et al.), as a marker for resistance to political oppression (hooks), and as a metaphor or replacement term for style, naturalness, persona, authority, essence, and a variety of other abstractions. (p. 236)

Composition studies, like teacher education, is multidisciplinary, and its definition of voice is no exception as it reflects psychological, philosophical, and writing theory. The understandings of voice forwarded by Belenky et al. and hooks are feminist and political and get closer to the explication favored in this book—a definition of voice that is a combination of personal expression and political empowerment. Vandenberg (1996) went on to write:

> No text has been more influential in advancing this sense of voice than *Women's Ways of Knowing*. In "in-depth" interviews with 135 women, Belenky et al. "found that women repeatedly used the metaphor of voice to depict their intellectual and ethical development; and that the development of a sense of voice, mind, and self were intricately intertwined." (p. 238)

Voice has long been understood as an important part of women's struggle for equality, in order to be adequately heard in a patriarchal culture.

In my study, Linda and Sandy provided good examples of discourse about how family and friends became helpful audiences that gave them opportunities to practice educational discourse and for this discourse to be heard. First, Linda described lengthy and elaborate family conversations about education. As noted previously, many of her family members were teachers or educators, or at the very least, interested in educational issues, and she told me how at holiday dinners they would talk about education:

> I have a very close-knit, as far as like, you know aunts and uncles and cousins. That's a very close-knit family, as far as that goes. So I see them all the time. One thing I've noticed is they're all so much older than me now, and I have new ideas, and sometimes they're kind of like just wait till you get out there, just—you know. But I still have my theories. I'm kind of headstrong that way. I know, I should listen to them. But the biggest debate, and this still goes on, one of my aunts is a learning disabilities teacher at Morgan City. She teaches a lot, and we used to get in the debate over Ritalin. And I've done lots of papers on Ritalin. ADD, ADHD. I had to do a research paper on that so I'm fascinated by it, because there were so many kids on Ritalin in my school. It was unbelievable to imagine. I'm not very much for Ritalin. In some cases I think it's fine, but there are so many now. Nobody really looks at these alternative methods for treating ADD. It's too fast. But my mom and my aunt have been teaching for a long time, and they're like, "You don't understand. These kids without Ritalin, they can't focus at all." And I'm like, " Well you haven't tried." (January 18, 2001)

And another example:

> It strengthens your belief sometimes about things to talk about them. I've always thought that. And you know that way I can affirm to myself what I believe. Just for example, one of my uncles who's a teacher believes very heavily in vouchers, and I don't, and we've gotten into that so much, and that was really interesting for me because it was really hard for me because he's a teacher, and from that standpoint I think he thought that I didn't know what I was talking about, but it really was affirming for me to be able to sit there and argue with him. (January 18, 2001)

Linda's family discussions and arguments about educational issues were clearly important to her as she became a new teacher. She even said that they were ways to "affirm" what she believed. She did not mention that any of these arguments changed her positions on topics or made her think differently. Interestingly enough, these examples of Linda's discourse contradict those in the section about discursive models in this chapter, because she was not imitating her mother's discourse about teaching, but was instead stating a dissenting opinion. However, this dissenting opinion was still understood in a rather uncomplicated way, and she seemed resistant to modifying it. Although it may not be an example of imitation, I posit that it is still an example of a resistance to the acceptance of cognitive dissonance or interrogation of previously held ideologies about education. Perhaps imitation is a parallel cognitive maneuver to flat resistance—both leave out the middle ground or the gray area. Both resist doubt, ambiguity, and dissonance.

Sandy also told stories about the importance of having an audience for her discussions about education. She shared with me her difficulties in continuing to develop her philosophies when she wasn't in English education methods classes and therefore didn't have a built-in audience of peers with whom to interact. This was similar to my discussion in the earlier section in this chapter about how, when Sandy and Karen were separated from peers, they had difficulty maintaining their beliefs and desire to be educators. In this example from Sandy, she discussed specifically how she missed educational *dialogue* with her peers that helped her in her professional identity development:

> I think the biggest one is just being detached from English methods. It's not that I feel like I'm losing anything by not doing it, it just feels like I'm, like, out of practice. When I was talking to Mike, Linda, and Donna [other preservice teachers], I just remember thinking, "I haven't talked about this kind of stuff in a long time." I mean, they were talking about things like "Oh, my students are doing this today." (November 8, 2001)

This might tell us something about how to structure English education curricula in the most effective way. Perhaps methods or education-specific courses might be staggered throughout a university education so that discussion with peers and mentors about educational issues will be consistently experienced throughout teacher education. Some cohort-based education programs are already working on this model, but other more traditionally designed programs, such as my own, only allow for short-term connection with a group of peers also in the program.

Participants often told stories of family and friends, although they were not as prevalent as were narratives of experience, tension, or embodiment. Bruner (2002) maintained, "A self-making narrative is something of a balancing act. It must, on the one hand, create conviction of autonomy, that one has a will of one's own, a certain freedom of choice, a degree of possibility. But it must also relate the self to a world of others—to friends and family, to institutions, to the past, to reference groups" (p. 78).

In this chapter I have provided examples of such narratives about relationships to family and friends and how they helped to make up the self-narratives of the participants in my study. The two participants who told the greatest numbers of narratives about friends and family were two who had not yet fully problematized their personal ideologies or experienced dissonance between these personal subjectivities and professional expectations: Sandy and Linda. The other four participants did problematize the personal to some extent, and this willingness to live in a state of tension while working toward growth was reflected in their narratives about family and friends. Janeen, while viewing her brother and grandmother as models of educational discourse and seeing her friend Linda as a sounding board for her discursive growth, still actively understood her personal subjectivities, personality, and working style as being important components in her professional identity development. Carrie and Karen both told stories of their family lives and communities in which they grew up or currently lived and how these communities affected their teaching selves in undeniable, and sometimes inflexible, ways. However, they also recognized this conflict, to a certain extent, and were aware of the struggle between their family or community memberships and their professional philosophies or goals. Just as when I discussed narratives of tension, narratives of experience, and narratives of embodiment in earlier chapters, participants who allowed themselves to experience discursive tensions and then engaged in borderland discourse were the ones who seemed most successful in learning to be teachers and who were the happiest and most comfortable choosing a teaching life.

I'm not arguing that simply because a person relies on family members for support it means that he or she is avoiding some aspect of crucial personal identity development. Of course, there are different ways of interacting with family and friends, and some of these ways are very healthy and necessary for emotional health. However, personal narratives about family and friends must be interrogated in much the same way as were the personal educational memories that I described in chapter 4, in order for complex and productive identify formation to occur. Such interrogation can be accomplished through classroom assignments, such as critically reflexive literacy autobiographies and providing narrative support for pedagogical decisions.

So, how can an awareness of the effect of family and friends help teacher educators? Perhaps in two ways: by helping us assist our students in nurturing an awareness of their home discourses and how these discourses affect their teaching selves, and by empowering them through this awareness when they realize that they do not have to unconsciously accept the ideologies inherent in their home discourses, but can and should critically examine them, choosing the discourses and associated subjectivities that they find convincing. As Stanton Wortham (2001) noted, "Work in many fields argues that people can construct and sometimes transform themselves by telling coherent autobiographical narratives that representationally foreground certain characteristics and by subsequently acting in terms of the characteristics thus foregrounded" (p. 7). In other words, once preservice teachers are aware of how both professional and personal discourses affect their lives, they can modify these discourses if they so choose and hence enrich their professional selves.

Chapter 7

Using Discourse to Create a Teacher Identity: Borderland Narratives

So what exactly is borderland discourse? Is it simply a catchy name for critical thinking, reflection, or analysis? Is it just another way of saying that new teachers need to be critically reflective practitioners? The concept of borderland discourse as it emerged from my data has similarities to these concepts; it does have something to do with critical thinking and reflection, because it often reflects or prompts such cognitive and affective responses. However, it is also *discourse,* and as such invites the teacher educator to encourage its expression in the university classroom, where new teachers are initially trained and mentored.

In addition to facilitating personal/professional development, the expression of borderland discourse can positively affect classroom practice. Secondary school teachers constantly translate philosophies and beliefs into actions in their classrooms—often almost simultaneously. Sometimes these thoughts and actions are a result of cultural definitions of a teacher's role or arise from habit or imitation. However, when engaging in borderland discourse there is an enhanced consciousness, a meta-awareness of thought and action that can incorporate the personal as well as the professional, and multifaceted, contextual, and sometimes contradictory ideologies and situated identities. Rather than asking preservice teachers to simply "reflect" on a lesson plan or teaching experience, facilitating their borderland discourse raises simple reflection to a higher level of complexity, to another level of consciousness and critical action.

Critical reflection is not something that can be learned through its application to isolated assignments, lesson plans, or class discussions; I argue that it must also be applied to the larger, more abstract discourses of teacher identity that affect and reflect our students' development as teachers. Accepting the centrality of borderland discourse to teacher education necessitates the rejection of the theory that either through knowledge of pedagogical or disciplinary content or through isolated and disconnected reflective exercises a young teacher can emerge from a teacher education program ready to begin a satisfying and successful teaching life. It isn't only about learning content, pedagogical technique, or research strategies for reflecting on practice; it's also about how to honor personal beliefs, life choices, and experiences that have value and meaning while enacting elements of the professional identity that society demands. It's sometimes about making hard choices that modify personal or professional discourses to facilitate and nurture the creation of a new discourse—a borderland discourse that may represent and affect positive growth and necessary political or systematic change.

This fifth narrative genre of teacher identity discourse might have been the most important (and complex) in the development of the participants' teacher identities. Borderland narrative discourse facilitated and reflected cognitive and emotional dissonance between multiple cultural-contextual understandings of "teacher," personal beliefs and experiences, and understandings of professional expectations and responsibilities. I argue that engagement in borderland discourse was important, perhaps even vital, to the preservice teachers' initial development of a professional identity and a personal pedagogy.

As I noted previously, the most traditionally successful teacher education students in this study (i.e., those who went on to take secondary teaching jobs the autumn after their graduation) were those who were given the opportunity and provided with guidance to recognize complex relationships among their educational memories, their university education, their practical teaching experiences, and their core ideologies. Of the six students in the study, the three who engaged in the most borderland discourse chose to become teachers immediately after graduation. The other three, although not ruling out the possibility of teaching later in their lives, initially chose different professional paths.

In *Disturbing Practice: Reading Teacher Education as Text* (2002), Avner Segall discussed the difference between the concepts of critical thinking and critical pedagogy in teacher education. He noted:

> The first [critical thinking] focuses on student teachers' ability to create learning environments that initiate, maintain, and foster critical thinking with their future students in school. The second [critical pedagogy] explores student teachers' ability to think critically *themselves* about the content and context of their own learning in teacher education, making pedagogical connections between how the ways one teaches and learns structure and determine what is learned. (p. 74)

I believe that the goal of teacher preparation programs should include both types of critical education, and that the two are not mutually exclusive. In fact, they seem to be inexorably linked, because the preservice teacher who has engaged critically with her own education will be much more likely to successfully implement a critical pedagogy in her secondary school classroom and encourage critical thought on the part of her students. I believe such critical education, as described by Segall, can be achieved, in part, through encouraging preservice teachers to engage in borderland discourse.

Such a critical pedagogy can also be called a "personal pedagogy," and this term seems preferable because it avoids possible confusion over the word *critical*. A personal pedagogy can be the result of a critical teacher education. Such a teacher education results in new teachers who are not only knowledgeable about theoretically sound, evidence-based practices in their discipline, but also have critically reflected on these practices and made philosophical and pedagogical choices based on this reflection. The educational beliefs new teachers hold have been developed through an interaction of professional, intellectual knowledge and the personal, affective, and/or corporeal intelligences central to their core identities. In this way, a professional identity as a teacher begins to form, and a personal pedagogy is the material, practical, classroom manifestation of this identity. In short, a personal pedagogy incorporates a teacher's multiple subjectivities or identity strands, including personal educational experiences, core beliefs and ideologies, and educational theory and research as a philosophical foundation for classroom decision making, at the levels of both curricular planning and daily practice.

The students in my study were, of course, new to the profession, so I did not yet see them enacting any systematic or political changes in the larger educational arena; however, some of them did begin to honor their selves, *and* be good teachers. This was a strong first step; they had learned to express transformative discourse that, in turn, affected their professional identities, and it was probable that they would continue to engage in borderland discourses throughout their careers in increasingly complex ways.

Helping preservice and new teachers create a personal pedagogy is more difficult than it might seem. There is a significant distinction between personal pedagogy and educational philosophy, as it is generally understood, that is often difficult for our students initially to grasp. Therefore, when asked to talk or write about their personal pedagogies, our students often revert back to sweeping, sentimental generalizations, clichés, and euphemisms that lack specific connection to their educational histories, memories, and personal ideologies. One example of a largely unsuccessful attempt to incorporate a holistic, critical pedagogy into teacher education involves the "reflective" paper (see Fig. 7.1).

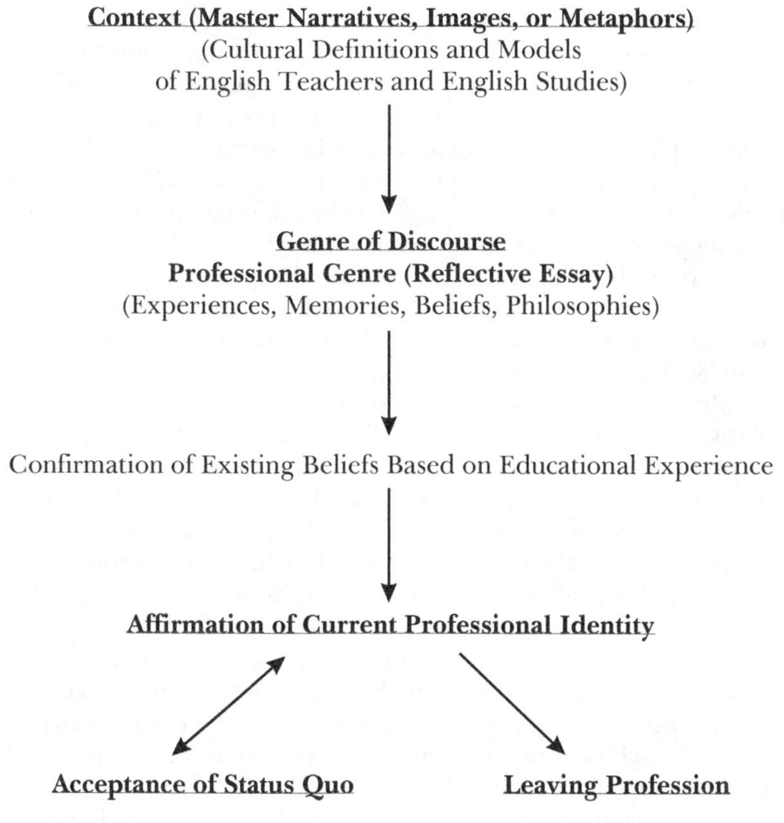

FIG. 7.1. Standard "reflective" assignment.

This figure is a model of what can happen when students respond to the traditional reflective assignment. Such an assignment can simply reinforce the existing beliefs and identity structures of students, rather than lead to cognitive dissonance and resultant critical engagement with their developing professional selves. As we know from this study and many others, students come to teacher education with preconceptions or experiential context concerning what it means to be a teacher. These master narratives, images, or metaphors guide the students as they take courses and complete assignments. If students are not prompted to interrogate these existing ideologies and subjectivities, there is an excellent chance they will simply reproduce them when asked to reflect on their teaching philosophies; they will write papers, for example, that reinforce existing beliefs or what they currently see as effective practice. Sometimes these beliefs and philosophies are consistent with what teacher educators teach, so the student might even be rewarded for such unreflective reproduction of ideas.

The problem with such unreflective reinforcement of existing beliefs and philosophies is that once student teachers are in the secondary classroom, they undoubtedly will face scenarios and situations that aren't adequately addressed by these ideologies and associated methods. Then, new teachers often select from choices, as represented at the bottom of Fig. 7.1: either accept the status quo in the current teaching context and teach as others around them do, even if such practice is contradictory to their existing philosophies and inconsistent with their professional identities, or quit teaching because they cannot resolve the conflict and frustration. Of course, there are individual teachers who are able to engage in transformative discourse and overcome this quandary on their own for whatever reason; however, many may not be able to resolve the crisis by themselves.

All of this is not to say that traditional reflection has no place in teacher education. In the 1980s, teacher educators and researchers discovered the benefits of "reflection" on practice and the writing of reflective pieces to accompany pedagogical projects. Consistent with the work of composition theorists Peter Elbow and Donald Murray, as well as educational researchers who found value in reflective thinking for the new teacher (e.g., Griffiths & Tann, 1992; Zeichner & Liston, 1996), teacher educators incorporated much written and oral reflection into their syllabi. However, as I've already mentioned, sometimes this reflection is assigned by teachers and completed by students rather automatically, and reflections may turn into generic statements that are recycled for each assignment, rife with buzzwords and educational jargon (e.g., *constructivism, student centered*, or *best practice*) that all too often plays well to the teacher educator. Although reflective assignments are not inherently ineffective, and the intentions behind them are often good, without overt attention to helping students make connections between various and competing identity strands or subjectivities, these assignments will not result in professional identity growth.

One of our goals as teacher educators should be to help in the creation and expression of such borderland discourse about teaching, to assist preservice teachers, as Gee (1999) said, in "weaving strands of ... multiple Discourses together" (p. 21) to create a new, albeit still recognized, discourse or professional identity. If we want teachers to enact real political change in our educational system, I believe borderland discourse is a necessity (see Fig. 7.2).

This figure is a diagram of the core argument about transformative discourse found throughout this book—beginning with the cultural context of the teacher and the teacher education student, the preservice teacher natu-

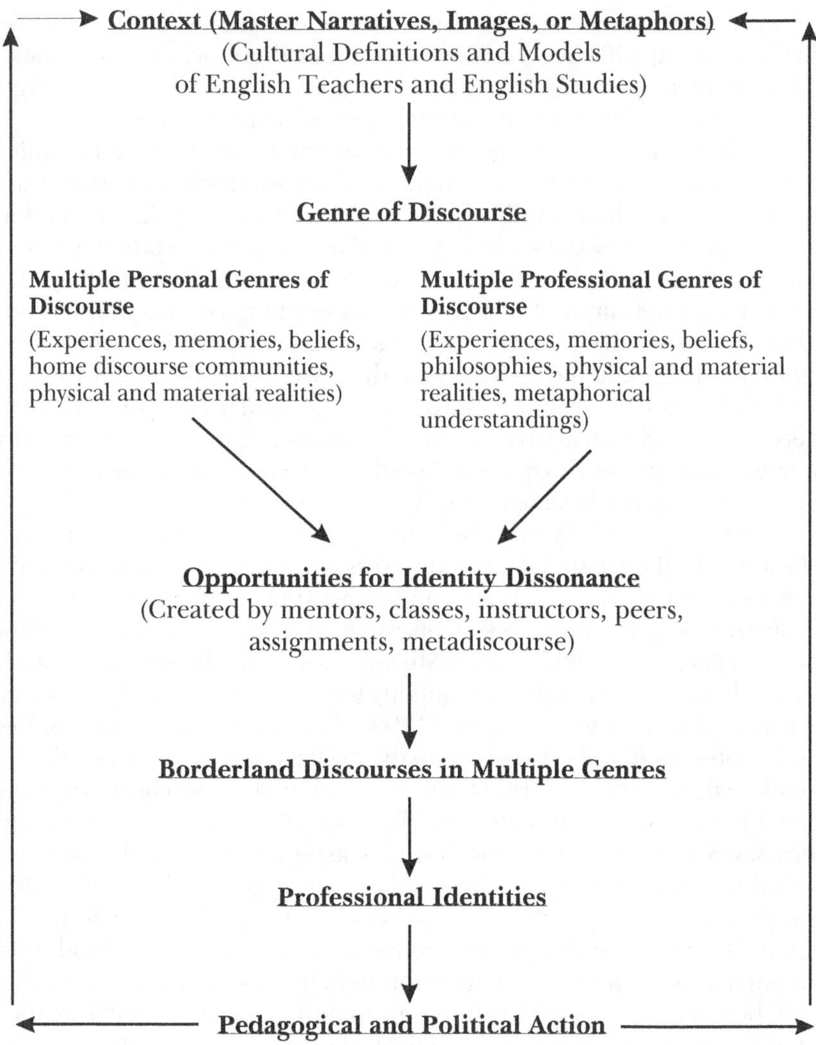

FIG. 7.2. Expression of borderland discourse.

rally engages in discourse about his or her professional and personal life. Then, if given the opportunity to critically analyze these discourses that represent and create ideologies and subject positions, the student may experience tension or cognitive dissonance that can lead to more complex, fulfilling, and politically active professional identities. Referring again to

Fig. 7.2, one can see that, at the end of the chart, arrows lead from "Pedagogical and Political Action" back up to "Context." Once teachers are in the process of developing and nurturing a professional identity, they can enact critical personal pedagogies and complementary political action that affect their understanding (and the understandings of others around them) of the cultural context or master narrative of teacher. In fact, these changes modify their teacher discourse and potentially begin to chisel away at stereotypical and harmful notions about teachers in our culture. However, engaging in this borderland discourse is not always automatic, and several contextual factors have to be in place prior to its occurrence. Particular types of field placements, university and school-based mentors, and university education had to occur in order to facilitate the discourse.

To make things more complex, engaging in borderland discourse is, to put it plainly, difficult. There are several easier paths, including (a) rejecting the teacher identity as simply incompatible with one's own, or (b) denying or suppressing any ideological tensions and molding oneself to "fit" the established model. The participants who engaged in borderland discourse were willing and able "to live with initial cognitive dissonance and conflicts" that were an essential part of professional identity formation and were "one of the leading edges of resistance and change" (Gee, 1990, p. 179). In addition to the necessity of living with dissonance, another reason that expressing and enacting borderland discourse is difficult is that an individual can feel hypocritical when participating in the discourse of the "other." Because borderland discourse is a merging of discourses, one of which is often the accepted or hegemonic discourse, individuals can judge themselves, or be judged by others, as giving up home discourses or personal ideologies in favor of privileged ones. However, such individuals might be engaging in hegemonic discourses in order to modify them or put them in direct and productive contact with home or individual discourses.

THE EXPRESSION OF BORDERLAND NARRATIVES BY THE PARTICIPANTS

In my study, borderland narratives had the following characteristics:

1. They were told most often by the participants who chose to become teachers or who were more successful in the early stages of their careers.
2. They typically described how secondary school and university mentors facilitated borderland discourse; how preservice teachers learned to connect university coursework with practical, field-based knowl-

edge; or were examples of metadiscourse describing students' awareness of their participation in borderland discourse.

3. The borderland discourse was sometimes difficult to express, because the students struggled with how to integrate various personal and professional subjectivities and still be successful during a graded student teaching.
4. The majority of borderland narratives concerned professional tensions—tensions between student versus teacher subjectivities and/or university versus practical orientations.

There was only one example, from Karen, of a narrative with characteristics of borderland discourse that concerned personal, ideological tension with professional expectations.

Lois, Linda, and Janeen told the greatest number of narratives with characteristics of borderland discourse. Lois told 15, Linda 12, and Janeen 7. All three students went on to take traditional teaching jobs the year after their graduation, whereas the other three students (Sandy, Carrie, and Karen) did not. A look back at Table 3.1 reveals that the four students engaging in the largest amount of transformative discourse were those who did not tell any narratives of personal versus professional tension. It seems that professional tensions were easier to navigate through borderland discourse than were more personal conflicts. Perhaps this is because traditionally we have trained students better in the area of the professional. We don't talk about the personal, the embodied, or the individual ideological crises or tensions that are sure to occur when one chooses teaching as a career. These issues don't seem to have a place in our sanitized professional worlds. However, these problems are clearly important for new teachers, as the students in this study demonstrated.

Lois' narrative borderland discourse concerned either negotiating the tensions of being a student versus being a teacher, or the tension between university and practical philosophies and practices. Lois engaged in a great deal of transformative discourse, discourse that expressed connections between student and teacher subjectivities and university coursework and practical field experiences. As previously mentioned, she told me a total of 15 narratives with characteristics of borderland discourse; in contrast, the two students who chose not to be educators, Carrie and Karen, told 0 and 1 borderland narrative, respectively. Lois' mentor teacher was a wonderful model of this borderland discourse and urged Lois to engage in it as much as possible. Additionally, Lois' open attitude about learning to teach and her lack of home discourses influencing her professional identity allowed her to feel less threatened and more open to cognitive dissonance than were some others in the study. Her narratives demonstrated how she willingly took suggestions and accepted guidance from her mentor teacher, while not giving up her own opinions.

At one point, Lois assigned a risky project that her mentor teacher, trying to protect her from possible failure, suggested she avoid. This following narrative tells the story of an assignment for which Lois asked her students to respond to an editorial in the high school newspaper criticizing the number of student teachers at the school. The assignment was risky, because Lois was a student teacher herself at the time, and she was, in a sense, inviting students to criticize her. However, the topic was relevant and timely to the students in her class; instead of ignoring the editorial and continuing to go about her teaching day as she had originally planned, Lois decided to confront the issue head on. With this assignment, she demonstrated recognition of how a teacher's pedagogy is variable based on immediate student needs and interests:

> I did one thing, Janet, this is really cool. I brought it so you could see it. There was an editorial in our school newspaper about student teachers. It was about how teachers leave their classroom to a bunch of rookies, and the students get the shaft. But I said, "Okay, guys," I did it with two of my three classes. I trusted two of them. I said, "You know, I'm going to read you all something." And I said, "You can do this anonymously," I said, "Don't put your name on it, or if you really want to put your name on it, you can." I said, "I want you to respond with an editorial back to this person." Then, I read it out loud. And I mean, some of the parts, the students were like, "Are you serious? They really think that?" And they were like, "Well, yeah," and then they were like, "Oh my God!" They were just totally talking back to me as I'm reading it. I said, "Okay you guys, honestly, if you want to go off on me [a student teacher], you can, but I would like you to not think about me as the student teacher. Think about the practice in general." There were mixed responses. But I thought it was a great activity. I was pretty happy with it, even though the responses weren't all positive. Some of the ones I learned from were the ones that agreed with it [the editorial]. Well, my mentor was kind of worried, and I said, "You know, I'm going to try it anyway." And I did. (Interview #4, December 4, 2002)

Giving this assignment demonstrated a great deal of confidence, because even Lois' mentor teacher was a little worried about the students' possible responses. It also demonstrated mutual respect between the two, because Lois was allowed to go ahead with the assignment even after her mentor expressed hesitation. Lois believed that the activity would work well, and she proceeded to give the students the editorial response assignment hoping for the best, despite doubts expressed by her mentor teacher. Embracing her own position as a student teacher, and fully aware that the students at the high school often worked with student teachers, Lois decided not to ignore this subjectivity, even though it was a position of reduced power and authority. Alternately, she directly confronted her student identity and invited her students to similarly analyze the role of student teachers in their school. In this way, Lois simultaneously interrogated her subjectivity as student teacher while also allowing her students to interrogate their positions as students of an inexperienced teacher.

These mutual interrogations took courage and spurred professional identity growth. Lois' narrative about this pedagogical choice is an example of borderland discourse and also metadiscourse, as she related how and why she came to take the risk. She told the story of integrating field-based and personal knowledge and identity positions to make a pedagogical decision. Furthermore, Lois was conscious of the process of making this difficult, and ultimately successful, choice.

Lois' mentor teacher often facilitated such borderland discourses through frank conversations encouraging Lois' pedagogical freedom, although, at other times, Lois took the initiative to build bridges between the various aspects of her self. Consequently, she had a very satisfying student teaching experience and went on to accept a secondary teaching job the following year. Here is a quote from an interview conducted with Lois on September 12, 2001, that exemplifies transformative discourse encouraged by her mentor:

> One of the first things she [her mentor] said was, "I don't want you to come in and model the classroom exactly the way I do." She said, you know, "If something I do works for you and that's the way you want to do it then go for it. But I want you to come in here, and I want you to do things the way you want to do them." She said, "I will help, you know, and I will offer you advice, but I want you to come and I want you to find your own way." Not necessarily my own way, but find what works for me. You know, if me being more strict with discipline is the way, you know, if I wanted to move those students then I would. I would move those students. But then, I would see how that worked for or against me.

Lois was in the process of developing a personal pedagogy, one that began to incorporate her multiple subjectivities or identity strands. One could say she *was* finding her own way, and her mentor teacher seemed to be encouraging this and providing her with a safe environment in which to do it. By engaging in narrative discourse about this development, her understanding of her own growth only increased, and with such enhanced meta-awareness, or reflexivity, Lois' professional identity might only have become richer, more complex, more effective, and more satisfying with time.

A personal pedagogy can be developed, in part, though the expression of borderland discourse and experiencing its reciprocal effect. Lois went on to describe how her mentor teacher helped her begin to develop her personal pedagogy:

> She [mentor] is willing to let me do stuff like that. And she says, "I don't want you to come in and mimic me," be exactly the way she is. She knows what she

> wants done while I'm here. And she has a sort of skeleton plan, which I can fill in. And that is what I wanted. She is really nice. I told her, "I will do what you want. I will get in front of the class when you want me to, but I was hoping you will work me in a little bit slower because I do have this problem, that I am, I'm not sure of myself." I'm not scared, but I get nervous when I deliver, sometimes. I could have the greatest lesson plan in the world. You know, infallible. The most wonderful lesson plan, but if you put me in there, I get scared. I just warned her that might happen. You know, I might stumble or I might get nervous being in front of the classroom. (September 12, 2001)

An early negative experience in a high school field placement led to these fears. Lois told me on January 25, 2001:

> My junior year I took a class called "literacy in the classroom." As a requirement for the course, we had to observe classes and teach a lesson to the students in the literacy lab at Washington High School. This was the absolute worst experience that I have ever had as a teacher. My group and I prepared what we believed to be an interesting lesson involving current hit song lyrics as forms of literature. At one point in the presentation, a child stole my lesson plan and proceeded to run around the room with it. I was not very happy, and shortly after that, I decided that I was not going to be a teacher.

Of course, Lois did decide to go ahead and become a teacher, and her mentor's willingness to work with her and support her during the difficult professional transition helped her to mature professionally. Furthermore, Lois was aware of her problem with nervousness or "stage fright" and how it developed, and this meta-awareness allowed her to move past it. She knew she was struggling with the aftereffects of a difficult and embarrassing teaching experience, and, therefore, she shared her concerns with her mentor. Many students might have kept such insecurities a secret from their mentor because of embarrassment or fears of negative evaluations. However, Lois came clean, and her initial honesty set the stage for future borderland discourse. To put it simply, she brought the personal firmly into the picture, so her mentor was aware of her willingness to confront it. Her mentor teacher recognized and respected Lois' fears, and works with her to conquer them by providing support and encouragement.

Perhaps the most striking example of transformative discourse from Lois is the following narrative excerpt, in which she described her attitude as a student teacher toward learning to teach. An individual's state of mind, mood, or general orientation toward situations, other people, or events affects subjectivities and identity orientations, which, in turn, affect discourse. Reciprocally, the expression of such discourse can influence the individual's state of mind or subjectivity. The attitude Lois brought with her to student teaching invited borderland discourse and positive professional identity growth. She told me during our final interview:

> I had no idea what I was doing, truly. I didn't feel like I was going be good in front of the classroom. I knew that I had to learn, and I had to learn fast. (Laughing) I wanted to learn. I didn't go in there thinking I was already a great teacher. I think maybe that was the difference. I didn't go in thinking, now I just have to show her what I know. I didn't go in thinking I knew what to do. And thinking that I could already be a teacher. Rather than think I know it, or go in with the attitude that I already thought I knew what student teaching was about, or thought I knew what to do, and then when I found out what it really was, not be able to recognize it, or not want to change my ways. And, you know—not want to totally scrap—like, an ideal, or admit that I was wrong—no, I just wanted to know how to really do it, and do it well. (April 16, 2002)

Lois' open attitude toward learning and acceptance of uncertainty and dissonance during the mentoring process qualitatively changed her experience as a student teacher and helped her experience more identity growth. I'm not sure how this recognition of an open attitude can help teacher educators; Lois seemed to come into the program with the attitude already in place. However, a recognition of its importance might help us see why we should encourage students who are resistant to change and afraid of ambiguity to take more risks.

Linda also told me a large number of narratives with characteristics of borderland discourse. Like Lois, her narratives were primarily about tensions between student versus teacher subjectivities or university and practical ideologies. She also told some stories that centered on issues of embodiment and family and friends. For Linda, it seemed that much of her teacher identity discourse stemmed from her relationship with her mother and learning about being a teacher from her. Although Linda's mentor was helpful in the professional development process, Linda's knowledge of the teacher identity provided (and modeled) by her mother appeared to be the most influential. Linda also engaged in metadiscourse about her own decision making as a teacher. Again, like Lois, Linda's borderland narratives concerned professional, not personal, tensions.

The following narrative is an example of Linda discussing how she changed her own practice based on that of her mentor. Earlier in this interview, Linda described how her mentor avoided group work and found individual work more effective most of the time. Linda had previously valued group work more than did Ms. Vanderholt, so she had to figure out how to integrate her mentor's expertise with her own beliefs:

> I kind of tended to believe that group work was real good, and then I've seen in classrooms, at times while observing, just chaos during group work. So I sit there and think, "How do I keep this from happening?" I think as far as the group work went, I had this paradise little scene [in mind]; everything would be fine, and all the kids were going to stay on task perfectly. So, then, I think what I really came up with for group work was that I just needed to come up with a way to introduce a little bit of accountability. Not so much that you'll fail

> if you don't stay on task, but a little bit of a check system or you know, 3 points here for participation. (January 18, 2001)

This narrative described some of the ways Linda thought she was different from her mentor, as well as other teachers she had observed, even though she could learn from them. It seemed that she took a middle ground between her old belief (all group work is good) and her mentor's ideology (group work is mostly ineffective). She decided that it is indeed good, but only if there is control and accountability. I believe Linda's narrative exemplifies Fig. 7.2, because she experienced dissonance that resulted in narratives with characteristics of borderland discourse and, eventually, modification of her professional identity. A model of Linda's transformative narrative discourse about group work can be seen in Fig. 7.3.

As you can see from the model, Linda began with her "context" or master narratives, images, and metaphors about teaching, many of which had been formed at home. Then, she engaged in genres of discourse that are discussed throughout this book, including those focused on student and teaching experiences, tensions, and beliefs. Once she was student teaching, she experienced cognitive dissonance concerning group work, engaged in so-called borderland discourse about group work, and eventually modified her beliefs about the practice. This change in belief resulted in a shift in one facet of her professional identity. Similar borderland narratives about professional tensions were evident during several interviews with Linda. For example, she described her mentor's approaches to "creative" assignments and classroom activities:

> She is still a little more structured than I would be. So that's probably one thing that would change because I still think I would probably be doing group work several times a week. It adds variety. Not just group work but any kind of creative activity that you do in class. And she feels kind of like a failure if she can't keep their attention on her constantly. And I know when you do more creative things, you can't. I mean you have to put up with a little bit of noise, and you have to put up with a little bit of weaving around to get to the point. I think if she were younger she would be teaching this way. (May 23, 2002)

Linda arguably exhibited a great deal of meta-awareness of her process of integrating her own ideologies that she had learned at home or in her teacher education with those of Ms. Vanderholt. She knew where they differed, and she seemed to be making decisions about how she would negotiate these differences and create her own professional identity. Linda even went so far as to hypothesize about her mentor's reasons for making the decisions that she did (i.e., "she feels kind of like a failure") and connected issues of embodiment (i.e., age) to this decision making. The issue of age came up again, as Linda discussed how conversations with a new teacher in

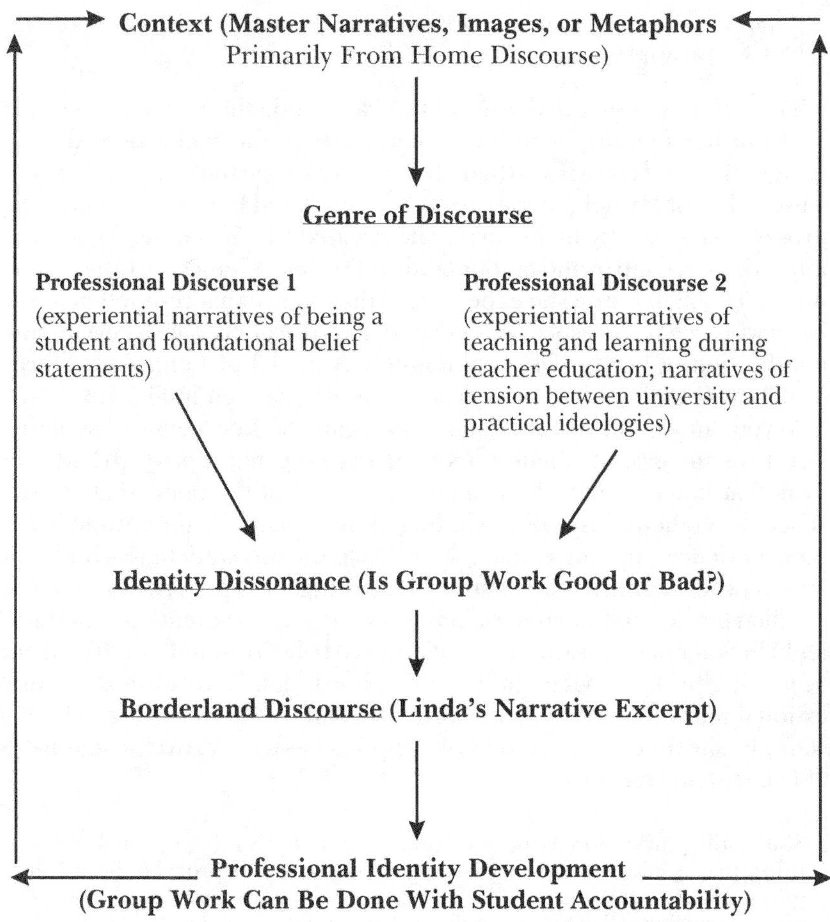

FIG. 7.3. Example of Linda's professional borderland discourse.

the school where she student taught helped her to figure out what her life as a teacher might be like the first few years:

> With student teaching you can't miss a minute. If you don't get everything done that you need to, you can't just give the kids a reading day or whatever. You're always being watched; you always want to be prepared. And have things done. And she [a young teacher in the building] was always there to remind me that you can, you do have that luxury sometimes [when you are actu-

ally employed as a teacher]. So, that was nice. To have somebody close in age. (May 23, 2002)

Linda described the benefits of speaking to a young teacher who was closer to her in age and level of experience than was her mentor. This relatively new teacher had credibility for Linda as someone who could tell her what it would *really* be like when she began to teach. Although not her actual mentor teacher, this new teacher provided a kind of mentorship for Linda, which helped her express discourse bridging her present situation as college student to her soon-to-be role as secondary school teacher.

In their book-length report of research with professional development groups for elementary school teachers, Rogers and Babinski (2002) discussed the importance of new teachers communicating with other new teachers. They asserted, "We found that other beginning teachers serve an important role in the professional development of their fellow teachers .... In our groups, because the role of expert was evolving and shared, these new teachers were, in effect, mentoring each other" (p. 85). This study supported such findings; Linda and Janeen described how new teachers helped them feel more comfortable and confident entering the profession, and Sandy and Karen both expressed concern that their teacher education was stunted when they did not consistently have classes with their peers in the English education program.

Linda's narratives with borderland characteristics were primarily about professional issues and tensions, rather than personal ideologies, subjectivities, or conflicts. Therefore, like the other students in the study who chose to become teachers, she did not seem to be experiencing much cognitive dissonance related to the integration of her personal or core identity with her developing teacher identity. When she discussed tensions and expressed borderland narratives, Linda mentioned only professional, classroom-based concerns and issues; she rarely brought up conflicts or tensions between her personal priorities or beliefs and what was expected of her as a teacher. These types of tensions simply didn't seem to be an issue yet for Linda, or at least not an issue she was comfortable sharing with me.

As I mentioned at the beginning of this chapter, expressing narratives with characteristics of borderland discourse can be difficult, because students might feel like they are making a choice between personal and professional subjectivities or situated identities, even when the discourse ideally represents a compromise of sorts. When they are learning to enact borderland discourse, students might feel like they are betraying their home discourse communities, or they may just cynically opt to do what they think is expected of them by their university supervisors or mentor teachers, even though they do not believe it is the right choice. Linda exhibited some of this cynicism when she discussed how she handled different expectations during student teaching:

> You have to juggle Mrs. Vanderholt's expectations, then your supervising teacher, and then of course your students who would be there anyway. And that's been stressful. Just like because Mrs. Vanderholt's thoughts are so much different than my supervisor's thoughts. Mandy (supervisor) wanted me to move two people, and Mrs. Vanderholt didn't. And so I didn't, because I figured it was her classroom, and I just can't move them. And so when Mandy came back and said, "Why aren't they moved?" and I was like, "Well, she told me not to because she tried it the other way, and she didn't like it." So she was okay with that, but then I feel like so ... who do I trust? Who am I going to please? Because I can't please both. Nobody seemed to care what I thought. (November 12, 2001)

Linda was struggling with how to handle conflicting advice from mentors, advice that came to represent field-based versus university knowledge. As I argued in chapter 3, Linda primarily selected field-based knowledge over the university-sanctioned approaches when they were in conflict. However, despite her pattern of selection, making such choices was clearly not easy for Linda, as the preceding excerpt demonstrated. She struggled with expressing her own discourse; unlike Lois, she didn't seem to feel completely comfortable taking risks or making decisions that might have contradicted the opinions of her mentors. She was caught in between two opinions, and expressed frustration that neither side seemed open to her input. She didn't share her opinion about moving the students; I learned Mandy's opinion and Ms. Vanderholt's, but Linda's remained a mystery, and the decision she made was based on what she thought she needed to do to satisfy the mentor teacher in whose classroom she worked.

Peter Sloterdijk (1987) discussed cynicism as being victim to "enlightened false consciousness" (p. 6). Linda seemed aware of the system of power and ideology around her and the contradiction between how her environment was and how she wished it could be, but chose to act in ways contrary perhaps to her own beliefs in order to secure external rewards (or simply to keep from rocking the boat). She seemed to know that making pedagogical decisions based on what others wanted her to do was not the best way to manage her classroom; however, she did what the most powerful person in her teaching context desired so that she could be successful in her student teaching. This apparent hypocrisy might also be read as political savvy, because Linda obviously wanted to graduate, get positive recommendation letters, and find a job. But her approach was cynical, because she knew that to some extent she was "playing the game." In short, this excerpt demonstrated that Linda sometimes struggled with borderland discourse as she searched for ways to take into account the opinions of others without losing her feelings of self-efficacy.

Janeen had the third-largest number of narratives with borderland characteristics, seven. Her narratives were similar to Linda's and Lois'. Like Lois, she felt like her mentor teacher allowed her to take risks and make her own decisions:

> She [mentor teacher] sounds like she has more of an idea of having lesson plans that are works in progress, and changeable, and they don't have to be totally exact and everything timed out. She said something like you look to see where you want to be at the end, and then decide what you need to do to get there. So it sounded like the lesson plans would be more dynamic. It sounded more like she would be guiding me, and we would just be working together. I think she won't impede me getting the full experience of it. She obviously knows a lot more than I know, so I think she's going to use everything that she knows to help me, but I don't think she's going to prevent me from finding out what it's like to be alone in the class. (January 22, 2002)

Janeen's mentor teacher wanted to assist her student teacher, but also urged her to make independent decisions and experience transformative discourse. Similar to Lois, Janeen expressed an openness to learning and an awareness that, as a student teacher, her job was to learn as much as possible from an experienced mentor. She didn't seem afraid of experiencing cognitive dissonance or admitting a lack of knowledge. As I mentioned when discussing Linda's experience with a teacher close to her own age, Janeen also found it helpful to work with a new teacher during a pre-student teaching field experience. Like Linda, Janeen discussed how this was good for her:

> But my middle school placement [for a methods course the 6 weeks prior to student teaching] is really good. The person I'm working with has only been teaching 2 years. So I walked in, and I was like, how more perfect could this be for me, for right now? To be working with somebody—I mean I wouldn't want to student teach, obviously, with somebody that young—but for this it's perfect to watch it—walk in and have it be somebody that's more my age, who's actually doing the things that I'll be doing. I was really excited about that. (January 22, 2002)

There seems to be a unique type of credibility for the teacher who is close in age and experience to the student teacher. In such a case, not only do the job expectations mesh with what the preservice teacher sees herself doing in the next few years, but the personal identity concerns, such as embodiment issues or ideological tension, also seem similar. Janeen and Linda both found working with someone their own age comforting, because these young teachers were models of how they might have enacted the identity of teacher when they finally entered their own classrooms. These models looked like them, acted like them, and had some of the same worries and fears; however, they were successful secondary teachers. The unique "bridge" younger teachers provided for Janeen and Linda helped them to begin their transition from a "student" to a "teacher" subjectivity more easily. Because contrasting identity markers, such as physical embodiment of professional identity and experiences with family and friends, were not as strongly felt when working with younger teaching mentors, Janeen and Linda could focus on other professional identity concerns, including pedagogical decision making and ideological conflicts. The preceding borderland discourse described the benefits Janeen garnered from such a professional collaboration as she continued to learn to be a teacher.

Last, her mentor helped Janeen build confidence by modeling a healthy response when things didn't go as expected. In this way, she modeled a part of the internal life of a career educator that often goes unseen during early apprenticeships of observation: "My mentor teacher's good about that. She laughs. You know, she laughs it off. Today, when the discussion was just pathetic, and she walked in, she laughed about it. She understands that you don't know [how something will go] until you do it with them. Some days it goes well, and some days it doesn't go well" (April 8, 2002).

The mentor's laughter was a corporeal response to a difficult class, a response that Janeen noticed and appreciated. She seemed to incorporate the necessity of not taking failure personally into her teacher identity, and it bolstered her willingness to take risks. Janeen's mentor, and subsequently Janeen herself, knew that to take a classroom risk or try a new pedagogical technique has uncertain results—but that's okay. Without such risks innovative ideas would never be nurtured or enacted, and many educational opportunities would be lost. Her mentor showed Janeen that laughter can be the most productive response to frustration. Although like the other students in the study—the majority of Janeen's transformative discourse concerned professional concerns, this example demonstrated the beginnings of borderland discourse about the personal. Janeen was learning how to live with disappointment and failure, two unfortunate realities of life for the teacher, without taking them as a personal affront or allowing such feelings to erode her confidence or desire to teach.

The last example of a narrative with characteristics of borderland discourse that I share in this chapter is from an interview with Karen. Her narrative was the only one I identified in the study that explicitly addressed a personal tension, not a professional one. Karen's narratives of tension were about personal versus professional identities and subjectivities, as I described in chapter 3. Her major conflicts concerned family and career responsibilities or teacher embodiment, namely as it related to race and ethnicity. Because Karen eventually chose not to be a secondary teacher, one might hypothesize that her tensions were overwhelming or too difficult to resolve. This isn't to say that Karen took the easy way out or made the wrong decision when she decided not to be a teacher. I don't think everyone should teach, and certainly there are many other wonderful careers from which to choose. However, I wanted to decipher why she made the decision that she did, and my data indicates that she was inundated with tensions between personal ideologies and professional expectations and models. This one example of transformative discourse suggests that Karen was trying to figure out how to integrate the personal and professional in productive ways, but didn't receive adequate support from her teacher education in order to do so effectively. This excerpt is from a letter she wrote to me on December 16, 2002, and sent via e-mail:

> I used to believe that teachers are always responsible for the performance of the students in their class. I believed that some teachers were underqualified to teach (i.e., those who flunk the tests they're required to take ... or scrape by in education courses). I watched some of the teachers in this school, though [the school where she was coaching middle school basketball]. I would be in before and after practices doing things ... and on the weekends, they were there. Most of them are working on their master's degree or already have one. I spoke to several of them. For example, one of my players, Lisa, was always ineligible. So after calling her mom ... and her mother not replying ... I went with Lisa to her teachers to see why she wasn't passing their classes. They explained to me that she was a constant problem in the classroom. She disrupted other students by talking to them. She never faced the board. She cussed at her teachers. She didn't turn in her homework, although she had it done. A few of the teachers even set up a weekly rewards system for her. Nothing seemed to work. I finally told Lisa that after 3 weeks of being ineligible that she would have to leave the team if she was ineligible again. Obviously basketball wasn't helping her with her schoolwork and that time should be spent doing homework ... or working on her attitude. Then she would be eligible. And by no means am I saying that putting these students into private schools [instead of public ones] is wrong or unjust. All students deserve the same education. But maybe the teachers in the schools where the kids aren't succeeding are doing their job, too.

Karen narrated how her attitude about teachers had changed after watching hardworking colleagues struggling with students and parents. She had rethought a personal ideology about ineffective teachers and their complicity in the "failure" of public schools. Her experience working as a middle school coach tempered her earlier harsh tones regarding teachers who aren't qualified or who don't work hard enough. Unfortunately, during her teacher education, Karen did not make similar realizations, nor was she prompted to investigate and interrogate foundational beliefs about education. Perhaps if she had engaged in such discourse prior to her graduation from college, she might have felt more prepared and motivated to pursue a secondary teaching career. She only coached the basketball team for one semester after graduating with her degree in English. She found the experience deeply unsettling, and it only seemed to solidify her decision to pursue a different profession.

HOW DO WE ENCOURAGE BORDERLAND DISCOURSE IN TEACHER EDUCATION?

M. M. Bakhtin has written extensively about speech genres and their use in discourse communities. He argued (1986) that mastering various speech genres can facilitate an individual's interaction within a community and eventual modification of genres that he or she finds unacceptable: "The better our command of genres, the more freely we employ them, the more fully and clearly we reveal our own individuality in them (where this is possible and necessary), the more flexibly and precisely we reflect the unrepeatable situation of communication—in a word, the more perfectly we implement our free speech plan" (p. 80).

Bakhtin's arguments about speech genres support my argument for the inclusion of borderland discourse in teacher education courses. If we want our students to be successful teachers who can not only communicate and interact effectively as educators in the educational community, but also have the ability and resources to modify the system and bring about necessary change, then they must have experience with transformational discourse that helps them integrate their various personal and professional spaces. As can be seen in this chapter, several of the students in my study engaged in such narrative discourse over the 2½ years of interviews and observations; however, the expression of this discourse didn't always result in an unproblematic merging of identity positions or a smooth and easy entrance into the teaching profession. Sometimes expressing so-called borderland discourse was explosive and difficult; other times it was satisfying and immediately enriching. Regardless, if it was successful, it did not result in the simple subsuming of one ideological position to another. Instead, the two (or more) identity strands coming into contact through discourse created a third that was both a compilation *and* an extension of the original. This isn't to say that students never abandoned ideological positions or pedagogical beliefs when engaging in borderland discourse; indeed, sometimes they did. However, such abandonment only occurred after critical interrogation of the possibilities and possible outcomes of such a decision.

If students were able to practice this transformative discourse in their education courses, they might begin to understand how it can be integrated into their professional lives. If what we want for our students is for them to become socially conscious, critical educators who question the system and make substantive changes when necessary, borderland discourse is essential. As Gee (1990) maintained, "Possible changes in Discourses and the emergence of new ones can open up possibilities for resistance to domination and hegemony" (p. 179). Only through the expression of new, integrative discourses can modified conceptions of teacher identity be introduced into—and eventually accepted by—the predominately conservative world of secondary education.

The creation and expression of borderland discourse occurred in this study in the form of narratives as described in this chapter, but also as metaphors and philosophy statements. In all cases, this discourse was neither the discourse of the old "regime" (i.e., the hegemonic discourse of the secondary English teacher) nor a completely new, unrecognizable, and therefore unaccepted discourse of a "new" professional teacher identity. Both of these extreme discourses would probably result in no real systemic change or meaningful professional growth for the teacher, because the first would only support the status quo, and the second would likely be rejected by the institutional system, along with the teacher him- or herself.

I suspect that Lois, Janeen, Linda, and Sandy will continue to engage in transformative discourse throughout their careers, but it will be modified as they grow and their teaching contexts change. Anecdotal, personal experience tells me that when teachers get older they begin to engage in more ideological or political debate. Perhaps Carrie and Karen engaged in this kind of discourse too soon. They had no confidence or experience on which to fall back, no way of being assured that they could be successful teachers despite their personal tensions or ideological conflicts. Their tensions overshadowed and buried other, more manageable professional tensions that then went unexamined as they decided not to be teachers. Therefore, the confidence they may have gained from effective negotiation of such tensions was lost.

It might seem like I'm arguing that the early experience of tension between personal and professional ideologies is preferred, because these more complex cognitive and emotional conflicts address aspects of professional identity that will eventually, and inevitably, be an issue. However, in the study, the students who experienced early tensions about their physical embodiment or between personal ideologies and professional expectations could not easily engage in transformative narratives to create discursive spaces for a professional identity to thrive. Perhaps only with age and experience can such tensions be experienced successfully, or perhaps other genres of discourse (e.g., metaphor) allow such experience more easily. Alternatively, it's possible that if these students had received greater support and wiser mentorship during their teacher education, they could have negotiated the tensions through narrative more successfully. I will have to continue to talk to the students about their professional experiences to see how their growth progresses and how they might experience such transformative discourse in the future. Perhaps Carrie, Karen, and Sandy will simply follow inverse pathways to Linda, Janeen, and Lois, with all six eventually reaching similar levels of personal and professional growth. This is yet to be seen.

Consequently, I'm not suggesting that teacher educators should facilitate the expression of various discourses of tension, experience, embodiment, or family/friends in any particular order to maximize effective and efficient teacher education. Each student will develop a professional identity in a different way. However, the goal of teacher educators should be to help students engage in various genres of potentially transformative teacher identity discourse whenever possible and relevant for the individual student. We can encourage and support engagement with cognitive and emotional dissonance to teach students how to grapple with tensions, or simply to assure them that grappling itself is okay, even inevitable, in their chosen profession. Education, as I explained at length in the chapter 2, is highly politically charged and culturally visible. Developing a teacher identity is difficult when it can seem like an identity has already been defined and modification is outside of a new teacher's control.

Is there a preferred route to teacher identity development? Is it better to grapple with pedagogical and institutional tensions before personal ones? Or vice versa? Are there some life paths that just make it harder to be a teacher because they foreground these personal conflicts too soon? I resist this final theory because it privileges one way of living over another. However, I suspect that the current structure of teacher education and the institution of secondary education favor one type of student, one kind of life path, over others. It seems to privilege and reward those students whose personal, core identities most closely match those of the culturally defined teacher figure. I find this realization troubling, and as a teacher educator I consider it my duty to reconfigure our practice to address this imbalance that often results in the elimination of some of the most promising teachers from our profession. The more self-awareness we can establish on the part of students about the complexity of the process of teacher education, the more practice we can give them with borderland discourses, and the better they should be able to establish and nurture both their professional and personal identities, no matter what life path they choose.

Chapter **8**

Teaching Is ... an Analysis of the Metaphor

Many people think of metaphor as something that only literature majors, poets, and English teachers consider. However, there has been much written in the last 30 years positing that metaphor is much more significant than widely believed, and that metaphorical discourse can create and reinforce personal and professional identities. George Lakoff and Mark Johnson are perhaps the best-known theorists of metaphor as a way to understand identity. In 1980, they published a seminal text, *Metaphors We Live By*, in which they argued that our relationship to the world is deeply metaphorical, and that metaphors form foundational, almost archetypal patterns we use to understand events and make decisions. They asserted, "a large part of self-understanding is the search for appropriate personal metaphors that make sense of our lives" (p. 233). They also noted, "We have found ... that metaphor is pervasive in everyday life, not just in language but in thought and action. Our ordinary conceptual system, in terms of which we both think and act, is fundamentally metaphorical in nature" (p. 3).

Lakoff and Johnson's book analyzed how fundamental cultural metaphors, such as "argument is war" or "love is a journey," affect human experience and the decisions that individuals make. Metaphors are not just creative ways to describe experience; they affect and influence that experience by changing how we perceive and understand various events, situations, and people. Furthermore, and perhaps most exciting of all, a change or modification in metaphorical discourse can alter material actions and concrete experiences.

Lakoff and Johnson warned that it is no easy feat to change metaphors, however, and hence modify philosophies, beliefs, and practices. Consequently, teacher educators should beware: Simply *telling* students to revise their personal metaphors will not result in identity growth. In fact, it may result in just the opposite—a deeper entrenchment in images or metaphors of teaching and learning from early experiences or cultural models. In order for change and growth to occur, students must first identify the metaphors that underlie and guide their pedagogies. Then, they can consider whether these metaphors that guide their practice are ones they wish to retain in the face of new knowledge and classroom experience. If not, then new metaphors can be created to take their place. Cognitive dissonance between old metaphors and new ideas or experiences can lead to modifications of the ideologies of the young teacher. My study demonstrated that, for the six participants, visual metaphors created connections between abstract ideas (i.e., philosophy statements) and narratives of tension, experience, embodiment, and family/friends. In this chapter, I provide examples of when student participants created metaphors to make sense of contradictory messages found in philosophy statements and narratives. These metaphors were often the clearest, most insightful expressions of the participants' developing professional identities produced during the study.

Since 1980, and building on the work of Lakoff and Johnson, interest has continued to grow about how the creation and analysis of metaphors can nurture teachers' self-understanding and professional growth (Bullough & Knowles, 1991; Connelly & Clandinin, 1988; Marshall, 1990; Russell & Johnston, 1988; Russell, Munby, Spafford, & Johnston, 1988; Taylor, 1984). Metaphors have been explored as tools to enhance teacher professional identity development, as theorists and researchers such as Zeichner and Liston (1996), Bullough and Stokes (1994), and Calderhead and Robson (1991) have explored how teacher educators might use metaphor to assist new teachers' entrance into the profession. Bullough, Knowles, and Crow (1992) addressed the importance of metaphors and teacher education:

> The meanings forming the teaching self are layered, and a goodly number of them, particularly those attached to the inner self, are tacit, unarticulated. In thinking about these characteristics of the meanings composing the teaching self and of the problem of how to access them, we have been drawn to the identification and analysis of teacher metaphors, specifically "root" metaphors, that capture a teacher's core self perception (Ball & Goodson, 1985a, 1985b) and that give coherence to the self. (p. 6)

In addition to metaphors expressed in words (i.e., through stories or in descriptive statements), metaphors as visual images are pathways to expression and increased understanding of the personal and professional self. According to many theorists, metaphors and images are closely related, because metaphors reflect visual images that teachers hold of themselves. The word *image* is used differently by various researchers and theorists; some use it to refer to metaphors (Clandinin, 1986), whereas others use the word to refer to an overall conception or understanding of teaching (Calderhead & Robson, 1991; Morine-Dershimer, 1979), and, finally, some use it to refer to particular incidents or educational memories that students recall very vividly as "snapshots in time." When I refer to visual images in this book, I mean metaphors that students in the study created in visual form (i.e., photographs) to represent their teaching philosophies.

Connelly and Clandinin (1988) determined that teachers in their research often acted in accordance with their teaching metaphors. Zeichner and Liston (1996) claimed that Connelly and Clandinin viewed teachers' practical knowledge as built on images, metaphors, and personal stories. They quoted Connelly and Clandinin as stating that an image is "something within our experience, embodied in us as persons and expressed and enacted in our practices and actions. Situations call forth images from our narratives of experience, and these images are available to us as guides to future action" (quoted in Zeichner & Liston, p. 35).

Calderhead and Robson (1991) also wrote about teaching images. They stipulated:

> In fact, being able to recall images, and to adapt and manipulate these images in reflecting about action in a particular context is possibly an important aspect of the task of teaching .... Images, whether representations or reconstructions, provide us with an indicator of teachers' knowledge and enable us to examine the knowledge growth attributable to different training experiences and the relationship between knowledge and observed practice. (p. 3)

The problem is that images or metaphors are usually not consciously articulated without some prompting by teachers or mentors. As Polanyi (1958) suggested, images represent tacit knowledge that must be made explicit in order to be reconstructed, and metaphors and narratives are two ways to make such knowledge explicit so that it can subsequently be examined. As Bullough et al. (1992) stated, "metaphors form the basis of the stories that are acted out and define the situational self when first becoming a teacher .... Emerging as a teacher is, therefore, a quest for compelling and fitting metaphors that represent who beginning teachers imagine themselves to be as teachers" (p. 8).

Overall, participants expressed fewer metaphors than narratives—15 metaphors, both textual and visual, in comparison to 354 narratives. Initially, because of the sheer number of narratives expressed, I expected the narrative to be the most powerful genre of discourse. Interestingly enough, metaphor—the genre of discourse that had the fewest instances of expression—seemed to have the greatest potential for eliciting borderland discourse and the greatest influence on teacher identity development. The power of metaphor to create a space for borderland discourse was a surprise to me as I analyzed the data, albeit a pleasant one—the study's participants benefited from metaphorical discourse as they developed professional identities. Over the time of the study, the metaphors of the participants became more sophisticated and reflective of nonunitary subjectivities and the complexities of a professional teaching life. In this chapter, I explain how the participants' metaphors were powerful, and I provide several examples of them.

The students created a textual metaphor at the beginning of the study (fall 2000) and a visual, photographic metaphor at the end (spring and fall 2002). Images and metaphors link the abstract with the concrete or the tangible, the theoretical or philosophical with the narrative. As was clear in the previous chapters, most of the six participants' narrative discourse of tension and the resultant borderland discourse concerned professional, not personal, philosophies. However, the visual metaphors demonstrated some grappling with ideological, oftentimes personal, contradictions with professional experiences that the students felt as they entered the teaching profession. When they were asked to create photographic images representing themselves as teachers, students consistently created and expressed metaphors that had characteristics of borderland discourse—or that seemed to reflect the meeting of divergent discourses or senses of self.

Was there something about the visual metaphor that led these students to take risks, to enter sites of ambiguity that the narrative genres of discourse didn't seem to invite? The visual metaphors appeared more effective in facilitating identity growth than did the textual metaphors, which the preservice teachers had created approximately 2 years previously. This increase in effectiveness might be due to the progression of time: The students simply had learned and grown during the 2 years, and thus their metaphors were more thoughtful. However, I hypothesize that some of the variability in effectiveness may have been due to the visual nature of the second metaphors. Perhaps creating the metaphors as photographs somehow enhanced the potential of the discourse to become borderland discourse.

Some believe that visual images are central to cognition and that visual thinking allows individuals to develop ideas that otherwise might not have been accessible. The centrality of visual thinking to the productive human mind is not a new idea. Very early, Margaret Mead (1951/1962; Mead & Cooke Macgregor, 1951) wrote about the power of images in popular culture to affect identity. Rudolf Arnheim (1969) wrote much about visual processes of thought, and, more recently, Howard Gardner (1983) included the visual thinker in his enumerated "intelligences" or preferred ways that individuals learn or approach new material. All of these scholars shared the belief that visual thinking is an important cognitive act and should not be underrated by psychologists, learning theorists, or teachers. Arnheim (1969) was among the first to argue that "visual perception is a cognitive activity" (p. V). He went on to assert, "cognitive operations called thinking are not the privilege of mental processes above and beyond perception but the essential ingredients of perception itself" (p. 13). Perceiving or forming images *is* thinking.

Arnheim's understanding of the image as both thinking and expression was relatively new in his day. However, others since Arnheim have valued visualization as a viable form of thought, including Gardner, who identified "spatial intelligence" as the ability "to perceive the visual world accurately, to perform transformations and modifications upon one's initial perceptions, and to be able to re-create aspects of one's visual experience" (1983, p. 173).

As I mentioned in chapter 1, Sandra Weber and Claudia Mitchell (1995) wrote about how images of teachers held by students (as well as parents, administrators, and the teachers themselves) affect the professional identities of teachers. They accessed these images by asking students and preservice teachers to draw pictures of teachers, and then Weber and Mitchell analyzed these images to discover what kinds of themes they reflected. Overall, they found that the traditional stereotypical images of teachers prevalent in Western nations since the 18th century prevailed: serious, conservative disciplinarians, usually White women, who wielded pointers or chalk sticks while lecturing to large groups of students. Interestingly enough, the preservice teachers in their study who did not wish to become this type of teacher also often drew this kind of image; then, when asked to reflect on their reasons for drawing such a representation of teacher, they realized that their subconscious minds continued to conjure images of teacher stemming from popular culture or their own early school experiences that they wished to reject. Therefore, the drawing and subsequent reflection were useful activities in their professional education. Accessing, reproducing, and reflecting on an image had psychological and emotional benefits.

Because metaphors often stem from ideologies, the imagistic metaphors created by the students in this study often constituted connective discourse between philosophy statements and narratives. When students' philosophy statements were disconnected from their narratively held and understood experiences, the expression of metaphors appeared to help them "translate" their ideologies into real-life experiences. As Bowers (1980) argued:

> Put succinctly, metaphors always have an ideological basis that gives them their special symbolic power to expand meaning ... metaphors carry or lay down, in Langer's phrase, "a deposit of old, abstracted concepts" that reflect the episteme or ideological framework from which they were borrowed. In this sense metaphors are carriers of meaning and images from one context to another. (p. 274)

As connecting discourse between narratives and philosophy statements, the metaphors confronted and addressed tensions among personal, ideological issues more frequently than did many of the other genres of discourse. The creation of a metaphor seemed linked to individual subjectivities and personal perspectives, more so than did most narratives. Of course, it's possible to reproduce a clichéd or "dead" metaphor that does not seem particularly personally relevant; however, if the preservice teachers in this study sincerely attempted to create an accurate and meaningful metaphor, they succeeded, and this metaphor facilitated identity growth.

In the paragraphs that follow, I describe the metaphors expressed by the student participants, focusing on how they have characteristics of borderland discourse. Some of the preservice teachers' metaphors appeared to be more influential in their professional identity development. For these participants, the metaphors represented more obvious ideological change as the participants became teachers, whereas for others, the metaphors reflected more minor indications of growth.

THE EXPRESSION OF METAPHORS BY THE PARTICIPANTS

Janeen's metaphors did not reflect a large amount of emotional or cognitive change over the time of the study. However, two of her visual metaphors, "the hand" and "the shoes," demonstrated reconsideration of the role a teacher should play in students' lives. Her early textual metaphor portrayed the teacher as the all-knowing purveyor of information; later, she realized that the teacher is more of a facilitator who "sets up" the classroom situation, or a motivator who urges students to intellectual action. Her first metaphor, which was composed in an e-mail message to her classmates and me on August 24, 2000, was as follows:

> Teaching is a puzzle. When all the pieces are dumped out of the box you are presented with a confusing and disjointed mess. You know all the pieces you need to complete the puzzle laying before you, but the opportunity to put them all together seems rather daunting. You are not quite sure of where to begin. This emotional beginning is much like that of a beginning teacher. She knows that within her mind lies all the information she needs to bring her students together with the power of knowledge, but she is unsure of where to start.

This metaphor put much faith in the knowledge of the teacher to create an appropriate and effective learning environment, and suggested that the teacher always has all of the knowledge and information at hand to do so, even if she is unsure how to use it ("You know all the pieces you need" and "she knows that within her mind lies all the information she needs"). The metaphor suggested that although the new teacher may be trying to figure out *how* to use her knowledge of content and teaching, all of the knowledge is nonetheless *there*, at her disposal. Furthermore, the implication was that such a set body of knowledge exists in the first place to be learned and used by the teacher.

In her later visual metaphors, Janeen appeared to rethink this rather simplistic perspective. One of her metaphorical photos was of a puzzle board, which she explained this way on April 8, 2002:

> It's [the photo] one of those little puzzle boards. This was to show the pieces of the puzzle. I wouldn't ever want to put the puzzle together for them. Like, with the newspaper assignment. I don't want to write the article for them. But yet I'm still going to type it out for them and give them the pieces of it, just because I wouldn't have time for them to type it out themselves, so I'll give them the pieces and let them assemble their own work, but I'm still heavily involved in creating the pieces of the puzzle. Hopefully I have a knowledge base, even though I'm reteaching myself things.

This later puzzle metaphor demonstrated some growth in Janeen's understanding of teacher identity in two possible ways: First, it recognized and accepted ambiguity in terms of the teacher's knowledge and readiness for every classroom situation ("Hopefully I have a knowledge base, even though I'm reteaching myself things") and second, it was more practical in orientation. In addition to discussing the theory behind her metaphor of how teaching is a puzzle, she related this theory to a real classroom situation from her student teaching (the newspaper assignment). With this metaphor, Janeen was connecting various subjectivities and orientations toward teaching that she had previously expressed through narrative, specifically her student and teacher subjectivities (because she was beginning to understand that the teacher is always also a learner) and university versus practical sources of knowledge.

I believe the most vivid examples of Janeen's borderland metaphors, however, came when she discussed two photos she took, "the hand" and "the shoes" (Figs. 8.1 and 8.2, respectively). When discussing the photograph of the hand in an interview on April 8, 2002, Janeen described how her understanding of this metaphor had changed since taking the photograph 3 months earlier:

> Janeen: This one with the hand was just more because I think of teaching as something like the teacher is to lead the students and to guide the students—rather than tell them exactly what to do, make them think for themselves.
>
> Janet: Okay. Would you think the same thing about the metaphor if you took the picture today?
>
> Janeen: Maybe I pull the students through things now—instead of leading.

Janeen's understanding of the hand as a metaphor for herself as a teacher had changed since her student teaching experience. She now saw

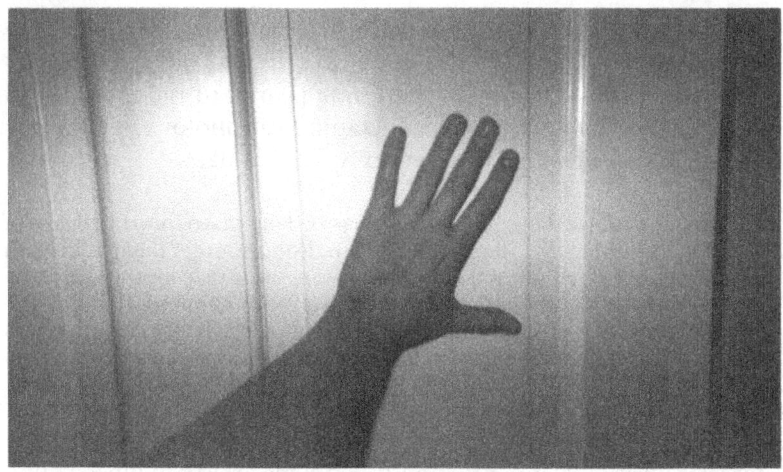

FIG. 8.1. Janeen's "hand" metaphor.

FIG. 8.2. Janeen's "shoe" metaphor.

herself as "pulling" more than "leading" or "guiding" students. Again, like in the puzzle metaphor, Janeen had started to combine practical and experiential teaching narratives with philosophies of teaching and her own experiential student narratives. Remember that Janeen had narrative memories of being a student forced to do meaningless busy work even though she was labeled gifted, so the idea of being *guided* to achieve greater academic heights instead of being *pushed* to do work that seemed irrelevant might have appealed to Janeen. However, the practical realities of classroom teaching had also led Janeen to understand the difficulty of motivating many students to achieve for primarily intrinsic reasons. Therefore, the "hand" remained, but its role had changed somewhat. It was still there to move students toward learning, but now it was somewhat more assertive.

Janeen's second borderland metaphor was her picture of a pair of shoes. In the same interview, Janeen described this metaphor, and again she explained how her understanding had changed since January, when she had taken the photo:

Janeen: This one was shoes. At the time, I was probably thinking more, you know, leading in the footsteps type of thing. Now I would think more of, like, put myself back in their footsteps, in their shoes, see what it's like from each other's perspective. Hopefully. Yeah. I'm not afraid to tell them that I'm tired; I was up late making your test last night, so that kind of thing. So they know what I'm doing for them. They have this idea that I am out here partying every night, but it's really not that at all, that I'm really doing work for them every night. So, you know, they feel more like I'm doing something for them, so you can do something for me.

Janet: So in that way, you're kind of getting closer to them?

Janeen: More understanding of what their position is, if they want to understand what mine is. Right. If they hand me something and they want me to look at it, it's like, well, I'll get to it when I can.

I believe Janeen's shoe metaphor had become more complex since its original creation. In her second explanation of it, it could be seen as an example of borderland discourse, discourse combining student and teacher subjectivities and taking into consideration both personal and professional identity positions. She was starting to understand how the teacher and student must have a reciprocal respect that recognizes each as an individual with various needs and responsibilities. Janeen's discourse reflected a recognition that teacher identity is not simply a professional identity, but also a personal identity that must negotiate and incorporate various subjectivities placing multiple demands on her time and energy. In this way, the shoe metaphor coiuld be understood as an example of borderland discourse that went deeper than pedagogical concerns and began to address issues of embodiment and personal ideology. The teacher is a human being with limited physical and psychological resources, regardless of her desire to see students succeed.

Karen's metaphors were equally interesting. Like Janeen, she created more than one visual metaphor reflective of her personal ideologies and philosophy statements. Her textual metaphor created and sent via e-mail on August 24, 2000, was already reflecting the complex ideas with which she struggled. It also demonstrated awareness of nonunitary subjectivities, or the multiple perspectives and stances of the teacher, as she compared teaching to a card game that is popular in Indiana, yet complicated—euchre:

> In a tedious attempt to come up with a metaphor for teaching, I found myself locked in the realization that it is a game of euchre. In careful consideration of how to explain my logic behind this, I found strategy, practice and talent, and luck. We all know (or those of us who have experienced this game know) that there is a great strategy behind the cards that one wants to play. I believe that strategy plays a big part in teaching in that we must take steps forward with planning and intent long before strategy becomes practice. As in anything, when we start we are unsure of what lies before us. We must get our feet wet. A new euchre player isn't going to know how to lead or what to lead; she must have guidance and time to know what to play. Even after she is let loose on her own, it takes practice to take on what others know. As teachers we are going to have to ask questions, watch other teachers, and try out our own ideas and solutions throughout our careers. And I believe that this leads to talent. No matter how much ability we have, we gain talent through practicing. One might be an excellent euchre player, but it didn't happen on the first or second time. And finally, as in all other things, there is luck. Every hand of euchre is dealt. One has no control over what they get. We are more than likely not going to be able to pick out the cards or children that we want in our classrooms. They are given to us. Euchre and teaching mix in this way because we must play each card with caution and care. It is not a game we're dealing with. We're dealing with kids' lives.

Through this metaphor, Karen recognized that many things go into the creation of a teacher identity, including hard work, strategy, and even luck. She also recognized that each student or classroom situation varies and therefore might change the proper teacher response. Finally, like Janeen, Karen realized that the teaching life is always in flux, and the teacher is always learning and growing ("As teachers we are going to have to ask questions, watch other teachers, and try out our own ideas and solutions throughout our careers."). Starting out with such complex insights about teaching, Karen's visual metaphors only became more interesting. Her photographs reflected ideological, not practical, concerns, and mirrored many of the personal tensions with the educational community that she described in narratives. For example, Karen took two photos in tandem to make a point about her understanding of teaching and learning: "the middle school" (Fig. 8.3) and "the river" (Fig. 8.4). Karen described the two pictures in this way on April 5, 2002:

FIG. 8.3. Karen's "middle school" metaphor. (Photo 1)

FIG. 8.4. Karen's "river" metaphor. (Photo 2)

About Photo #1: I think I took a picture of the school just because it's everything that I don't want to be. Just institutionalized teaching; I think that it's censored, and it's politically correct, and it's just everything that I don't want to be. I don't want to have certain hours; I don't think that teachers are on a clock. It's just not me. And I don't like the hierarchy of schools, like, "I am the teacher, you are the student." There are just a lot of things about the actual school and how institutionalized it is that I don't like. The status differences between the students, you know? The cliques. Not showing the students exactly what it is that they are doing. I think that society has its own cliques and everything, but the school doesn't do anything to intertwine people, and that's what I want to do.

> *About Photo #2:* Well, I was thinking about water, actually. And how, you know, it's always changing forms. Sometimes it's evaporated, it's frozen, it's liquid. It's always moving, it's always changing in some way, almost spontaneously. It travels all over the world and it's in this huge cycle, and I chose to take a picture of a river, because that transports it [water]. Takes it from the streams to the river to the ocean, where it's evaporated and comes over the land again. I was just kind of thinking that's what I want to be. I want to be different forms to different people, and I want to try to move through the waterways and get to different people and show them what I believe. I took those [pictures] back to back.

Karen saw the two photographs as binary opposites: the first was what she didn't want to be as a teacher, and the second was what she did want to be. These metaphors were bridges, of a sort, between her philosophies of education and her narratives of experience, embodiment, and tension. I believe she was working out, though the metaphors, how she might be and what she might do as a teacher. She was exploring how she could make her beliefs about education consistent with her personal experiences as an educator. Her conception of teacher was bigger than a school building, and she saw herself as a teacher outside of the school walls, rather than inside. Bringing cultural awareness and "intertwining people" was important to her; she saw herself as being a different type of teacher to different students and being unrestricted by building policies, political correctness, censorship, or time. Karen's paired visual metaphors demonstrated her acceptance of cognitive dissonance and her first, best attempt to bridge the divide between contrasting societal expectations for teachers and her own educational philosophies. She viewed herself as a teacher, but not in a traditional way.

Karen's school and river metaphors were also examples of "root" metaphors as discussed by R. H. Brown (1978) and Lakoff and Johnson (1980). Brown identified three kinds of metaphors: analogic metaphors, which make comparisons and describe relationships; iconic metaphors, which provide an image of what things are rather than creating a new meaning with a comparison; and root metaphors, which represent previously unrecognized assumptions and ideologies of the metaphors' creator. These root metaphors reflect the ideological positions and subjective stances that must be accessed as part of transformative teacher education. Lakoff and Johnson (1980) talked about "deep" versus "surface" metaphors, and their deep metaphors were similar to Brown's root metaphors. Of the five students who created visual metaphors, three of them—Karen, Linda, and Lois—created metaphors that could be called root metaphors. Karen's school and river images were root metaphors because they reflected some of her underlying ideologies about teaching, learning, and interacting with other human beings. She represented these beliefs abstractly with two images that had meaning specific to her—these images could not be explained identically by anyone else. (This is in contrast, I believe, to Janeen's explanation of the metaphor such as the "hand," which someone else might guess at correctly without a great deal of difficulty.) I believe these understandings, reflected in the visual metaphors, formed the basis for much of Karen's other professional and personal discourse excerpted in this book.

Linda also expressed metaphors with characteristics of borderland discourse involving personal beliefs, even though she had trouble expressing narratives about anything except practical, classroom concerns. Like Janeen and Karen, some of her visual metaphors moved past the practical and accessed personal tensions. Other metaphors reflected perspectives similar to those expressed in her narratives of tension, experience, embodiment, and family/friends. For example, Linda took two photos to represent the importance of diversity in teaching; these portrayed uncomplicated and uninterrogated notions of multiculturalism. These two photos were of a multicolored scarf and a group of CDs by different artists who perform various genres of music. These seemed to be superficial representations of diversity and reflected a version of multiculturalism that simply urges the inclusion of texts by and about many groups of people. This approach, although better than some alternatives, is sort of a "buffet" approach to diversity—put it all out there at some time or another, and sensitivity will result. However, as postmodern theorists of diversity teach us, building understandings of race, gender, ethnicity, sexual orientation, and other human difference is much more complex and requires self-reflection as well as simple exposure. Linda's first textual metaphor also mirrored this oversimplified view of diversity, and demonstrated the reductive potentiality of metaphor. She wrote on August 24, 2000:

> Teaching is a kaleidoscope. There is much diversity in teachers, students, types of schools, abilities, and so on. Every student in each classroom is different in some way; teachers must learn to deal with these differences and then shape them into a working form just like the beautiful arrangements of the kaleidoscope. There are different types of teachers in each school, which also can make up the arrangement of the kaleidoscope. Different teachers, with different teaching styles, can form the most beautiful, beneficial, and diverse school. Also, abilities of students are also like the many colors of a kaleidoscope. Just like each color serves its own purpose in the picture, each student has some ability to serve the flow of the classroom. Each student has some talent, just like each color has some beauty.

Linda's understanding of classroom (and human) diversity was similar to early conceptions of diversity and multiculturalism that, according to Rita M. Kissen (2002), "drew on the 'melting pot' theories of the 1950s and 1960s: Diversity and difference are real and valuable, but the ultimate goal was to create a homogeneous society that assumed that everyone was equal" (p. 5). In other words, everybody is really the same deep down, so everyone should be valued equally. Although this version of diversity is certainly preferable to discrimination or bigotry, it ignores identity politics, which argue that each identified minority group, and even each person within it, is unique—to put it simply, equal under the law or in the classroom isn't equivalent to a bland sameness.

However, Linda did create two visual metaphors that I believe were examples of transformative discourse and that confronted educational issues more thoughtfully: the "leopard" (Fig. 8.5) and the "knife" (Fig. 8.6). The leopard metaphor was one of Linda's first forays into ideological ambiguity or cognitive dissonance concerning teaching, a state of mind mostly avoided in her narrative discourse. On April 9, 2002, she said to me about the photo:

> This one was kind of like a wild world. Kind of like the wild feel the classroom has sometimes. You can go into it and it will be just overwhelming—and so different from everything else around it, and, you know, you walk out and it's like, "Okay. Deep breath." You walk back in and it's crazy. I don't know. I'm having a hard time explaining some of these. Because you can leave—when you leave, it doesn't—you know, you don't—you can't grasp the feel of it like you can when you're actually in there, and so that's kind of all around you.

Linda had a difficult time explaining the metaphor, and I think her difficulty signaled that she was walking on new terrain. She wasn't just engaging in transformative discourse about pedagogy, but also about incongruities between personal and professional life. She described how there is a palpable difference between life inside and outside the classroom. She even described it concretely and spatially—literally walking in and out of the classroom allows the teacher to experience different worlds. The leopard print photo was a metaphor for the wildness, the activity, the stress, the energized feeling in the classroom that is unlike anything else that Linda had ever experienced. For the first time of which I am aware, Linda expressed personal reactions to her new teacher identity that were uncertain, ambiguous, and focused on corporeal reactions to the high-energy classroom environment.

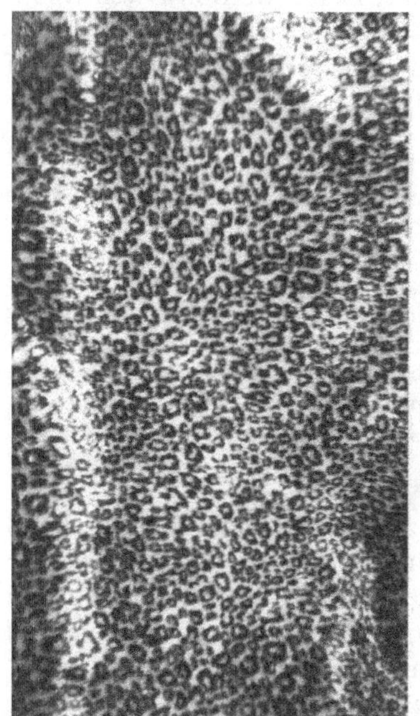

FIG. 8.5. Linda's "leopard" metaphor.

FIG. 8.6. Linda's "knife" metaphor.

Her knife photo was possibly another example of a transformative, visual metaphor that had a similar purpose: Through the metaphor, Linda expressed how it felt to be a teacher—the stress, the uncertainty, the trepidation:

> This one was my cutting edge one. I do remember that one. Because I remembered that [metaphor] long after [creating it]. It's the cutting edge of education because you're always on the cutting edge. You could always make a mistake that could affect you, or you could always do something that will positively affect somebody for the rest of their life. Or negatively affect somebody for the rest of their life, you know? You're right on that edge all the time. Because everything that comes out of your mouth is important in one way or another. And while half of what you say may go in one ear and out the other, it could be one sentence, one word that could affect you—or them, either way. I think because you so easily could do something to damage yourself or a student really—I mean, or, you know, vice versa, you could do something great to really help. And either way, you just have to be thinking of that all the time. Which was really scary sometimes. Like during student teaching I think—I mean, it was good because that was one of the best things about student teaching; it got me prepared to be up in front of the class all day. Not just for one class, but all day. But it does take a toll on you. Kind of the pressure of being on display and everything. It's one of those necessary evils for us. It's like, look at me, but ! (laughing) don't look at me! (April 9, 2002)

I believe this was a pivotal example of discourse for Linda. It was the first example of borderland discourse I identified in which she talked about her feelings of fear and insecurity concerning her new professional role. Instead of reverting to the habitual discourse of confidence stemming from her years raised in a "teacher family," Linda expressed some fear about the influence she might have over students. The image of the knife was telling—a knife can be both a useful tool and a harmful weapon, depending on how it is used. Linda still explained the teaching situation as something she may or may not have had control over at any given moment ("You could always make a mistake that could affect you"), which may not have been an exactly accurate description. Regardless, she seemed awed by the influence she would have over students. She was also aware of how the cultural expectations for teachers made her job more difficult than other professions and made it almost too easy for her to politically "damage herself" unknowingly. Linda was opening to cognitive dissonance about her teacher identity; she was not resettling into preestablished beliefs and subjective stances about a teacher's role, nor was she oversimplifying the difficulty of the job. Additionally, she also again confronted issues of embodiment in much more complex ways than she did in her narratives, in which she mostly discussed professional dress and age. Here she talked about being "on display" and the personal pressures that being the object of such a gaze created, day after day.

Lois' visual metaphor was likewise interesting and could be seen as an example of borderland discourse. She took only one photo demonstrating her understanding of the subjectivity of the teacher as nonunitary and multidimensional. Her textual metaphor, created before the visual one, was much more simplistic:

> Teaching is like the weather—sure, we're going to have our sunny days where we are all excited and happy to be a teacher, when we have reached that unreachable student, when we have delivered the lesson plan of our careers. But there are also going to be our stormy days, where all hell breaks loose, and the days when everything seems to snowball at us. Like the weather, teaching is unpredictable. As much as we plan for the day or as much work as we put into a lesson, there is no guarantee that it will work in the classroom. (August 28, 2000)

Similar to Linda's "knife" metaphor discussed earlier, this metaphor did not recognize very much agency on the part of the teacher. Instead, Lois described teaching successes and failures as almost being out of the teacher's control, like the weather: We can report on it, but we can't change it. Although this metaphor did not assume that the teacher is the purveyor of all knowledge or the unproblematized center of the classroom context, it was missing some of Lois' later insights when she admitted that although, yes, teaching is not dependent on the teacher alone, the teacher does have some say in the matter—her subjectivity or positioned identity in the classroom affects the success of the teaching and learning that happens there. Her visual metaphor demonstrated this growing awareness. Lois took a picture of 2-liter soda bottles on a ladder in Wal-Mart (Fig. 8.7) to make her point. Lois explained her visual metaphor to me this way on February 4, 2002:

> My metaphor is three bottles of pop. One is 7-Up, one is Sprite, and one is some sort of other Sprite-like item. They are all a caffeine-free beverage of

FIG. 8.7. Lois' "soda" metaphor.

the "clear" choice. They're different, some little bitty difference in flavor, but they're basically the same thing. So, my teaching style is the way I taught, you know, three different classes of communications, and two of composition. In none of those classes was I the same person. I got across the same message. We did the same things in class. I taught them the same things as I taught the rest of the kids. But I did it in distinct flavors, distinct ways, and I had subtle differences with each class. Because of the students, because of the way they responded either to me or to the material, I mean, just small variations in things. So, I'm a different person with every class, but I'm the same teacher.

Here we see a rich example of metaphorical discourse expressing Lois' understanding of the complex and many-faceted professional life of the teacher. In comparison to the early metaphor created 2 years ago, this second metaphor revealed aspects of Lois's professional identity that were not evident then, including her increased feelings of control over her professional demeanor and classroom environment and how her pedagogical decision making could (or even had to) be specific to a particular class or educational context.

Sandy's metaphors are the last that I describe in this chapter, because Carrie, due to her late entrance into the study, did not create any visual or textual metaphors. Sandy's textual metaphor of August 24, 2000, was as follows:

> Teaching is a marriage of countless different and complicated things. It involves devoting extra time to grading papers, preparing lesson plans, attending school plays or games, or helping the student council with the bake sale when we would rather be sleeping in on Saturday morning. It involves conflicts of all kinds: emotional, personal, economic, and political. It involves sacrificing yourself for the sake of your students, your school, your career, and your future. The marriage between a teacher and his or her profession is much like the one he or she may have with a spouse. There will always be things one spouse absolutely has to do, but the other simply refuses to go along. There is give and take, compromise involved on both sides. All people involved in the educational system share some type of love for knowledge, teaching, empowerment, and kids. Without that love, there would be

no marriage, and therefore no compromising, and therefore no hope for our students.

This metaphor was interesting for several reasons: first, this early understanding of teaching seemed based on personal sacrifice, which is a troubling metaphor for both teaching and marriage. It seemed to assume that the choices the teacher makes for her students (and spouse) are done unquestioningly; there is only one right thing to do, so that's what is done. There was little ambiguity or questioning of the teacher's role or responsibilities. Sandy's later, visual metaphor complicated this notion of teacher identity somewhat, as she was beginning to understand the value of reflective thought and the idea that decisions are not predetermined, but instead are decided on a case-by-case basis as the teacher does his or her job and develops a progressively stronger professional identity. Sandy demonstrated this growth in identity development through her photo of a mirror (Fig. 8.8). Sandy described this metaphor on April 5, 2002:

> I look in and see totally different person than before. When I talk to my boyfriend, all I talk about and what occupies all of my time is teaching. I've changed in so many ways—as teacher, student, and sibling. I have more respect for all teachers—like my brother. I come home in a bad mood more often. My roommates are my refuge. I come home and complain to them. It's important to look at changes because if you don't think about how you've changed, you aren't learning and evaluating the change.

FIG. 8.8. Sandy's "mirror" metaphor.

Here Sandy was speaking about the power of true reflection, which resulted in material change and continued reflection in a cyclical process of professional development. She described how she now looked at herself in a different way, as a new person, now that she was a teacher.

The visual metaphors were an especially powerful genre of teacher identity discourse for the preservice teachers in this study. I was surprised by the power of the visual metaphors and the extent to which they reflected cognitive dissonance and increased reflectivity on the part of the participants. These metaphors seemed to narrow perceived gaps between narratives of experience and connected perceptions of the teacher's role and the ideologies expressed in philosophy statements of teaching and learning. By narrowing the gap between the perceived demands of professional identity and ideologies central to the students' core identities, the visual metaphors played an important role in teacher identity development. To put it simply, the metaphors prompted cognitive dissonance that often led to the integration of personal and professional spaces.

Chapter 9

What Do I Believe? Statements of Philosophy

Philosophy or belief statements are a genre of discourse familiar to teacher educators. Many methods instructors ask their students to create philosophy statements at various times during a semester and even at intervals during students' university education. Crafting a thoughtful philosophy statement is seen as an important part of developing a personal pedagogy and a useful teacher identity. The theory is that without a well-thought-out philosophy of teaching, a new teacher will be unable to implement pedagogical strategies effectively. Although I also believe in the importance of developing critically reflective philosophies of teaching, I am skeptical of the value of such statements if they do not exhibit characteristics of transformative discourse or evidence of critical interrogation and reflection.

According to my definition, a philosophy statement encompasses a series of beliefs about different teaching practices and is often generalized to the educational system as a whole or to the role of teachers within this system. A philosophy statement may include commentary concerning what teachers believe about specific classroom practices; however, more often philosophy statements in my study consisted of abstract epistemological assumptions about teaching and learning.

I remember writing a philosophy statement when I was a senior in my teacher education program, and I was amazed at what I produced. It certainly sounded really good; the problem was I wasn't exactly sure what it meant! I used all the right words—*student-centered curriculum*, *reader response theory*, and *constructivism*, to name a few—but I never took these words and phrases down the ladder of abstraction to give them real-world, classroom referents. What would a student-centered curriculum *look like*? What kinds of literature assignments would qualify as examples of reader response?

What lessons are truly constructivist? Actually, the problem wasn't really that the philosophy statement itself didn't contain the answers to these questions, but rather that I didn't know what those answers were.

I do not believe that my experience drafting a philosophy statement was unique; many students in undergraduate education courses write philosophy statements that simply reproduce educational jargon and politically correct clichés, rather than reflect thoughtful interrogation of past experiences or ideological tension. The act of assigning a written philosophy statement does not inherently produce thoughtful, critically reflective statements about pedagogical beliefs; as with the genres of narrative and metaphor, it is only with the encouragement of borderland discourse that a statement of philosophy reaches its transformative potential. Like the other genres of discourse described in this book, an unexamined philosophy statement can be, at best, an exploratory genre allowing the professor and preservice teacher access to the nature of a student's current thinking patterns; at worst, it can be a vehicle for the reinforcement of unexamined beliefs and the enactment of unreflective pedagogies.

During data analysis, I coded 77 philosophy statements uttered by the participants in my study. Given the nature of most philosophy statements, it was perhaps not surprising that there was little substantive change in these statements over the time of the study. Of the six student participants, only two—Karen and Lois—expressed philosophy statements demonstrating significant identity growth or exemplifying borderland discourse. Only one of these students, Lois, decided to teach after graduation. Interestingly, their development of philosophic discourse can be linked to their creation of metaphors connecting these philosophy statements to selected narratives examined in chapters 3–7. Additionally, Karen and Lois were the two students who stated that their philosophies included the notion that teachers are always learning and growing and don't possess all of the answers. These two participants were beginning to understand that being a teacher necessitated attending to their *own* professional identity, in addition to analyzing and responding to students' needs.

The identified philosophy statements expressed themes as diverse as the importance of engaging with students, the preferred purpose for teaching literature, and how teachers should use authority. The major themes that reoccurred in all six students' philosophy statements are summarized in Table 9.1. The philosophy statements emerged naturally from the data, except for those that arose when I asked students to create two pie charts describing "What do you think an English teacher should know/be able to do?" and "What do you believe about teaching English?" For these prompts, the students were given an empty circle on a sheet of

TABLE 9.1
Major Themes Emerging From Philosophy Statements

Theme	*Number of Occurrences*	*Preservice Teacher Expressing Theme*
It's important to connect/relate to students.	5	Janeen, Karen, Linda, Carrie, Sandy
A teacher should be interesting and engaging.	4	Janeen, Karen, Carrie, Sandy
A teacher should be confident.	4	Janeen, Karen, Lois, Sandy
A teacher should understand students' lives.	4	Janeen, Karen, Linda, Sandy
A teacher should connect content to students' lives.	4	Janeen, Karen, Linda, Sandy
A teacher should be a professional/personal role model.	3	Karen, Linda, Sandy
The purpose of teaching literature is to allow students to explore ideas/cultures/beliefs.	3	Karen, Carrie, Linda
A teacher should know the disciplinary content.	2	Karen, Janeen
A teacher is always learning and in a continual process of growth.	2	Karen, Lois

paper and asked to divide the "pie" into segments that they would label with ideas or skills they believed are important for the English teacher and an ideal classroom (e.g., content knowledge, relating to students, encouraging writing as expression, etc.).

Western philosophy, as it has been traditionally understood, is being rethought in a postmodern world, and this rethinking should influence how we assign philosophy-writing assignments to our students. As I described in chapter 2, postmodern theorists are moving away from viewing the world in terms of binaries—subject/object, male/female, mind/body—and moving toward a more holistic conception of identity that perceives interactions among these ways of being and knowing as essential to the human experience. Foucault (1972) saw knowledge as produced by individuals through discourses that are "practices that systematically form the objects of which they speak," not "groups of signs ... signifying elements referring to contents or representations" (p. 49). Discourse in this sense creates material subject positions for an individual to occupy, such as communities of "clinical discourse, economic discourse, the discourse of natural history, [and] psychiatric discourse" (p. 107) and, I would add, educational discourse. Anthony Petrosky (1994) wrote about the application of Foucault's theories of discourse to the teacher:

> The key moves, then, in describing and analyzing an individual's creation, or production, of knowledge have to do with (1) defining the discourse, the discursive structures and practices, in which the individual locates himself or herself, and (2) developing the terms, the language, to describe and analyze the individual's knowledge production as discourse. (p. 25)

The individual teacher's creation and production of knowledge is analyzed by examining the discourse of the teacher, or the various genres of discourse in which he or she engages. Then, by naming these genres (as I have done in this book) and interrogating them or subjecting them to critical analysis, the new teacher can develop professionally and personally. Therefore, when writing a philosophy statement, I argue that it must be consciously grounded in an analysis of various genres of discourse through which student teachers understand their practice. At the end of this book (in appendix A) I include some assignments for the teacher educator to assist the new teacher in this process, including one for creating a "discourse map" analyzing teaching philosophy through a close reading of various discourses that have affected the student's various understandings of self.

In this chapter I discuss in more depth how the participants' philosophy statements were connected to narrative genres through metaphors, as noted in the previous chapter. The metaphors created ideological and discursive links between seemingly contradictory philosophy statements and narratives. Because two of the three students who chose not to teach experienced tension between or among narratives reflecting personal/professional ideology and stated philosophies of teaching, awareness of such a potential function for metaphor could help teacher educators assist students in developing a workable professional identity and meaningful educational philosophy. Perhaps most important, the discourse of the participants reveals that philosophy statements alone, disconnected to narratives and/or metaphors, did little to enhance their professional identity development because they usually merely reproduced uninterrogated beliefs or imitated educational discourses. I give examples in Appendix A of assignments that ask students to create philosophy statements grounded in real-world experiences and connected to various understandings of self. I argue that such "grounded philosophy statements" or "statements of personal pedagogy" can result in reflective thinking and identity growth, rather than the superficial and reductive summaries of educational jargon that usually result when teacher educators give the ubiquitous "philosophy statement" assignment.

THE EXPRESSION OF PHILOSOPHY STATEMENTS BY THE PARTICIPANTS

Karen told the greatest number of philosophy statements in interviews, with a total of 22. This large number was not a surprise, because her discourse throughout the study was consistently ideological and political. The themes of her philosophy statements ranged among statements of the importance of relating content to students' lives, of working to keep students interested, of teaching literature to make students think, and of becoming a role model as a teacher. The most interesting example of Karen's philosophic discourse was about teacher identity, role expectations, and responsibilities. This discourse also demonstrated modification of Karen's philosophy statements over the time of the study. In order to understand this change and the increasingly transformative nature of her philosophy statements, I share an early philosophy statement from an e-mail dated August 19, 2002:

> The students who don't want to learn need to be in those classrooms more than anyone else. As educators, we know the pay when we go into the classroom. We know that it's low. And perhaps teachers don't get paid enough to put up with all that crap, *but* they know what to expect before they go into the classroom. The agreement that they make to the world when they become a teacher isn't that they will teach certain kids. A teacher's responsibility is to teach all students and not leave any behind. To create a learning environment that tailors to all students needs. I feel very strongly about this. The problem is not the students, it is the teachers. Whether it is the training that teachers get in college or their own laziness, the problem lies in teachers not performing as well as they should. Some take the easy way, which is how they were taught.

In this e-mail message, Karen blamed teachers for the failure of students because teachers should work harder, should not expect high pay, and should recognize their responsibility "to teach all students and not leave any behind," language reflective of current political discourse. Quite a tall order, although it sounded heroic. Later, on December 16, 2002, after being a middle school coach for a semester, Karen's opinion changed as she integrated teacher experiential discourse with this philosophy statement:

> So, what have I observed from this. (1) Some people use race and judge race. (2) Not every kid can be motivated. (3) Parents have such a huge role in their kid's attitudes about learning. (4) Teachers aren't always in the wrong. (5) Despite your efforts, not everyone will always appreciate or agree with what you're trying to do. (6) In sports, and maybe in other things, individual ac-

> complishments are intangible. So ... do I think that the teachers are still responsible for their students' performances? Absolutely. But I am not such a big advocate now of charter schools. What I mean by this is that when I looked at this program before, I thought that it was totally the teacher's fault that the student wasn't passing, or couldn't read, or couldn't do math. Now I know that it only takes one student to disrupt the learning environment of other students.

Karen demonstrated through this statement that she now understood the role of the teacher more deeply and recognized the complexity of the teaching task more clearly. A teacher subjectivity, based on narratives of teaching experience and of tension between university and practical orientations, had entered her discourse and affected her professional identity. As I said earlier, Karen and Lois were the only two students who engaged in philosophy statements with characteristics of borderland discourse, and, interestingly enough, the statements in both cases explicitly concerned issues of teacher identity (e.g., societal expectations, integrating the personal with the professional, or responsibilities to students).

As mentioned in the previous chapter, I believe Karen's metaphors of "the school" and "the river" acted as intermediaries between her philosophy statements and her narratives of teaching experience. For example, Karen told the following story of frustration working in a public school environment (you might remember this story from chap. 3):

> So then the very next day I go to teach at Washington High in the class for the "Tiger-ettes." Tiger-ettes is like this dance club they have, where they wear next to nothing and do half-time shows. The class is a time for them to practice, and it's offered 7 hours a day. So I'm thinking, you know, we can fund these things, but we can't take care of these other kids [in alternative schools]? So yeah, I think about teaching a lot. I think about what I *don't* want to be a part of. And that's what I don't want to be a part of. (January 23, 2002)

I coded this narrative as a "narrative of tension" between Karen's personal ideologies of education and her understanding of the current educational climate. She couldn't seem to reconcile what goes on in public schools with her beliefs about teaching and learning expressed in her philosophy statements, such as those told to me on September 10, 2001:

> I thought it would be a good idea if teachers in college, learning to be teachers, would take classes like, I'm taking an African American literature course right now, so, if you took those classes and learned about the cultures—the different cultures—that way you'd be so diversified [and ready] to go into a classroom with a diverse class.

And on January 23, 2002:

> I was thinking about how we're taught culture in our actual schools and stuff, and how you really don't deal with the hard issues. You know, like what really happened during slavery and stuff. You don't really deal with that too much .... And that was something I would want to take on.

Her beliefs included an emphasis on teaching "hard issues" and multicultural awareness (predictable, perhaps, based on her personal struggles with this issue) and seemed opposed to the way she saw schools being run when she was substitute teaching. Instead of bringing students of various races, classes, and ethnicities together, she saw schools supporting their differentiation and placement into class and racial hierarchies. Whereas one group of students was privileged with a special dance class, another was relegated to a prisonlike school building without access to any extracurricular benefits.

How did Karen make sense of these opposing discourses? You may remember that, when analyzing her narratives, I came to the conclusion that she didn't—the tensions were so great among them that she chose to leave the profession and not teach high school English after graduation. However, when looking closely at Karen's metaphors, I realized that they provided one way for her to begin to connect divergent philosophy statements and associated personal ideologies with experiential narratives of teaching. Karen's metaphors of the river and the school reflected the development of an understanding of teaching and learning that, although perhaps impossible in many public school settings, might be possible in other educational contexts: bookstores or adult education outreach services, for example, two career paths that Karen considered. I believe Karen's metaphors began to connect her dreams with her perceptions of reality.

Linda had the second-highest number of philosophy statements, with 17. Unlike Karen's, Linda's statements did not change very much over time. The philosophic themes and issues reflected in Linda's statements included the themes that all kids should be able to learn to write, literature should connect to students' lives, students will rise to teachers' expectations, realism should be tempered with idealism (as far as pedagogical practices), and teachers should act and dress professionally. Like Karen, Linda's metaphors sometimes provided bridges between philosophy statements and narratives of teaching experience. Also like Karen, the teaching experience narratives in particular emphasized such philosophic tension—there was something about working in a school, during student teaching or substitute teaching, that created frustration. Linda included the following statement of philosophy in her student teaching application. In it, she described how she believed she knew a lot about teaching because of her family background, and was prepared to teach because of this home-based knowledge:

> The success of my students will be my highest priority as an educator. I have learned by watching my mom, a fifth-grade teacher, and some of my favorite

> teachers, that it is the way the teacher approaches the lesson that helps the students learn the material. I feel that my experience in observations provides me with many different types of lesson plans to keep my class interesting for students.

Linda's confidence, based on her home discourse, has been discussed in several previous chapters. This confidence, although not inherently harmful, sometimes caused Linda to avoid discourse that might have allowed interrogation and true reflection on educational ideologies. Although Linda did take a teaching job after graduation and is currently a secondary school teacher, at the end of the study she had yet to engage in much real ideological investigation involving conflicts between personal and professional ideologies. However, once again, metaphor seemed to be successful in creating such discourse when narratives could not. To demonstrate, I share the following narrative of professional experience that Linda narrated on November 12, 2001. Then, I show how one of her visual metaphors provided a discursive, ideological connection between the narrative and her previous philosophy statement:

> They were [in] this college comp class, and this was only the second week I had them. And they were talking about parallel constructions. And they were supposed to write directions from the auditorium to their house, because that's where graduation is for the high school. And so they were supposed to pretend that they had a graduation party right after commencement, and they were supposed to write them [the directions] in parallel construction. You would have thought that the world was coming to an end. And it was only two kids, but they were the most vocal students in the class. They didn't see how it [the assignment] had any purpose. And I think looking back on it, it makes sense, but I don't think there was anything I could have done about that. Also, the grades for the 9 weeks had been posted that day, and those two students were failing the class. If they fail English they can't graduate. So all that made sense afterwards, but I didn't know grades were going to be posted that day. They threw a big fit.

Linda recognized that she was involved in a difficult situation, and if she had had more knowledge about when grades were to be posted, she may have changed the assignment. Asking students to write about a graduation party the same day they realize that they may not graduate is perhaps not the best idea. However, this narrative showed how Linda's knowledge was not sufficient to take care of every situation or scenario—she still had many things to learn about interacting with students and planning lessons (as should be expected, of course).

Her metaphor of the knife was an example of a new transformative discourse that integrated her earlier philosophical discourse of confidence with the previous narrative discourse of insecurity and occasional failure. The knife metaphor, as discussed in the previous chapter, described how Linda felt "on edge" or nervous about her authority and power as a teacher. She was a little afraid of making important decisions every day, and somewhat nervous about being on display in front of students who, like the ones described previously, were not always sympathetic to her efforts. The metaphor did not necessarily demonstrate a loss of confidence but instead a more realistic and balanced understanding of it; yes, Linda was prepared to teach, but she also had to continue to learn and explore her teacher identity.

Janeen and Sandy each uttered 12 philosophy statements. Janeen's statements did not reflect much change over time; she even said on April 8, 2002, that the only modifications in philosophy she'd noticed had been "because of structural constraints," but the basic things were still the same. She also told me that her philosophy "always was to help them [students] become good communicators." Themes running throughout Janeen's philosophy statements included engaging with students, teaching communication skills, fostering an "open" environment, relating to students on their level, making sure not to assign busy work, exuding confidence as a teacher, and demonstrating an openness to student ideas.

Like the other participants, Janeen's visual metaphors reflected cognitive dissonance and increasing dialogue between personal ideologies or subjectivities (expressed as philosophy statements) and perceived professional responsibilities or knowledge (expressed as narratives). In Janeen's case, her narratives about her experiences as a gifted student were directly connected to her philosophies concerning the banning of busy work. Following is a narrative from Janeen's educative experience, which reflected her unsatisfying student experiences:

> When I was in the seventh grade I was in a gifted program. I had two friends, and we were on a future-problem-solving team, and it was run through the gifted program. So she [the teacher] would give us the English assignment and just say, "Go out of the room, and do it," and we would sit down and do it in 3 minutes where the rest of the class would take the whole hour to do it. So, yeah, I mean, even then what we were doing seemed really trivial to me. I went to Catholic school for grade school, so it was tons of repetition and tons of busy work. It was absolutely ridiculous. (September 10, 2001)

Janeen's memory of being a student asked to do trivial busy work remained with her and informed her educational philosophy, as she articulated to me on the same day: "Probably the best [teacher] would be the teacher that can most easily relate to them, be on their level, the lessons are going to be interesting, there's not going to be a lot of busy work—what they're doing is engaging."

However, in another experiential narrative from her student teaching, Janeen realized that not all students are as intrinsically motivated or prepared for challenging work as she was:

Janet: So, how did the newspaper project go?

Janeen: It's not done, yet. I didn't think that it would go fast. We did a lot with "who, what, when, where, why, and how." I tried to do that with real newspapers. Didn't go so well. Nobody could do it, so—

Janet: Nobody could pick those things out?

Janeen: Not very easily. They could, but they kept asking a lot of questions. They were very unsure of themselves. Like, the facts are fine, but then when you get to why and how, it totally threw them. So we did that first, and that kind of went okay, sort of, and then we started doing that for our own articles. So we've done a lot of that. One day we did just the facts, and then the next day we did the why and the how. Everything together. So right now we are writing the paragraphs of the articles. So two different people—they're not doing it together, but two different people are writing on the topic of the fire. A paragraph on that, and then two different people are writing about the murder. And so then they're turning all that in to me, and I'm editing them and giving them back. So then today they turned in a final draft, and I'm going to type it into sections, and then we're going to assemble everybody's, hopefully. (April 8, 2002)

Her real experience teaching secondary students did not parallel her experiences as a student or even support her philosophy statement concerning busy work. Janeen's description of the newspaper assignment reflected her surprise at the trouble her students had with a relatively simple concept (who, what, where, when, and why), and described how she very slowly guided students through the newspaper analysis and writing processes. One can imagine that if Janeen had experienced such a project as a student, she would have found it boring and unnecessarily meticulous.

How did Janeen justify such pedagogies, given her philosophies? It seemed that she might have had to admit to assigning her own students "busy work," the very type of assignment she despised. However, her visual metaphor of the hand provided a clue about how she balanced her philosophies about assignments with her real-life teaching experiences. As she discussed changes in her understanding of the photo—remember that now she "lead" or "pushed" students as much as she "guided" them—it's clear she hadn't given up on the idea of teacher as motivator and intellectual leader; she had simply modified the nature of this motivating or leading. Some students have difficulty learning without a structured series of activities, activities, and assignments that Janeen would have found unbearable.

Like Janeen, Sandy uttered 12 philosophy statements during the study, and little change was evident over time. Sandy discussed the importance of being sensitive to student feelings, understanding that students have lives outside of school, being fun and interesting as a teacher, enjoying one's job, and having both passion and poise. Many of Sandy's philosophy statements could be connected with her own experiences as a tutor or a student. In general, Sandy's philosophy statements were much "deeper" and more reflective than were her experiential narratives or narratives of tension. Consequently, there was a disjuncture between what she *said* she believed about teaching and learning and what she actually *did* in the classroom. The following philosophic excerpt was from her student teaching application:

> There are several factors, which have influenced my decision to become a teacher, but the most powerful one would be my desire to be a role model for students. I have always enjoyed and taken pride in being someone that people can look up to and can look to for guidance. I take comfort in knowing that I may be influencing and developing young lives by teaching them to not only be good students, but also productive citizens, critical thinkers, constructive individuals, and successful adults. I am motivated by the idea of being a source of guidance and respect for my students and my colleagues. Another factor that has influenced my becoming a teacher is the school that I graduated from. The teachers in that school demonstrated their strong love of teaching and their students. I believe that if I emulate some of the same positive attributes that they possessed, I will be as influential in my students' lives as my teachers were in mine.

This philosophy statement is very large, ambitious, and abstract; Sandy discussed things like being a "role model," teaching students to be "good citizens," and being "influential in students' lives." In contrast, her narratives of teaching experience and tension were much narrower and more concrete, focusing on specific classroom events and scenarios. Remember that Sandy engaged in no identified narratives of tension between personal and professional perspectives and only one "embodiment" narrative. The majority of the stories she told were about assignments she gave to students, how they responded, and how her mentor teacher responded to her teaching. However, Sandy's visual metaphor of the "mirror" made a connection between her abstract philosophies and her concrete experiences by focusing on reflection, a cognitive strategy that might have helped Sandy link these two discourses. A great deal of reflection would have been necessary to cultivate her understanding of the classroom applications of her philosophy statements. Borderland discourse is also *reflective* discourse, a type of discourse requiring metacognitive thought about discursive practices and related ideological tensions. To begin to integrate her personal experiences with her professional goals, Sandy needed to do as the mirror metaphor commanded: reflect on her developing self.

Carrie told me eight philosophy statements that didn't really change over time but, similar to Karen's, consistently reflected the ideological tensions with which she struggled. Themes in Carrie's statements included the importance of "keeping students awake," being willing to talk to students after class, creating a diverse and open environment, and doubting the possibility of studying queer and women's issues in the secondary school. All of these philosophy statements, with the exception of the tongue-in-cheek "keeping students awake," were connected to Carrie's focus on issues of diversity and making classroom space for the marginalized student. These are the very issues that Carrie experienced as a marginalized preservice teacher and that eventually led to her decision to choose another vocation. Because Carrie created no visual metaphors, I have no evidence of productive cognitive dissonance between experiential narratives and philosophy statements—no identifiable borderland discourse resulting in professional growth.

Finally, Lois engaged in the fewest philosophy statements, with six. One might have predicted that she would have uttered more given the success she had with borderland or transformative discourse. However, I argue that her openness to cognitive dissonance and ambiguity and her readiness to view herself as a learner made it less likely that Lois would create so-called philosophy statements, which are traditionally blanket judgments about fundamental beliefs. Perhaps Lois would have engaged in more discourse of her *personal pedagogy* if she had been asked to do so and if the distinction between philosophies and personal pedagogies had been explored with her.

However, Lois' six philosophy statements did demonstrate some growth over time. Like Karen, Lois produced philosophy statements with characteristics of borderland discourse. Both she and Karen began to realize by the end of the study that the teacher is in a continual process of learning, and they embraced the idea that they didn't (and couldn't) know everything about how to teach. They realized that they had to participate in multiple personal and professional discourses and understand their teacher subjectivities as being many faceted and often contextually enacted. Their philosophy statements were often about the teacher's professional self, the teacher's role, and the complexity of the teacher identity.

Lois discussed how she had learned after her student teaching experience that she was a lifelong learner as well as a teacher, a realization that was central for both her personal and professional identities. This complex understanding of teacher identity was an example of transformative discourse expressed on April 16, 2002:

> Rather than think I know it, or go in with the attitude that I already thought I knew what student teaching was about, or thought I knew what to do, and then when I found out what it really was, not to be able to recognize it, or not want to

> change my ways ... not want to totally scrap an ideal or admit I was wrong—no, I mean, I just wanted to know how to really do it and do it well.

Lois seemed to have learned much about the complexity of a teaching life, and she appeared prepared for the challenge. Her philosophy statements did not theorize what she hoped students would literally do (e.g., group work, literature circles, or process writing) in the classroom, but they described how *she* would be in the classroom, and outside of the classroom, as an education professional always in a state of reflective self-analysis and identity growth.

Consistent with her other philosophy statements about continuous professional growth, Lois' statements describing her preferred theoretical approach to teaching literature and writing changed over the time of the study. Early in the study, Lois spoke of her understanding of herself as a "language as artifact" teacher who valued language learning as text analysis, an idea she explored in a pie chart and also in an interview with me on April 19, 2001. At this time, Lois believed that teaching English primarily centered on teaching texts and teaching students to appreciate, understand, and emulate them. This philosophy statement was graphically communicated in her first pie chart, which she created for a methods class she was then taking. Lois dedicated a full half of her symbolic pie to the language teaching philosophy centered on the study of textual artifacts (i.e., literary works).

Approximately 8 months later and after another semester of coursework, she realized that this emphasis on the study and creation of textual artifacts no longer dominated her teaching. Lois told me through a revised pie chart and related interview discussions that she was now also a so-called "language as expression" and "language as social construct" teacher (see *Language and Reflection: An Integrated Approach to Teaching English,* by Anne Ruggles Gere et al., 1991, for a thorough discussion of these categories). Valuing these different philosophic categories represented an ideological change for Lois; although she didn't reject the notion of teaching students to value and interpret texts, her new pie chart gave almost equal space to language as expression (using reading and writing for personal growth) and language as social construct (understanding that writing is learned when writing for real audiences, and both reading and writing tasks are better understood while interacting in a specific discourse community). Lois' philosophy of teaching had modified to become more complex, as additional approaches and points of view were integrated with her original beliefs.

Lois' metaphor of the "soda bottles" connected her increasingly reflective philosophy statements to her classroom teaching experiences. The following narrative of practice told by Lois described a classroom situation demanding an awareness of nonunitary subjectivity and reflective decision making:

> I would like to run my classroom the way she [mentor teacher] does. She is very laid back. After the last class she asked me what I thought. And I said, well, there is a group of boys up in the front, and they just talked the entire period, distracted the other kids on the other side [of the room] and she let it go. It wasn't really bad but it was something that would of drove me nuts. There were some kids in the back that had some senior pictures out and were passing them around. And that got on my nerves as well. She ran her class kind of laid back but everybody responded to her. And, so that's what I said. I said, "I don't know, well Miguel and somebody, the first thing that entered my mind was to separate them. But, you know, put one over here and one over there because they were so distracting." And she said, "Yeah, but they are 18 years old, you know. You can't necessarily treat them like middle schoolers anymore." And I said, "Yes, but the senior pictures they would have had to go away." I said I couldn't have done that. I wouldn't have made a big deal about it. I would have gone back there, as I was talking. I've done that before, just take them and put them in the bag or take them up to the desk and say you can come get them after class or something. I've done that. I've done that once when I was in a field experience. And I did it when I substitute taught. She said, "I couldn't have [taken the pictures], that would have interrupted the whole class." I said yeah, but if you did it a different way, you know, something like that. But, she said her philosophy is you pick your battles. She says if she's really strict all the time or she embarrasses the kids then maybe they won't want to respond in the classroom. And they weren't really bad. She said you could have a lot worse. (September 12, 2001)

Here Lois was disagreeing with her mentor, although they seemed to be able to have a collegial discussion about the disagreement. This real-life teaching experience could be ideologically connected to Lois' philosophy statements by examining the visual metaphor of the soda bottles, which recognized the various subjectivities and practical pedagogies that come into play when a teacher makes daily classroom decisions: She was the same Lois, but also different based on her classroom context and student needs or behaviors. In this particular case, Lois may have moved the students, but she remained open to her mentor teacher's analysis of the situation and respected her pedagogical decisions. (She even began her statement by saying, "I would like to run my classroom the way she does.") She was open to learning, a concept that was central to her philosophy, but she was also aware that sometimes on-the-spot decisions must be made to establish a productive learning environment, decisions that may not always be those advised by mentors, teacher educators, or students.

The reason for the "empty" or ineffectual nature of philosophy statements as assigned in many methods courses may be that students are far too comfortable and confident uttering them. If that is the case, one job of teacher educators may be to complicate the notion of the educational philosophy statement to encourage the expression of such statements with characteristics of borderland or transformative discourse. For Karen and Lois, philosophy statements eventually demonstrated characteristics of borderland discourse as a result of pivotal teaching experiences that prompted critically reflective discourse about prior philosophy statements that no longer "worked" as they began to own their new teacher identities. However, for several of the other participants, the philosophy statements were most influential when they were ideologically connected to the visual metaphors. For these student participants, when their philosophy statements contradicted experiential narratives, they felt ideological tension; however, for the five students who created them, the visual metaphors facilitated productive interaction between the seemingly disparate experiential narratives and philosophy statements. Even if the philosophy statements themselves did not reflect characteristics of borderland discourse, they were foundational discourse for the visual metaphors. These philosophy statements helped the preservice teachers to consciously identify their current philosophic positions and belief structures about teaching, and this metacognitive turn enabled the creation of transformative visual metaphors, which significantly enriched their teacher identity development.

Chapter **10**

To Know Thyself: Final Thoughts About Teacher Identity

After the qualitative analysis of the preservice teacher discourse, 10 general themes or findings emerged. These characteristics are summarized in the sections that follow. They have been discussed in detail in the previous seven chapters, where supporting examples of participants' discourse were also provided. I hope that this summary helps the reader process the wide-ranging analysis and many discursive examples found throughout this book.

1. NONUNITARY SUBJECTIVITIES ARE ESSENTIAL FOR HOLISTIC IDENTITY FORMATION

An awareness of nonunitary subjectivities was important to holistic professional identity formation of the participants. Leslie Rebecca Bloom (1998) examined nonunitary subjectivities from a feminist perspective. She asserted that women's narratives will not follow a "traditional" structure moving from exposition, through climax, and to a more or less neat resolution that usually puts the narrator in the role of hero. Instead, she claimed that women's narratives generally include many subplots, complexities, twists, and turns, and often do not contain a clear climax or neat resolution. Bloom hypothesized that such narratives represent what she calls the nonunitary subjectivities of women.

In this study, the participants who were more confident in their growing professional identities told stories describing their ability to embrace a variety of different ways of approaching classroom decision making and a number of context-specific strategies they might use when responding to students. The students who were able to believe that there was not always a single correct way to teach, or one rigid cultural model of teacher—no matter what media images may present—were able to make decisions that were based on student needs and were more consistent with their professional priorities and personal ideologies. They were able to see the identity of teacher in a broader way than the cultural model would seem to allow them. Therefore, they had an easier time assuming a teacher identity. Being a teacher is, to some extent, playing a role; but good teaching also exhibits the quality of improvisation. The teacher has to respond to the environment and be aware of the unfolding classroom scene in order to improvise successfully. In other words, a teacher must be aware of diverse classroom demands (e.g., intellectual, social, behavioral) present at a given moment and be ready to respond to those demands with any number of actions chosen from a repertoire of possibilities (e.g., spending more time on a problem, changing the focus of an activity, or focusing briefly on a single student).

One of the problems faced by some students in this study is that although their personal identities were multiple and diverse, their perception of the professional identity of the teacher was not. They saw the teacher identity as rigid and unchangeable. Although this view has grown out of long-held cultural scripts and therefore had some validity, such a perception often made the assumption of a teacher identity seem difficult, if not impossible. The opposite type of problem was also evident: The student teacher who saw her personal identity as being fairly uncomplicated and coherent, yet found the teacher identity overwhelmingly complex and many-faceted. The disjunction between an awareness of the multiplicity and complexity of personal and professional identities often increased tension and unease when the participants were transitioning from student to teacher.

The three types of preservice teachers who moved fairly smoothly from student to teacher were (a) those who were able to begin to see the identity of teacher as nonunitary and therefore not completely at odds with their personal identities; (b) those who view their personal and professional identities in similarly uncomplicated or unitary ways (these students had little ideological conflict when taking on a rigidly perceived teacher identity); and (c) those whose tensions were primarily professional in nature, instead of personal. It seemed that professional contradictions and tensions were easier to resolve for the students, and they received better and more consistent mentorship about engaging in professionally oriented borderland discourse. However, the recognition of both personal *and* professional nonunitary subjectivities, which happened primarily for one participant in the study (Lois), resulted in the richest, most reflexive teacher identity development.

2. TENSION BETWEEN DISCORDANT SUBJECTIVITIES AND ASSOCIATED IDEOLOGIES LESSENS THE CHANCE OF DEVELOPING A SATISFYING PROFESSIONAL IDENTITY

I found that the number of narratives of tension told by the preservice teachers was associated with the level of difficulty they had developing a teacher identity, whether these narratives were describing tensions between student and teacher subjectivities, personal and professional ideologies, or university and practical orientations. The students with the most occurrences of narratives of tension actually chose not to take secondary teaching jobs following graduation. The three students who chose not to be secondary school teachers told 34, 27, and 16 narratives of tension, respectively; the three students who took teaching jobs told 13, 8, and 14 such narratives, respectively.

I do not want to imply that tension is always bad. Davies (2000) noted, "Since many stories can be told, even of the same event, then we each have many possible coherent selves. But to act rationally, those contradictions we are immediately aware of must be remedied, transcended, resolved, or ignored" (p. 102). Tension between subjectivities can actually provide the site or impetus for important identity development—a type of transcendence—to take place. However, when tensions were too great for the students and there was little mentorship or support for negotiating the dissonance, students couldn't translate these "noisy" contradictions into identity growth.

It was disturbing that those participants who most complicated the identity issue were the least likely to become secondary teachers, even though they were doing important identity work. Thinking or acting outside "the box"—the accepted ideological and behavioral space for the teacher—caused ideological tension; however, some students were not comfortable with the status quo and found it impossible simply to remain in the box. The resultant tension was often unexpected and difficult to manage, especially if it was about personal ideologies and core subjectivities. The preservice teachers had chosen to become teachers because they were good students themselves and had found some of their own secondary teachers to be helpful, even inspirational. They had learned about teaching during a 12- to 16-year apprenticeship of observation, during which they absorbed the practices of their teachers. Most had little knowledge of the internal, invisible life of the teacher prior to their teacher education and student teaching. To make things more difficult, because teacher educators are often not comfortable talking about their own or their students' emotional lives, they may not always do a good job of helping students negotiate the difficulties of establishing a professional identity.

3. EDUCATIONAL DISCOURSE IS POLITICAL, ERGO TEACHER EDUCATION MUST ALSO BE POLITICAL

Historically, education has had a political bent, and in educational debates various discourses often compete with each other. Depending on the political climate of a school administration or state board of education, different discourses and associated ideologies are privileged. There are two ways of understanding the word political: social and cultural power and prestige; and governmental laws, rules, and regulations. Education in the United States is political in both senses of the word.

Teacher education students have the opportunity to choose among competing educational discourses. These choices have significant ramifications in terms of professional identity and the formation of a personal pedagogy. Students soon learn that certain discourses carry greater social value and prestige in certain contexts, as compared with others. However, the preferred discourse might be very different in the university than it is in the public school, or in their hometown versus at a professional teaching conference.

Because education is political and educational discourse holds cultural and disciplinary capital for school administrators and politicians, teacher educators must be political in our pedagogies. We must enlighten students about the political nature of education as well as help them understand how to engage in teacher identity discourse that will provide them access to ideological borderlands, and empower them to change the educational system through transformative discourse.

Discourse analyst Normal Fairclough (1989) viewed language and discourse as being connected to power:

> I have written it [his book] for two main purposes. The first is more theoretical: to help correct a widespread underestimation of the significance of language in the production, maintenance, and change of social relations of power. The second is more practical: to help increase consciousness of how language contributes to the domination of some people by others, because consciousness is the first step towards emancipation. (p. 1)

In this extract, Fairclough made a very powerful statement about the potential of language to critically examine power hierarchies and modify oppressive communities of discourse. I hope this book increases awareness of the importance of discourse vis-à-vis teachers' identity development.

4. THE TELLING OF POSITIVE STORIES ABOUT TEACHING AND LEARNING SEEMS TO RESULT IN MORE POSITIVE EDUCATIONAL EXPERIENCES

Perhaps not surprisingly, the students in this study who told positive stories seemed to live them. There were two main types of experiential stories:

"success" stories and "failure" stories. As previously noted, much narrative theory says that stories *are* our identity, so it follows that if a preservice teacher tells positive stories about educational experiences, then she or he might actually experience a more positive teaching life. Wortham (2001) argued that narratives affect the lives of the tellers: "While telling their stories, autobiographical narrators can often enact a characteristic type of self, and through such performances they can become that type of self" (p. xii). He calls this narrative becoming, "narrative self construction" (p. xi).

In my study, the number of teacher success stories was associated with a higher rate of success integrating into the profession—success as defined by taking a teaching job after graduation and expressing continued interest in being a teacher. One student who told 32 success stories about teaching took a successful teaching job after graduation; another told 26 success stories about being a teacher and also began a successful career. In contrast, the three students who chose not to take traditional teaching jobs told the highest number of teacher failure stories.

5. DEVELOPING TEACHER IDENTITY INVOLVES EMBODYING THE DISCOURSE OF TEACHER

Most contemporary poststructuralist theorists and educators have noted the value of the "embodiment" of identity. It is from Hocking et al. (2001) that I borrow the word *embodiment*, which they defined as "a seamless though often elusive matrix of bodymind-world, a web that integrates thinking, being, doing, and interacting within worlds" (p. xviii). When one claims or performs a particular identity or subjectivity, this performance takes place within a physical body, in a corporeal form. The participants in my study who had the most difficultly visualizing themselves in the teacher body—a body that looks and acts like the culturally preferred model of a teacher—experienced difficulty in developing a teacher identity. However, rarely do teacher educators ask preservice teachers to interrogate their own materiality or corporeal subject positions when they are in methods classes or student teaching. The students in this study often cited embodiment issues as being important to the development of teacher identities; these issues included body size, age, dress, social class (e.g., where they grew up and lived, occupations of their family members, jobs they have held), gender, sexual orientation, and race/ethnicity. Two students in this study who told the most narratives about embodiment tensions decided not to teach after graduation. These students told 12 and 8 embodiment narratives, respectively. The remaining four students told five, one, one, and seven narratives of embodiment.

Concerning the embodiment of teacher identity, Hocking et al. (2001) asserted:

> The idea of combining body and mind into one word is not new. John Dewey (1929) using a hyphenated version of the term argued that "Body-mind simply designates what actually takes place when a living body is implicated in situations of discourse communication and participation ... 'body' designates the continued and conserved, the registered and cumulative operation of factors continuous with the rest of nature, inanimate as well as animate; while 'mind' designates the characters and consequences which are differential, indicative of features which emerge when 'body' is engaged in a wider, more complex and interdependent situation." (p. xvii)

Such embodiment of identity was difficult when the preservice teachers could not negotiate the divide between the characteristic embodiment of their personal identities and the perceived teacher body; the two seemed contradictory and uncomfortable to inhabit. The issue of embodiment is linked to the concept of "dispositions," which is becoming a common addition to teacher education standards across the nation. For example, The Indiana Professional Standards Board (IPSB) as well as the National Council for Accreditation of Teacher Education (NCATE) have issued standards for preservice teachers seeking licensure in Indiana. These standards are broken into three areas: knowledge, performances, and dispositions. The IPSB defined dispositions as "the habitual behaviors, which communicate the qualities or traits valued by the teaching profession" (www.IN.gov/psb/standards/preface.html). However, what are these "behaviors" and what exactly are the "qualities and traits" valued by the profession? At the institution where I teach, this statement has been translated into guidelines concerning punctuality, leadership, desire to help students learn, and the ability to be collegial with peers, instructors, and mentors. Genet Simone Kozik-Rosabal (2001) noted:

> The National Council for Accreditation of Teacher Education (NCATE), which rates teacher education programs on these same qualities [dispositions], specifically highlights the need for teachers to have a "professional conscience" which NCATE defines as "commitment to inquiry, knowledge, competence, caring and social justice." (p. 102)

Although I also value these qualities, when teacher educators recognize the importance of the embodiment of teacher identity, they will have to lobby for the creation of disposition standards that are more complex and multidimensional. In addition to preservice teachers who respect diverse learners and multicultural approaches and who care about student learning, perhaps we could strive for a more complex understanding of preservice teachers' own racial/ethnic/gender identity and how that might intersect with the variety of subjectivities of their future students. Perhaps in addition to simply following school rules and showing up on time, education students could be assisted as they make connections among their bodies, their personal/political ideologies, and the role of "teacher." Kozik-Rosabal (2001) argued, "Dispositions must be embodied or authentically drawn into or out of our human being. Working on dispositions requires intention, will, risk-taking, awareness, and the ability to change course when things are not working out" (p. 103). Without a doubt, these qualities are difficult to teach and assess. I hope viewing teacher education through the lens of discourse might provide a way to address them.

6. STUDENTS MUST HAVE THE OPPORTUNITY TO *SPEAK* AS TEACHERS AND DISCUSS THEIR DEVELOPING PROFESSIONAL IDENTITIES WITH INFORMED AND INTERESTED OTHERS

Dwight L. Rogers and Leslie M. Babinski (2002) wrote about a study they conducted with elementary school teachers who were placed in support groups:

> In our exit interviews, the teachers mentioned again and again the importance of having the groups made up of all beginning teachers. The participating teachers overwhelmingly stated that the single most valuable attribute of the New Teacher Groups was that it offered the opportunity to engage in dialogue with other new teachers. The groups helped to lessen their feelings of isolation. (p. 75)

New teachers needed to talk to other new teachers and/or knowledgeable others about their teaching lives. The closer the listeners were to the new teachers in age or experience, the better. In the study discussed in the present volume, the participants told narratives about having "voice." The narratives described in chapter 6 as "narratives about family and friends" explored various ways that significant others affected the participants' teacher identity development, including acting as empathetic listeners. These stories did not comprise a large percentage of the total narratives; the six students told 10, 30, 7, 3, 3, and 1 of these narratives. As previously noted, when new teachers engage in discourse to describe an experience, feeling, or idea, the language simultaneously influences their understandings of this experience, feeling, or idea. Therefore, talking through beliefs, philosophies, or ideologies with others can be commensurate with increased self-understanding.

7. STUDENTS WHO ENGAGE IN BORDERLAND DISCOURSES ARE ABLE TO BEGIN THE DEVELOPMENT OF A TEACHER IDENTITY

Borderland discourse includes language (narrative, metaphor, and philosophy statements), actions, emotions, feelings, ideas, and appearances in which preservice teachers engage; interactions among these affect-related discourses help the preservice teachers make connections across subjectivities and nonunitary identities. Such connections help new teachers integrate personal and professional identities and beliefs, and heighten metacognitive awareness of self. Britzman (1994) described what I call borderland discourse in this way:

> Those of us in teacher education need to engage in dialogue with student teachers about each of our ideological processes of becoming, in order to open spaces for a discourse that, while concerned with slippage and displacements, can move beyond the normative discourse of who a teacher is and can become, and on to the critical awareness of the constructedness of knowledge and how these images set the terms for and boundaries of identity. (p. 72)

Elizabeth Rankin (1994) called engaging in such discourse "embracing contraries," Gee (1996) labeled it being "bi-Discoursal," and Davies (2000) explained that authority can be thought of as:

> a sense of oneself as one who can go beyond the given meaning in any one discourse and forge something new, through a combination of previously unrelated discourses, through the invention of words and concepts that capture a shift in consciousness that is beginning to occur, or through imagining not what *is*, but what *might be*. (p. 67)

This creation of new discourse (and associated "shifts in consciousness") is what I'm calling the creation of borderland discourse. Those students in the study who did not regularly engage in such discourse experienced more tension between personal and professional subjectivities that could not be managed or understood productively. This engagement in transformative discourse was central to beginning the development of a professional identity.

There were three different kinds of narrative borderland discourse that the preservice teachers in my study engaged in: stories about secondary school and university mentors and how they facilitated borderland discourse, stories about how preservice teachers connected university coursework and theory to practice, and metanarratives about how preservice teachers successfully negotiated various tensions through a conscious use of borderland discourse. Not all of the students in this study expressed borderland discourse. The students who were most successful in assuming a teacher identity and who decided to pursue a teaching career engaged in the most examples of such discourse. The three students who chose not to teach told 2, 0, and 1 borderland narratives, whereas those who became secondary teachers told 12, 7, and 14 such stories, respectively. Other genres in which borderland discourse occurred were metaphors and philosophy statements. Visual metaphors were the genre of discourse most likely to have characteristics of borderland discourse, because students created visual metaphors demonstrating cognitive dissonance and reflecting increased metacognitive awareness.

8. METAPHORS HELP STUDENTS CRITICALLY EVALUATE AND REFLECT ON INTERNALIZED BELIEFS ABOUT TEACHING AND LEARNING

Metaphor is a genre of discourse that has been shown in research to enhance teacher education and identity formation (Ball & Goodson, 1985a; Bullough & Stokes, 1994; Calderhead & Robson, 1991; Lakoff & Johnson, 1980). In response to my request, students in the study created written and visual metaphors representing their teaching philosophies. They created a textual metaphor at the beginning of the study (fall 2000), and a visual, photographic metaphor at the end (spring and fall 2002). These metaphors provided opportunities to rethink beliefs and philosophies about teaching and learning.

The use of metaphor to encourage ideological reflection is closely related to the use of narrative; both genres ask individuals to reconceptualize abstract beliefs or ideas as concrete discursive forms. This act of reconceptualizing the abstract in either visible language or imagery is essential for critical examination of philosophies to occur, because implicit knowledge must often be made explicit in order to be reconstructed. Similar to narratives, metaphors are a way in which human beings create their identities and explain these identities to themselves and others; hence, metaphors can determine how people interact in different settings, such as the classroom. Additionally, narratives can often be metaphorical (e.g., the memory of the classroom practices of my ninth-grade math teacher comes to represent poor classroom management), and metaphors can sometimes provide links between images and narratives (e.g., metaphor creation can add narrative meaning to an otherwise isolated, but often powerful, singular, remembered image). Some educational theorists believe that the analysis of deeply held images of teaching can be important in developing teacher identity.

In chapter 8, I shared several examples of such metaphors and described how the second metaphor assignment reflected important changes in personal pedagogy and growth in an understanding of professional identity. Over the time of the study, the metaphors of participants became more complex, sophisticated, and reflective of the difficulties of a teaching life.

9. TRADITIONALLY DEFINED STATEMENTS OF PHILOSOPHY OFTEN SERVE TO SOLIDIFY UNEXAMINED POSITIONS RATHER THAN ENCOURAGE CRITICAL EXAMINATION OF IDEOLOGIES AND PERSONAL PEDAGOGIES

The writing of philosophy statements is a common assignment in education methods classes. However, they often become euphemistic and jargon-filled texts that are forgotten as soon as they are composed. The participants in this study spontaneously provided statements of philosophy during the six interviews; I define philosophy statements primarily as abstract statements of belief about education, epistemology, and pedagogy.

There was little significant change in the content and vocabulary of the philosophy statements over the 2 years of the study. There was virtually no distinguishable change among four of the six students; the remaining two students did exhibit some enhanced metacognition through the expression of philosophy statements. I believe these mixed findings suggest that the genre of the philosophy statement may need to be reexamined by teacher educators and introduced into methods classes in modified ways that help students explore and articulate their complex developing identities.

10. APPRENTICESHIPS OF OBSERVATION POSTPONE COGNITIVE DISSONANCE AND BORDERLAND DISCOURSE

As I discussed in chapter 2, Dan Lortie's book-length ethnography *Schoolteacher: A Sociological Study* (1975) identified the "apprenticeship of observation" as teaching based on imitation, not on individual decision making. Lortie found that teachers in his study often imitated their former teachers, colleagues they admired or found successful, or even cultural conceptions of what a good teacher should be, rather than evaluating their own classrooms and students and applying personal pedagogies to make decisions. Such apprenticeships of observation can be helpful segues to independent professional identity; alternatively, they can lead to stagnation in professional development, as teachers act out of habit or imitative ritual rather than from a state of intellectual curiosity and reflection. Creating and using a personal pedagogy is dependent on the expression of transformative discourse, and such discourse can be emotionally and cognitively difficult. Borderland discourse necessitates confrontation among contrasting ideologies and subjectivities and accepts cognitive dissonance as a pathway to rich identity growth, pedagogical creativity, and the creation of new, innovative educational discourses.

In this study, the students who most frequently made professional decisions based on apprenticeships of observation engaged in less borderland discourse, expressed fewer narratives of personal versus professional tension, and were less open to experiences of cognitive and ideological dissonance, intellectual doubt, or ideological ambiguity. Therefore, their professional identity development was delayed or inhibited, at least for the time being.

AN ATTEMPT TO CONCLUDE

Helene Cixous (1993) addressed endings in *Three Steps on the Ladder of Writing:* "I am trying to conclude. Suddenly, as it was page 158—and the third hour was ending, I realized that perhaps there must be 'conclusions' to my journeys, because these sheets I'm walking across with my hand are 'lectures.' But there is no 'conclusion' to be found in writing ..." (p. 156).

I am equally confounded by the idea of concluding, and fear that oversimplification and reductionism will result. The thesis set out in this book is deeply important to me. This project is not just a research study I conducted to secure professional advancement. Simply put, it is the culmination of my life's work as a teacher. By beginning this book with a narration of my early days as a teacher, I hoped to communicate a small sense of my own struggles in developing a teacher identity—struggles that, of course, don't ever "conclude." Sometimes I still wonder what I'm doing standing in front of all these intelligent college students under the guise of being able to teach them something. This all-too-familiar "imposter syndrome" has not yet deserted me, especially in times of fatigue or stress. And I know I am not alone in my insecurities; many of my teacher friends tell similar stories.

In the course of writing this book, I have learned much about my own identity as a teacher and the role that my discourse plays in its ongoing formation. Working with Lois, Linda, Janeen, Sandy, Carrie, and Karen has enlightened me about narratives, metaphors, and philosophy statements that I have told others (and myself) over the years and how these discourses have created and communicated my professional self. Sometimes this discourse has been powerful and life changing; other times it has stifled my growth by allowing me to replay old tapes over and over again that emphasize negativity or reinforce insecurity. Often I have needed an outside mentor, friend, or instructor to give me that nudge toward often-frightening interrogation or cognitive/affective dissonance. Only then have I confronted tensions among discourses and eventually enacted change in my life—heightening my metacognitive awareness of my teacher self and its connections to my core identity. To all these nudging mentors, I express my sincere gratitude. It is partially through them that I have learned to be a better teacher of my own students who are entering our demanding profession.

Given the narrow cultural definition of the secondary school teacher, professional identity development for the educator is arguably more difficult than it is for professionals in other fields. American teachers are often expected to teach in certain ways, conform in speech and dress, and take on a narrowly defined identity corresponding to the implicit and explicit characteristics of a "good" teacher. As schools and teachers find themselves placed more and more often under the microscope of a critical society, new teachers in particular struggle with assuming a professional identity that both respects their personal ideologies and functions in the professional arena. And as this research has demonstrated, establishing such a rich, multifaceted identity is difficult—it requires the acceptance of ambiguity, multiple subjectivities, shifting contexts, and uncomfortable tension among ideological perspectives. Therefore, if preservice teachers are to become successful, self-actualized teachers, they require guidance and support from mentors and teacher educators as they transition into their careers.

Throughout this book, I have explored the occurrence of three genres of teacher identity discourse as expressed by six preservice teachers moving from their last years at the university to the first year of their teaching lives. The preservice teachers engaged in teacher identity discourse throughout their preservice education, and this discourse was both prompted by teacher educators and mentors and self-initiated by the student teachers themselves. Through various types of teacher identity discourse, the participants explored aspects of their professional identities; sometimes these explorations marked the beginning of a satisfying teaching life, and other times the discourse revealed confusion, trepidation, and frustration. Borderland discourse was the most transformative type of teacher identity discourse, because it allowed student teachers to begin integration of personal and professional subjectivities while creating a professional identity and personal pedagogy. The genre of visual metaphor had the most potential to stimulate identity development, although all genres of discourse played a role in the formation of a professional identity: Narrative allowed the student teachers to interrogate or analyze deeply held memories and cultural models; and philosophy statements helped teacher education students make connections among experiences, memories, and their developing professional selves. Each type of discourse accessed a different part of the student's intellect and affect, and hence influenced professional identity growth in distinct, yet significant, ways.

The borderland discourse described in this study occurred in all three of the genres I identified, but perhaps the most surprising finding for me was the raw power of the visual metaphor as borderland discourse. The photographs that the students took during the study to represent their teaching selves allowed them to experiment with professional identities and personal pedagogies more effectively than did any other genre of discourse that I identified. Based on this conclusion, teacher educators should surely incorporate metaphor into their syllabi if they are interested in fostering professional identity development and recognize that *visual* representations of metaphors in particular have the capability to access intellectual and emotional knowledge in ways that written language alone cannot.

Creating and expressing discourse with borderland characteristics can be a risk to preservice teachers as they relinquish the security of long-held beliefs and related narrative constructs. Similar to critical theorists in composition and literary studies who advocate pedagogies of liberation or transformation, a critical teacher educator focusing on the expression of transformative discourse doesn't always create a classroom that is comfortable for students. Preservice teachers who are confident that they know what good teachers are and what they will be like as teachers may resist rethinking these assumptions and interrogating their young professional identities. However, it is the role of the teacher educator to encourage questioning, cognitive dissonance, and even emotional discomfort in order for new teachers to emerge as happier, healthier, more effective educators who may remain in the field longer than 5 years.

In appendix A, I provide sample assignments for teacher educators to use in their classrooms to encourage student experimentation with teacher identity discourse and eventually create borderland discourses. These assignments are intended to create a shift in the thinking of preservice teachers—a shift toward critical analysis of their traditional or comfortable notions of education. Additionally, I contend that a paradigm shift is overdue for English educators themselves. As teaching professionals, *we* must experiment with some of our own discourse and rethink our personal pedagogies, just as we are asking our students to do. We, like our students, can become too comfortable with our long-held educational beliefs and philosophies, our internalized narratives of good teaching, our standard methods course syllabi, and our habitual ways of conducting classes. It's safe to say that when teaching our courses becomes too easy, it is a sign that we may be acting out of habit or imitation, not from a place of critical reflection or questioning. In short, I suggest that teacher educators also complete some of the assignments I have suggested throughout this book, and resume work on their own professional identities.

Monica Miller Marsh (2003) discussed what she viewed as the implications of a discursive understanding of teacher identity development for teacher educators:

> We need to understand that the ways we choose to render our identities as teacher educators provide limits and possibilities for the prospective teachers with whom we work as well as the children who will inhabit their future classrooms. Once we are able to recognize the discourses that permeate our speech and actions, we can begin to make choices actively and responsibly about the pedagogy that we enact in our teacher education programs. (p. 154)

In other words, if teacher educators are to help their students experience so-called "borderland teacher identity discourse," they should also become meta-aware of their own teacher discourse and related professional identity. They should realize that their identity is also in flux—always developing, always with the potential for growth and development.

Another reason for teachers to pay attention to their professional identities is related to the political climate of education—if educational reform is to take place, teachers should have a say in what changes occur. Teachers must be confident enough in their own personal pedagogies and comfortable enough in their own teacher bodies to take a stand and herald their educational beliefs. All too often, teachers are oppressed and suppressed to the point of powerlessness, eventually becoming what Mark B. Ginsburg (1988) called "curriculum delivery service workers" (p. 119) rather than active, thoughtful teachers. Preservice teachers should reflect on how they can fit into and even transform a world that encourages them to be such service workers, a world dominated by prepackaged curriculum materials, standardization, and multiple-choice tests. Australian educator John Smyth (2001) argued that teachers should be seen as intellectuals, not as technicians. He contended that the intellectual engages in close questioning and reflective analysis when confronting a problem or challenge; the technician simply reacts automatically, without such critical analysis, doing as the institution demands. A self-actualized, politically aware teacher is such an intellectual, and borderland teacher identity discourse can help new teachers achieve this intellectual status.

Related to the idea of teachers as service workers is Ginsburg's notion of the "deskilling" of teachers, a contemporary educational and economic problem:

> Recent analyses have discussed the proletarianization/deskilling as well as reskilling of educators. Thus, our attention has to be directed not only to the private sector economy, but also to the public sector or the state. For instance, Apple describes teachers' deskilling, which results from the introduction of prepackaged curricular forms ... and their reskilling in techniques for controlling students. (p. 101)

Through deskilling of the job of teaching, more people with less preparation can become classroom teachers. Such accelerated deskilling and deprofessionalization is evidenced by the increasing number of alternative licensure programs permitted by state departments of education that reduce the pedagogical and theoretical preparation (as well as hands-on experience) that teachers receive before entering the classroom to teach. Such a shift in the professional education of teachers will eventually influence the quality of education in our country. Research studies about the effectiveness of alternative or fast-track licensure programs are few and contradictory; more research must be done in this area to discover exactly how a decrease in preparation will affect teacher quality and student achievement, and to determine which type of alternative programs are most effective. However, anecdotal evidence and my personal experience tell me that the less preparation and education that new teachers receive, the more they struggle in the classroom and the more often they will rely on prepackaged curriculum materials instead of creating contextually appropriate lessons and activities. Hence, the push to get more teachers into classrooms as quickly as possible increases the rate of teacher deskilling.

In my state of Indiana, an alternative licensure bill was passed in 2001 that required all teacher education programs in the state to offer an alternative licensure program of no more than 21 credit hours for elementary teachers and 18 credit hours for secondary teachers. Although I believe in the need to provide teacher education to nontraditional students who wish to enter the profession later in life, this top-down control of curriculum and the implication that professional education coursework is dispensable are alarming developments that teacher educators at my institution resisted.

Most teachers, both new and experienced, are cognizant of and often vocal about the problems of such a factory approach to education. But being vocal does not always prompt institutional change, and teachers are often left feeling frustrated and ignored, and can even be viewed by the lay public as complainers who don't want to be held accountable. So what are the teachers' choices? Do they give up their personal opinions and ideologies to play the required role? Or do they become teacher-rebels who eventually burn out and leave the profession?

I hope neither. I hope that teachers can find ways to craft their teacher discourse so that administrators, the public, and even politicians will listen and enact some positive change. Although this might be a pie-in-the-sky goal, and undoubtedly teachers are faced with incredible challenges, teacher educators must understand that transformative teacher identity discourse is central to the professionalization of new teachers and to the general health of our educational system. Teacher educators can no longer simply teach how to structure a lesson plan or outline the basics of reader response theory; we have to assist our graduates in developing professional identities that leave them feeling happy and satisfied, but that also result in good teaching and systemic improvement. As long as teachers are the ones left behind, as long as they are rendered powerless by educational systems that continue the long tradition of treating teachers as unprofessional, unqualified service workers, many schools and students in the United States will struggle. Teacher educators have a responsibility to nurture professional identities that can counteract such attacks on teachers and help them regain their agency.

As James Gee (1996) contended, "Bi-Discoursal people (people who have or are mastering two contesting or conflicting Discourses) are the ultimate sources of change" (p. 136). I contend we need bidiscoursal teachers in our 21st-century classrooms, in the age of No Child Left Behind, the resurgence of phonics and programmed instruction, teachers who are relegated to the role of service employee or security guard, and students who grow up amid rampant anti-intellectualism. Teacher quality is not simply an issue of completing coursework or meeting licensure requirements; it's also dependent on an intellectual and emotional readiness to function in the professional role. As Parker Palmer (1998), in *The Courage to Teach: Exploring the Inner Landscape of a Teachers's Life*, eloquently asserted, "In our rush to reform education, we have forgotten a simple truth: reform will never be achieved by renewing appropriations, restructuring schools, rewriting curricula, and revising texts if we continue to demean and dishearten the human resource called the teacher on whom so much depends" (p. 3).

I began this book by asking: What does a successful teacher need to know and be able to do? One of the fundamental arguments of this book is that the definition of teacher knowledge must be expanded to include self-knowledge. I don't only mean knowledge about one's personal likes or dislikes, spiritual and moral beliefs, or family history. I also mean knowledge about how one processes, sees, or makes sense of the world—how and why, for example, do I tend to have strong feelings about independent reading, or journal writing, or the research paper? Why do I get horribly angry whenever anyone makes a racist or sexist joke? Why is collaborative work so important to me? Many of the ways we respond to our worlds and structure our classrooms can be traced to narrative memories or metaphorical understandings of experiences that underlie our beliefs and philosophies. Interrogating as much as possible the discursive foundations of how we position ourselves as educators can help us develop richer, more consistent, and more professionally satisfying personal pedagogies. In addition to knowing disciplinary content, pedagogical theory, the basics of educational research, and the fundamentals of adolescent psychology, we teachers should follow the advice of the philosopher and teacher Socrates, who told his pupils to, first and foremost, "know thyself."

Appendix A: Sample Assignments

In addition to the following assignments, which intend to facilitate professional identity development, I believe that individual conferences held with preservice teachers once or twice per semester could be extremely beneficial. During my research, I interviewed each student twice per semester over 2½ years. At the end of the study, the students all reported that these conversations, in which we discussed professional development issues and concerns, were extremely helpful to them as they figured out who they would be as teachers. In these interviews, the students engaged in transformative discourses facilitating their growth, and I often prompted such discourse (sometimes knowingly; sometimes by chance) with my questions and comments. Although I understand that teacher educators have many students each semester and it may not be possible for them to conference with each one, I want to encourage this one-on-one communication when it is possible. I believe it could be transformative for our students as they leave behind their student subjectivity and begin to live as teachers.

ASSIGNMENTS USING NARRATIVE TO ENCOURAGE PROFESSIONAL IDENTITY DEVELOPMENT

In this section, I include four assignments that encourage students to use narratives to develop their professional identities and engage in transformative discourse. Assignments 1 and 3 build on experiential narratives and narratives of tension; assignments 2 and 4 tap into the potential of embodiment narratives.

Narrative Assignment 1: The Pedagogical Discussion With Anecdotal Evidence

This assignment asks students to lead a pedagogical discussion about the teaching of a particular literary text of their choice. Prior to initiating the class discussion, students provide the rest of the class with a complete lesson plan and write a 1–2 page reflexive essay explaining why they made the pedagogical choices they did concerning the teaching of the selected text. Specifically, the essay should include:

1. Discussion of research or theory from texts the student has read in class that support his or her pedagogical choices.
2. Anecdotal or narrative evidence from past classroom experiences (either as a student or teacher) demonstrating the appropriateness of these choices.
3. Discussion of the student's teaching philosophy (personal pedagogy) and how it is consistent with his or her pedagogical choices.

To begin the discussion, this reflexive essay is summarized and shared orally with the student's peers, and the discussion leader poses questions to the class such as, "What do you like/agree with concerning my choices?" "What suggestions/ideas might you add?" or "What narrative or anecdotal evidence do you have that is similar or different than mine?" The questions that are posed are based on the leaders's interests and concerns, and should prompt discussion not only of the lesson, but also about why the discussion leader chose to structure it as he or she did.

Narrative Assignment 2: Role Playing or "Situated Performances"*

In this assignment, students choose a classroom scenario or situation and role play various reactions to it based on their knowledge of and experience with middle and high school classrooms. In this way, they will enact, or embody, the role of teacher, student, parent, administrator, and so on.

Students are grouped, and scenarios with associated roles are placed in a basket (sample roles include that of a new teacher, an experienced teacher, a high school student, and a parent; sample scenarios include a parent–teacher conference, a student "acting out" in class, or an evaluative conference between a principal and teacher); a representative from each group se-

*The phrase *situated performances* comes from "Learning from Experience: Using Situated Performances in Writing Teacher Development" by Shirley K. Rose and Margaret J. Finders (1998). In this essay, Rose and Finders described their strategy of situated performances or role-playing scenarios that allow students to experience problematic teaching situations and experiment with possible reactions or solutions, all within the safe context of a pedagogy class.

lects a scenario with roles. After selecting scenarios and roles, each group of students enacts the parts they drew in the selected context.

Afterward, students reflect on the embodiment experience with a brief reflective writing and class discussion. Questions the teacher might ask to facilitate the writing and discussion include: How did it feel to play the role? Did you feel nervous? Anxious? Uncomfortable? Comfortable? Did you experience any physical symptoms of these feelings, like a headache, tension in your shoulders, or tightness in your stomach? Can you reflect on why you might have had these emotions or feelings? Did the role playing go as expected? Did anything surprising or unexpected happen?

Narrative Assignment 3: The Reflexive Paper

The idea for this paper comes from an assignment created by Bullough and Stokes (1993) called a "Life History Assignment" (p. 221), in which the authors asked students to identify "critical incidents" that affected their decisions to become teachers. This paper is an alternative to the reflective essay or educational philosophy paper that often becomes a place where clichés, foundational narratives, and cultural stereotypes are reproduced rather than a place where personal pedagogies can be explored. This essay assignment asks students to reflect on their foundational beliefs and narrative scripts about teachers and teaching, and consider how these notions affect their current teacher education and personal pedagogies. I have chosen to use the word *reflexive* and not *reflective* because *reflexive* indicates a type of critical rethinking that incorporates revised action, discourse, or attitudes in addition to critical thought.

The prompt for my suggested reflexive essay is as follows:

> Write an essay in which you reflect on your educational memories as a student and preservice teacher. What events stand out to you from your middle or high school education or from field experiences you have had teaching in classrooms? Narrate these events, and then consider why you might remember them. Are they good memories? Bad memories? How do you think they have affected your beliefs about teaching and the qualities of a good teacher? Last, identify any conflicts you can identify between these beliefs and the content of your teacher education program, including information you have learned in field experiences. Consider how you might address these conflicts as you continue your teacher education.

Narrative Assignment 4: Reflection Through the "Five Aggregates"

This assignment is an example of a way students might reflect on practice or field experience teaching more effectively using the concept of "the five aggregates" from Buddhist philosophy. Sandra Hammond (1998) wrote that the five aggregates are form (bodily form, materiality), sensations/feelings, consciousness, perceptions (recognition of sensation), and intentionality/actions/reactions (mental formations). She went on to assert that "we do not exist apart from the aggregates which compose us" (p. 1). The five aggregates combine qualities of body and mind, and the day-to-day interplay of the aggregates composes the self or identity.

Ask students to apply the concept of the five aggregates to their developing teacher identities. After teaching a practice lesson to their peers or a lesson in a middle or high school class, they should sit down and reflect on the experience using the five aggregates as a guide:

1. *Form:* Describe the classroom context in which you taught and your own physical presence as a teacher. What was the room like? How many students were present? How old were they? What did they look like? What were you wearing, and how did you feel standing/sitting in front of the class?
2. *Sensations/feelings:* What do you remember hearing, seeing, touching, tasting, or smelling during or after the teaching? How did you feel about any of these sensations? Did anything make you angry? Happy? Sad? Confused?
3. *Consciousness:* During the teaching experience, were you ever conscious of any of these sensations or feelings? Did you ever *notice* them in addition to experiencing them? If not, try to take note of them now. Instead of allowing yourself to be lost in a feeling or sensation, take a step back and reflect on how it felt. For example, if you became angry as a result of a student comment, step outside the anger and consider why the comment was infuriating. Be curious about the anger.
4. *Perceptions:* Try to connect feelings or sensations to forms. In other words, reflect on what was going on in the room when the student comment made you angry. Where were you standing/sitting? What was the student doing? What exactly did he or she say? Perception is an important component of consciousness.
5. *Intentionality/actions:* What did you say during the teaching? (Be as specific as possible.) How did you move about the room? Did you modify anything during your lesson, based on the situation? How did you respond/react to student questions, comments, or actions? What did you do directly after the lesson ended?

Reflecting through the five aggregates is one way in which students can use narrative discourse to consider the challenges of embodying a teacher identity. Attention to the five aggregates can encourage mindfulness about the practice of teaching. A related assignment would be to ask students to videotape themselves teaching and then reflect on their feelings, thoughts, and so on by using the previous questions. With a videotape, students could actually review their teaching as many times as desired instead of relying solely on memory.

ASSIGNMENTS USING METAPHORS AND PHILOSOPHY STATEMENTS TO ENCOURAGE PROFESSIONAL IDENTITY DEVELOPMENT

Often, teacher educators ask their students to write philosophy statements or reflective essays without understanding the complexity of identity development or without revealing this complexity to their students. As I've argued throughout this book, such a process of identity formation involves the analysis or interrogation of preexisting ideologies and educational experiences as well as the integration of personal and professional selves. Oftentimes, however, assignments incorporating belief and philosophy statements are viewed as relatively simple exercises in transcribing what is already inside young teachers' minds. As teacher educators, how can we use metaphors and philosophy statements to provide preservice teachers with opportunities to begin developing professional identities and personal pedagogies during their teacher education program? What follows are four examples of assignments that could be given in a teacher education course to encourage such critical thinking about learning to be a teacher and, hence, the development of a personal pedagogy.

Assignment 1: Visual Metaphor Assignment—Photographic Philosophies

In this assignment, students use metaphor to help them deconstruct previously unexamined ideologies about teaching and learning. Students take digital photographs of images that they see as metaphors for their beliefs about teaching English in the secondary school. Although this assignment also includes a written component (in the genre of the student's choice) that explains or unpacks the photo, the original metaphorical thinking required of students takes the form of an image.

1. Using a digital camera, ask students to take three to five photos that they will use as a visual representation of themselves as teachers. There are various ways that students can take the pictures—if they are working in a group, each person could be responsible for one photo, or they could talk as a group and decide together what pictures they will take. The photos are to be metaphorical images that represent the students' philosophies/beliefs about English language arts teaching. Encourage students to think of their photos as answering the following questions (although these are simply a guideline):

A. Why do we teach literature/writing/media studies/grammar/language?
B. Why do I think people should read or write?
C. How do books or writing make me feel?
D. Why is it important to read books and/or be a writer?
E. How might I explain this importance to adolescents?
F. What is the best way to teach literacy skills/strategies to adolescents?
G. What memories do I have of English in my life or education?
H. What do I think my role as a teacher should be?
I. What aspects of teaching seem the most/least difficult to me?

2. Ask students to download or save the pictures in a word file and write text about what these pictures mean. The text can be in any genre: prose, poetry, fiction, drama, or a combination thereof. Encourage students to be creative; but above all encourage them to write text that accurately describes the meanings of the picture(s) and that "pulls" the photos together into some sort of coherent whole.
3. Ask students to turn in a hard copy and an electronic copy. The instructor can put the projects on a course Web site, if desired.

Assignment 2: Making an Identity Discourse Map

I found the idea for this assignment in a book by Monica Miller Marsh, *The Social Fashioning of Teacher Identities* (2003). She wrote about getting the idea from James Gee (1990/1996), who was "asking students to construct autobiographies in the form of a discourse map, working from the outside in rather than the inside out" (p. 155). In this way, students can trace the origins of their beliefs and pedagogies and how they are often connected to previously unexamined assumptions or foundational narratives.

The assignment takes place in two stages: a group stage and an individual stage. Marsh described the first two steps in the process of the assignment; the third and final step is my addition.

1. Students will be divided into small groups, and list aspects of popular culture (TV, movies, magazines, music, popular books), educational influences (textbooks, novels, projects, assignments), and historical events that have been significant to them. (It is better if the students in each group are approximately the same age.) Then, students are asked to think about the "societal messages" (Marsh, 2003, p. 156) that they received through these discourses, primarily about race, class, gender, and sexuality. The students then share their findings with the whole class.
2. Each student individually examines the group-generated information and makes a list of messages that he or she has received through more

personal, family, or home discourses related to religion, ethnicity, race, geographic locale, family, class, and sexuality.

3. Students then write a statement in which they compare and contrast messages from each set of discourses and examine/evaluate how they believe these discourses have affected what they feel about teaching and learning. Do they notice any competing discourses? Do they wish to interrogate or "test" any of the assumptions underlying these discourses?

Assignment 3: The Grounded or "Reflexive" Philosophy Statement

Reflexivity assumes concrete, material action or change as a result of reflective thought. In this philosophy statement, students will not only describe what they believe about the effective teaching of English language arts, but will also take these beliefs down the ladder of abstraction to the material, the concrete, and the specific.

Direct students to begin by writing an educational philosophy statement as they would usually create one—they can pretend they are writing it for a student teaching or job application. Next, ask students to reread this statement and underline or highlight words, phrases, sentences, or even entire paragraphs that exist purely in the realm of the abstract, hypothetical, or ideal. Finally, ask them to think of memories or experiences they have had that provide empirical evidence or concrete referents for the abstract words, phrases, or sentences. Encourage the students to add as many of these examples as possible to their statements. Students may find that they need to eliminate some abstract parts of their statements for lack of concrete referents or space.

Assignment 4: What Is Your Personal Pedagogy?

The purpose of this assignment is to encourage students to interrogate the phrase *personal pedagogy* and explore its significance to their professional identities. Ideally, this assignment is conducted at the beginning and again at the end of a class, or even at the beginning and end of a degree program.

Students brainstorm in class the meanings of the words *personal* and *pedagogy*. What are their definitions? How do they intersect with each other? How do they seem at odds with each other? The goal for the teacher is to encourage an awareness of the public/private or personal/professional split that occurs in so many teachers' lives.

After this class discussion, students complete two in-class writing assignments. In the first, they are to write about a classroom activity, pedagogical method, or assignment that they either experienced or have seen done in a middle or high school class that they liked very much. In the second, they are to write about a classroom activity, pedagogical method, or assignment that they either experienced or have seen done in a middle or high school class that they disliked very much.

Students take their two writings to a small group where they share or read their descriptions and discuss the following: Why did the student like/dislike the activities or methods? How might the student modify the activities or methods he or she disliked to make them more palatable? Have the students attempt to incorporate personal preferences and beliefs while also meeting perceived school or curricular demands.

To end the activity, students write a one- or two-page statement of personal pedagogy that describes how their personal subjectivities and philosophies might be integrated with perceived school demands. They should try to use specific examples of this pedagogy whenever possible.

Appendix B: Glossary

borderland discourse	Discourse in which disparate personal and professional subjectivities are put into contact toward a point of integration. Such integration can lead to cognitive, emotional, and corporeal changes, resulting in identity growth or increased metacognitive awareness.
core identity	The underlying, more "fixed" sense of self that is the foundation for multiple, context-specific situated identities or subjectivities.
embodiment	The critical awareness of the physicality of human life. An individual expresses discourse through or with the body (e.g., clothing, body size, race or ethnicity, disability, etc.). In this book, embodiment is often expressed through narratives.
identity	A general sense of selfhood or understanding of the self; a set of distinguishing characteristics of an individual that emerge from this sense of selfhood. Identity is not singular or unchanging; instead, it can shift over time and vary depending on context.
identity development	Occurs when an individual experiences discursive tension and cognitive dissonance leading to heightened understanding (meta-awareness) of the intersections among personal and professional subjectivities.
ideology	A system or set of beliefs or ideas that determines how one interacts in the world. In my view, ideologies are both affected and reflected by discourse.
mentor teacher	A secondary school teacher who volunteers or is recruited to mentor preservice teachers during their required field experiences or student teaching internships.

personal pedagogy	A choice of classroom methods resulting from the expression of borderland discourse and critical identity work.
philosophy statement	A stated set of abstract principles or beliefs that often allude to the educational system, epistemological assumptions, and/or the role of the teacher.
preservice teacher	A university student who is being educated to become an elementary or secondary teacher.
professional identity	A subjectivity or situated identity relevant to an individual's professional life and necessary for the successful meeting of her or his professional responsibilities.
professional identity discourse	Any discourse that both reflects and influences the professional identity; borderland discourse is one type of teacher identity discourse that facilitates the creation of a professional identity.
subjectivity (situated identity)	One of multiple possible identity positions that varies dependent on context and an individual's perceptions. Subjectivities are brought to a discursive act and are also affected by it.
tension	When various subjectivities or identity positions come into conflict.

References

Alcoff, L. (1988). Cultural feminism versus post-structuralism: The identity crisis in feminist theory. *Signs, 13,* 405–436.

Alsup, J. (2000). Washing dishes or doing schoolwork? Reflective action as renewal. In R. F. Fox (Ed.), *Updrafts: Case Studies in Teacher Renewal* (pp. 65–84). Urbana, IL: National Council of Teachers of English Press.

Anzaldua, G. (1987). *Borderlands/la frontera: The new mestiza.* San Francisco: Aunt Lute.

Apple, M. (1993). *Teachers and texts: A political economy of class and gender relations in education.* New York: Routledge.

Archibald, G. (2003, February 26). Report finds nation still "at risk" in education: Follow-up study faults teachers unions. *The Washington Times,* p. A06.

Arnheim, R. (1969). *Visual thinking.* Berkeley: University of California Press.

Bakhtin, M. M. (1986). *Speech genres and other late essays.* (V. W. McGee, Trans.). Austin: University of Texas Press.

Bal, M. (1999). *Introduction to the theory of narrative* (2nd ed.). Toronto: University of Toronto Press.

Ball, S., & Goodson, I. F. (Eds.). (1985a). *Teachers' lives and careers.* London: The Falmer Press.

Ball, S., & Goodson, I. F. (1985b). Understanding teachers: Concepts and contexts. In S. J. Ball & I. F. Goodson (Eds.), *Teachers' lives and careers* (pp. 1–26). London: Falmer.

Baumlin, J. S., & Baumlin, T. F. (Eds.). (1994). *Ethos: New essays in rhetorical and critical theory.* Dallas: Southern Methodist University Press.

Belenky, M. F., Clinchy, B. M., Goldberger, N. R., & Tarule, J. M. (1986). *Women's ways of knowing: The development of self, voice, and mind.* New York: Basic Books.

Bell, B., & Gilbert, J. (1994). Teacher development as professional, personal, and social development. *Teaching and Teacher Education, 10,* 483–497.

Bennett, W. J. (1983). *A nation at risk: A report to the President and the American people.* Washington, DC: U.S. Department of Education.

Berkenkotter, C., & Huckin, T. N. (1995). *Genre knowledge in disciplinary communication: Cognition/culture/power.* Hillsdale, NJ: Lawrence Erlbaum Associates.

Bizzell, P., & Herzberg, B. (1990). *The rhetorical tradition: Readings from classical times to the present.* Boston: Bedford Books.

Bloom, L. R. (1998). *Under the sign of hope: Feminist methodology and narrative interpretation.* Albany: State University of New York Press.

Bodenhausen, J. (1989). Advanced placement instruction: Teacher credentials and student outcomes. *College Board Review, 153,* 48–51, 55–56.

Borko, H., Eisenhart, M., Brown, C. A., Underhill, R. G., Jones, D., & Agard, P. C. (1992). Learning to teach hard mathematics: Do novice teachers and their instructors give up too easily? *Journal for Research in Mathematics Education, 23,* 194–222.

Bourdieu, P. (1991). *Language and symbolic power.* Cambridge, MA: Harvard University Press.

Bowers, C. A. (1980). Curriculum as cultural reproduction: An examination of metaphor as a carrier of ideology. *Teachers College Record, 82,* 267–289.

Bracey, G. W. (2003a). April foolishness: The 20th anniversary of a nation at risk. *Phi Delta Kappan, 84*(8), 616–621.

Bracey, G. W. (2003b). *What you should know about the war against America's public schools.* Boston: Allyn & Bacon.

Brimelow, P. (2003). *The worm in the apple: How the teacher unions are destroying American education.* New York: HarperCollins.

Britzman, D. P. (1991). *Practice makes practice: A critical study of learning to teach.* Albany: State University of New York Press.

Britzman, D. P. (1994). Is there a problem with knowing thyself? Toward a poststructuralist view of teacher identity. In T. Shanahan (Ed.), *Teachers thinking, teachers knowing: Reflections on literacy and language education* (pp. 53–75). Urbana, IL: National Council of Teachers of English Press.

Britzman, D. P. (1998). *Lost subjects, contested objects: Toward a psychoanalytic inquiry of learning.* Albany: State University of New York Press.

Brown, R. H. (1978). *A poetic for sociology.* Cambridge, UK: Cambridge University Press.

Bruner, J. (1986). *Actual minds, possible worlds.* Cambridge, MA: Harvard University Press.

Bruner, J. (2002). *Making stories: Law, literature, life.* New York: Farrar, Straus & Giroux.

Bruner, J., & Weisser, S. (1991). The invention of self: Autobiography and its forms. In D. R. Olson & N. Torrance (Eds.), *Literacy and orality* (pp. 129–148). Cambridge, UK: Cambridge University Press.

Bullough, R. V. (1987). First year teaching: A case study. *Teachers College Record, 89*(2), 39–46.

Bullough, R. V., & Knowles, J. G. (1991). Teaching and nurturing: Changing conceptions of self as teacher in a case study of becoming a teacher. *Qualitative Studies in Education, 4,* 121–140.

Bullough, R. V., Knowles, J. G., & Crow, N. A. (1992). *Emerging as a teacher.* London: Routledge.

Bullough, R. V., & Stokes, D. K. (1994). Analyzing personal teaching metaphors in preservice teacher education as a means for encouraging professional development. *American Educational Research Journal, 31*(1), 197–224.

Butler, J. (1993). *Bodies that matter: On the discursive limits of "sex."* New York: Routledge.

Calderhead, J., & Robson, M. (1991). Images of teaching: Student teachers' early conceptions of classroom practice. *Teaching and Teacher Education,* 7(1), 1–8.

Carson, C. C., Huelskamp, R. M., & Woodall, T. D. (1991). *Perspectives on education in America: Annotated briefing—third draft.* Albuquerque, NM: Sandia National Laboratories, Systems Analysis Department.

Carnegie Forum on Education and the Economy. Task force on teaching as a profession. (1986). *A nation prepared: Teachers for the 21st century.* New York: Carnegie Forum on Education and the Economy.

Cixous, H. (1993). *Three steps on the ladder of writing* (S. Cornell & S. Sellers, Trans.). New York: Columbia University Press.

Clandinin, D. J. (1986). *Classroom practice: Teacher images in action.* London: Falmer.

Clandinin, D. J., & Connelly, F. M. (2000). *Narrative inquiry: Experience and story in qualitative research.* San Francisco: Jossey-Bass.

Clifford, G. J. (1989). Man/Woman/Teacher: Gender, family, and career in American educational history. In D. Warren (Ed.), *American teachers: Histories of a profession at work* (pp. 293–343).

Clift, R. (1990). *Encouraging reflective practice in education: An analysis of issues and programs.* New York: Teacher's College Press.

Connelly, F. M., & Clandinin, D. J. (1988). *Teachers as curriculum planners: Narratives of experience.* New York: Teachers College Press.

Crow, N. A. (1987a, April). *Pre-service teachers' biography: A case study.* Paper presented at the Annual Meeting of the Educational Research Association, Washington, DC.

Crow, N. A. (1987b). *Socialization within a teacher education program.* Unpublished doctoral dissertation, University of Utah, Salt Lake City.

Danielewicz, J. (2001). *Teaching selves: Identity, pedagogy, and teacher education.* Albany: State University of New York Press.

Davies, B. (2000). *A body of writing: 1990–1999.* Walnut Creek, CA: AltaMira.

Deleuze, G., & Hurley, R. (1988). *Spinoza, practical philosophy.* (R. Hurley, Trans.). San Francisco: City Lights.

Denzin, N. (1978). *Sociological methods: A sourcebook.* New York: McGraw-Hill.

Dewey, J. (1938/1963). *Experience and education.* New York: Macmillan.

DuBois, W. E. B. (1903). *The souls of Black folk: Essays and sketches.* Chicago: A. C. McClurg.

Ebert, T. L. (1996). *Ludic feminism and after: Postmodernism, desire, and labor in late capitalism.* Ann Arbor: University of Michigan Press.

Ellis, K. (1989). Stories without endings: Deconstructive theory and political practice. *Socialist Review, 19*(2), 37–52.

Emig, J. (2001). Embodied learning. *English Education, 33*(4), 271–280.

Fairclough, N. (1989). *Language and power.* London: Longman.

Feiman-Nemser, S. (1983). Learning to teach. In L. S. Shulman & G. Skyes (Eds.), *Handbook of teaching and policy* (pp. 150–170). New York: Longman.

Feller, B. (2003, August 27). American teaching force experienced but lacking diversity. SFGate.com (p. 1). Accessed June 15, 2005, from www.sfgate.com/cgi-bin/article.cgi?file=/news/archive/2003/08/27/national1450EDT0661.DTL

Ferguson, C. (2003, August 25). High school for gay students draws criticism from conservatives, civil libertarians. Retrieved June 3, 2003, from http://www.cnn.com/fyi/

Ferguson, P., & Womack, S. T. (1993). The impact of subject matter and education coursework on teaching performance. *Journal of Teacher Education, 44*(1), 55–63.

Fischer-Rosenthal, W. (1995). The problem with identity: Biography as solution to some (post)modernist dilemmas. *Comenius, 15*(3), 250–264.

Flesch, R. F. (1955). *Why Johnny can't read—and what you can do about it.* New York: Harper.

Foucault, M. (1972). *The archeology of knowledge.* London: Tavistock.

Foucault, M. (1973). *The birth of the clinic: An archaeology of medical perception.* New York: Pantheon.
Foucault, M. (1977). *Discipline and punish: The birth of the prison.* New York: Pantheon.
Foucault, M. (1978). Politics and the study of discourse. *Ideology and Consciousness, 3,* 7–26.
Freedman, S., Jackson, J., & Boles, K. (1983). Teaching: An imperiled profession. In L. Shulman & G. Sykes (Eds.), *Handbook of teaching and policy* (pp. 261–299). New York: Longman.
Freire, P. (1970/1993). *Pedagogy of the oppressed.* New York: Continuum.
Fuller, F. F. (1969). Concerns of teachers: A developmental conceptualization. *American Educational Research Journal, 6*(2), 207–226.
Galvarro, P. A. (1945). *A study of certain emotional problems of women teachers.* Unpublished doctoral dissertation, Northwestern University, Evanston, IL.
Gardner, H. (1983). *Frames of mind: The theory of multiple intelligences.* New York: Basic Books.
Gee, J. P. (1990/1996). *Social linguistics and literacies: Ideology in discourses* (2nd ed.). New York: Routledge Falmer.
Gee, J. P. (1999). *An introduction to discourse analysis: Theory and method.* London: Routledge.
Geertz, C. (1973). *The interpretation of cultures: Selected essays.* New York: Basic Books.
Gere, A. R., Fairbanks, C., Howes, A., Roop, L., & Schaafsma, D. (1991). *Language and reflection: An integrated approach to teaching English.* Englewood Cliffs, NJ: Prentice-Hall.
Gergen, K. (1994). *Realities and relationships: Soundings in social construction.* Cambridge, MA: Harvard University Press.
Gergen, K., & Gergen, M. (1983). Narratives of the self. In T. Sarbin & K. Schiebe (Eds.), *Studies in social identity* (pp. 254–273). New York: Praeger.
Gilligan, C. (1982). *In a different voice: Psychological theory and women's development.* Cambridge, MA: Harvard University Press.
Ginsburg, M. B. (1988). *Contradictions in teacher education and society: A critical analysis.* London: Falmer.
Giroux, H. (1997). *Pedagogy and the politics of hope: Theory, culture, and schooling: A critical reader.* Boulder, CO: Westview.
Glaser, B. G., & Strauss, A. L. (1967). *The discovery of grounded theory: Strategies for qualitative research.* Chicago: Aldine.
Goldhaber, D. D., & Brewer, D. J. (1998). When should we reward degrees for teachers? *Phi Delta Kappan, 80*(2), 136–138.
Goodson, I. F. (Ed.). (1992). *Studying teachers' lives.* New York: Teachers College Press.
Gordon, S. P. (1991). *How to teach beginning teachers to succeed.* Alexandria, VA: Clearinghouse.
Grant, C. A., & Zeichner, K. M. (1981). Inservice support for first-year teachers: The state of the scene. *Journal of Research and Development in Education, 14*(2), 99–111.
Griffiths, M., & Tann, S. (1992). Using reflective practice to link personal and public theories. *Journal of Education for Teaching, 18*(1), 69–84.
Grossman, P. L. (1989). Learning to teach without teacher education. *Teachers College Record, 91*(2), 191–208.
Hammond, S. (1998). *The five aggregates and impermanence as the basis of individual personality.* Retrieved on June 15, 2005, from www.prairiesangha.org/articles/displayArticles

Hawk, P., Coble, C. R., & Swanson, M. (1985). Certification: It does matter. *Journal of Teacher Education, 36*(3), 13–15.

Herbst, J. (1989). Teacher preparation in the nineteenth century: Institutions and purposes. In D. Warren (Ed.), *American teachers: History of a profession at work* (pp. 213–236). New York: MacMillan.

Hermans, H .J. M. (1993). *The dialogical self: Meaning as movement.* San Diego: Academic Press.

Hermans, H. J. M., Rijks, T. I., Harry, J. G., & Kempen, H. J. G. (1993). Imaginal dialogue in the self: Theory and method. *Journal of Personality, 61*(2), 207–236.

Hocking, B., Haskell, J., & Linds, W. (Eds.). (2001). *Unfolding bodymind: Exploring possibility through education.* Brandon, VT: Foundation for Educational Renewal.

Hoffman, N. (2003). *Women's "true" profession: Voices from the history of teaching.* Cambridge, MA: Harvard Education Press.

Holmes Group. (1986). *Tomorrow's teachers.* East Lansing, MI: The Holmes Group.

Holt-Reynolds, D. (1992). Personal history-based beliefs as relevant prior knowledge in course work. *American Educational Research Journal, 29,* 325–49.

hooks, b. (1989, April). The politics of radical black subjectivity. *Zeta Magazine,* pp. 52–55.

hooks, b. (1994). *Teaching to transgress: Education as the practice of freedom.* New York: Routledge.

Huling-Austin, L., Odell, S., Ishler, P., Kay, R., & Edelfelt, R. (1989). *Assisting the beginning teacher.* Reston, VA: Association of Teacher Educators.

Indiana Professional Standards Board. (1999, September 21). "Standards preface." In *Standards.* Retrieved from www.IN.gov/psb/standards/preface.html

Jahn, M. (1999). "Speak, friend, and enter": Garden paths, artificial intelligence, and cognitive narratology. In D. Herman (Ed.), *Narratologies: New perspectives on narrative analysis* (pp. 167–194). Columbus: Ohio State University Press.

Jenkins, R. (1997). *Social identity: Key ideas.* London, Routledge.

Johnson, T. S. (2004). "It's pointless to deny that that dynamic is there": Sexual tensions in secondary classrooms. *English Education, 37*(1), 5–29.

Kestner, J. L. (1994). New teacher induction: Findings of the research and implications for minority groups. *Journal of Teacher Education, 45*(1), 39–45.

Kilcher, J. (1994). "Pieces of you." On *Pieces of you* [CD]. San Diego, CA: Atlantic Recording Company.

Kirsch, G. (1999). *Ethical dilemmas in feminist research: The politics of location, interpretation, and publication.* Albany: State University of New York Press.

Kissen, R. M. (Ed.). (2002). *Getting ready for Benjamin: Preparing teachers for sexual diversity in the classroom.* Lanham, MD: Rowman and Littlefield.

Knowles, J. G. (1992). Models for understanding pre-service and beginning teachers' biographies: Illustrations from case studies. In I. F. Goodson (Ed.), *Studying teachers' lives* (pp. 99–152). New York: Teachers College Press.

Knowles, J. G., & Holt-Reynolds, D. (1991). Shaping pedagogies through personal histories in preservice teacher education. *Teachers College Record, 93*(1), 87–113.

Koerner, J. D. (1963). *The miseducation of American teachers.* Boston: Houghton Mifflin.

Kozik-Rosabal, G. S. (2001). How do they learn to be whole? A strategy for helping preservice teachers develop dispositions. In B. Hocking, J. Haskell, & W. Linds (Eds.), *Unfolding bodymind: Exploring possibility through education* (pp. 100–117). Brandon, VT: Foundation for Educational Renewal.

Labov, W. (1972). *Language in the inner city.* Philadelphia: University of Pennsylvania Press.

Labov, W., & Waletzky, J. (1967). Narrative analysis: Oral versions of personal experience. In J. Helms (Ed.), *Essays on the verbal and visual Arts* (pp. 12–44). Seattle: University of Washington Press.

Lakoff, G., & Johnson, M. (1980). *Metaphors we live by.* Chicago: University of Chicago Press.

Lakoff, G., & Johnson, M. (1999). *Philosophy in the flesh: The embodied mind and its challenge to western thought.* New York: Basic Books.

Lessinger. L. (1970). *Every kid a winner: Accountability in education.* New York: Simon & Schuster.

Lieberman, A., & Miller, L. (1991). *Staff development for education in the '90s: New demands, new realities, new perspectives* (2nd ed.). New York: Teacher's College Press.

Lieblich, A., Tuval-Mashiach, R., & Zilber, T. (1998). *Narrative research: Reading, analysis, and interpretation.* London: Sage.

Lincoln, Y. S., & Guba, E. G. (1985). *Naturalistic inquiry.* Newbury Park, CA: Sage.

Lipka, R. P., & Brinkthaupt, T. M. (Eds.). (1999). *The role of self in teacher development.* Albany: State University of New York Press.

Lortie, D. C. (1975). *Schoolteacher: A sociological study.* Chicago: University of Chicago Press.

Luke, A. (2003, July 5–8). *Critical literacy and English.* The Garth Boomer Address at the 8th International Federation for the Teaching of English Conference, Melbourne, Australia.

Lyons, N., & LaBoskey, V. K. (Eds.). (2002). *Narrative inquiry in practice: Advancing the knowledge of teaching.* New York: Teachers College Press.

Marsh, M. M. (2003). *The social fashioning of teacher identities.* New York: Peter Lang.

Marshall, H. H. (1990). Metaphor as an instructional tool in encouraging student teacher reflection. *Theory into Practice, 39,* 109–115.

Maslow, A. (1962). *Toward a psychology of being.* Princeton, NJ: Nostrand.

McLaren, P. (1995). *Critical pedagogy and predatory culture: Oppositional politics in a postmodern era.* New York: Routledge.

McAdams, D. P. (1993). *The stories we live by: Personal myths and the making of self.* New York: William Morrow.

Mead, M. (1951/1962). *The school in American culture.* Cambridge, MA: Harvard University Press.

Mead, M., & Cooke Macgregor, F. (1951). *Growth and culture: A photographic study of Balinese childhood.* New York: Putnam.

Miller, C. (1984). Genre as social action. *Quarterly Journal of Speech, 70,* 151–167.

Miller, R. (1997). *What are schools for? Holistic education in American culture.* Brandon, VT: Holistic Education Press.

Morine-Dershimer, G. (1979). *Teacher plan and classroom reality: The S. Bay Study, part 4* [Research monograph]. Ann Arbor: Institute for Research on Teaching, University of Michigan.

National Center for Education Statistics. (2000). *The condition of education,* p. 128 (NCES 2000-062). Washington, DC: U.S. Department of Education Office of Educational Research and Improvement.

National Commission for Excellence in Teacher Education. (1985). *A call for change in teacher education.* Washington, DC: American Association for Colleges of Teacher Education.

National Commission on Excellence in Education. (1983). *A nation at risk: The imperative for educational reform.* Washington, DC: U.S. Department of Education.

National Consortium for Educational Excellence. (1984). *An agenda for educational renewal: A view from the firing line.* Report to the Secretary of Education, U.S. Department of Education. Nashville, TN: Vanderbilt University, Peabody College of Education.

NEA Research. (2003, August). *Status of the American public school teacher 2000–2001.* Washington, DC.

Newcomer, M. (1959). *A century of higher education for American women.* New York: Harper & Row.

No Child Left Behind Act of 2001. Public Law 107-110-January 8, 2002. 115 STAT. 1425. 107th Congress.

Paley, V. G. (1979). *White teacher.* Cambridge, MA: Harvard University Press.

Palmer, P. J. (1998). *The courage to teach: Exploring the inner landscape of a teacher's life.* San Francisco: Jossey-Bass.

Perkins, L. M. (1989). The history of Blacks in teaching: Growth and decline within the profession. In D. Warren (Ed.), *American teachers: History of a profession at work* (pp. 344–369). New York: Macmillan.

Petrosky, A. (1994). Producing and assessing knowledge: Beginning to understand teachers' knowledge through the work of four theorists. In Timothy Shanahan (Ed.), *Teachers thinking, teachers knowing: Reflections on literacy and language education* (pp. 23–38). Urbana, IL: National Council of Teachers of English Press.

Polanyi, M. (1958). *Personal knowledge: Towards a post-critical philosophy.* Chicago: University of Chicago Press.

Polkinghorne, D. E. (1991). Narrative and self concept. *Journal of Narrative and Life History, 1,* 135–154.

Popkewitz, T. (1991). *A political sociology of educational reform.* New York: Teacher's College Press.

Pulliam, J. D. (1991). *History of education in America* (5th ed.). New York: Merrill.

Rankin, E. (1994). *Seeing yourself as a teacher: Conversations with five new teachers in a university writing program.* Urbana, IL: National Council of Teachers of English Press.

Reynolds, C. (1996). Cultural scripts for teachers: Identities and their relation to workplace landscapes. In M. Kompf, W. R. Bond, D. Dworet, & R. T. Boak (Eds.), *Changing research and practice: Teachers' professionalism, identities, and knowledge* (pp. 69–77). London: Falmer.

Rinehart, A. D. (1983). *Mortals in the immortal profession: An oral history of teaching.* New York: Irvington.

Rogers, D. L., & Babinski, L. M. (2002). *From isolation to conversation: Supporting new teachers' development.* Albany: State University of New York Press.

Rose, S. K., & Finders, M. J. (1998). "Learning from experience: Using situated performances in writing teacher development." *WPA: Writing Program Administration, 22*(1/2), 33–52.

Rosenthal, G. (1997). National identity or multicultural autobiography. *Narrative Study of Lives, 5,* 1–20.

Rosiek, J. (1994). Caring, classroom management, and teacher education: The need for case study and narrative methods. *Teaching Education, 6*(1), 21–30.

Rury, J. L. (1989). Who became teachers? The social characteristics of teachers in American history. In D. Warren (Ed.), *American teachers: History of a profession at work* (pp. 9–48). New York: Macmillan.

Russell, T., & Johnston, P. (1988). *Teachers learning from experiences of teaching: Analyses based on metaphor and reflection.* Unpublished manuscript, Faculty of Education, Queen's University, Kingston, Ontario, Canada.

Russell, T., Munby, H., Spafford, C., & Johnston, P. (1988). Learning the professional knowledge of teaching: Metaphors, puzzles, and the theory–practice relationship. In P. P. Gimmett & G. L. Erickson (Eds.), *Reflection in teacher education* (pp. 67–89). New York: Teachers College Press.

Ryan, K. (1970). *Don't smile until Christmas: Accounts of the first year of teaching.* Chicago: University of Chicago Press.

Schell, E. E. (1997). *Gypsy academics and mother-teachers: Gender, contingent labor, and writing instruction.* Portsmouth, NH: Boynton Cook.

Schon, D. A. (1983). *The reflective practitioner: How professionals think in action.* New York: Basic Books.

Schon, D. A. (1990). *Educating the reflective practitioner: Toward a new design for teaching and learning in the professions.* San Francisco: Jossey-Bass.

Segall, A. (2002). *Disturbing practice: Reading teacher education as text.* New York: Peter Lang.

Seidman, I. (1998). *Interviewing as qualitative research: A guide for researchers in education and the social sciences* (2nd ed.). New York: Teachers College Press.

Shor, I. (1987). *Critical teaching and everyday life.* Chicago: University of Chicago Press.

Sloterdijk, P. (1987). *Critique of cynical reason.* Minneapolis: University of Minnesota Press.

Smyth, J. (2001). *Critical politics of teachers' work: An Australian perspective.* New York: Peter Lang.

Taylor, W. (1984). *Metaphors of education.* London: Heinemann.

Tillema, H. H. (1998). Stability and change in student teachers' beliefs about teaching. *Teachers and Teaching, 4,* 217–228.

Tisher, R. P., & Wideen, M. F. (1990). Review, reflections and recommendations. In R. P. Tisher & M. F. Wideen (Eds.), *Research in teacher education: International perspectives* (pp. 255–268). London: Falmer.

Toolen, M. J. (1998). Narrative: *A critical linguistic introduction.* London: Routledge.

Tremmel, R. (1999). *Zen and the practice of teaching English.* Portsmouth, NH: Boynton/Cook.

U.S. Department of Education. (1999). NCES, Schools and Staffing Survey (SASS). *Public Teacher Questionnaire, Charter Teacher Questionnaire and Private Teacher Questionnaire and Public School Questionnaire, Charter School Questionnaire, and Private School Questionnaire 1999–2000.*

U.S. Department of Education. (1999). NCES, Schools and Staffing Survey (SASS). *Table 29.1: Percentage distributions of full-time public and private school teachers according to years of teaching experience by selected characteristics: 1999–2000.*

Vandenberg, P. (1996). Voice. In P. Heilker & P. Vandenberg (Eds.), *Keywords in composition studies* (pp. 236–239). Portsmouth, NH: Boyton/Cook.

Veenman, S. (1984). Perceived problems of beginning teachers. *Review of Educational Research, 54*(2), 143–178.

Villaneuva, V. (1993). *Bootstraps: From an American academic of color.* Urbana, IL: National Council of Teachers of English Press.

Warren, D. (Ed.). (1989). *American teachers: Histories of a profession at work.* New York: Macmillan.

Weber, S., & Mitchell, C. (1995). *"That's funny, you don't look like a teacher": Interrogating images and identity in popular culture.* London: Falmer.

Weedon, C. (1987). *Feminist practice and poststructuralist theory.* New York: Basil Blackwell.

Wise, A. (1979). *Legislated learning.* Berkeley: University of California Press.

Wortham, S. (2001). *Narratives in action: A strategy for research and analysis.* New York: Teachers College Press.

Young, K. (1999). Narratives of indeterminacy: Breaking the medical body into its discourses; breaking the discursive body out of postmodernism. In D. Herman (Ed.), *Narratologies: New perspectives on narrative analysis* (pp. 197–217). Columbus: Ohio State University Press.

Zeichner, K. M. (1987). The ecology of field experience: Toward an understanding of the role of field experiences in teacher development. In M. Haberman & J. Backus (Eds.), *Advances in teacher education* (Vol. 3, pp. 94–114). Westport, CT: Greenwood.

Zeichner, K. M., & Liston, D. P. (1996). *Reflective teaching: An introduction.* Hillsdale, NJ: Lawrence Erlbaum Associates.

Author Index

Note: *n* indicates footnote

Subject Index

Note: *f* indicates figure, *n* indicates footnote, *t* indicates table

O

P

R

S

T